T0196960

"You Still ROC"

Encouraging Yourself through Sickness

Teresha A. Sutton

authorHOUSE®

AuthorHouse™
1663 Liberty Drive
Bloomington, IN 47403
www.authorhouse.com
Phone: 1 (800) 839-8640

P.O. Box 344
Edgewood, Maryland 21040
youstillroc@yahoo.com

Illustrations by Philip McCorkle.

Published by AuthorHouse 02/12/2016

ISBN: 978-1-5049-6741-9 (sc)
ISBN: 978-1-5049-6742-6 (e)

Print information available on the last page.

This book is printed on acid-free paper.

KJV
Scripture quotations marked KJV are from the Holy Bible, King James Version
(Authorized Version). First published in 1611. Quoted from the KJV Classic
Reference Bible, Copyright © 1983 by The Zondervan Corporation.

NIV
Scripture quotations marked NIV are taken from the Holy Bible, New
International Version®. NIV®. Copyright © 1973, 1978, 1984 by International
Bible Society. Used by permission of Zondervan. All rights reserved. [Biblica

MSG
Scripture quotations marked MSG are taken from THE MESSAGE.
Copyright © 1993, 1994, 1995, 1996, 2000, 2001, 2002, 2003 by Eugene
H. Peterson. Used by permission of NavPress Publishing Group. Website.

DEDICATION

I would make no other dedication than to God Almighty.
I dedicate my first work back to him. "It is in him that
I live, move, and have my being (Acts 17:28)." It was
he that caught my every tear and rocked me to sleep
countless nights and calmed my many storms. In His
loving presence is where I found the strength to endure.
He was the one who told me that my latter would be
greater and to have faith in him. He told me that he
would never leave me, and he didn't.

CONTENTS

Acknowledgements

I wish to thank my family who has always been there for me and supported me throughout this entire journey. To my beloved son Jaren, I love you and thank you for allowing me to be me even when you did not understand me.

A very special embrace to my spiritual leaders Bishop Ralph L. Dennis and Lady Deborah S. Dennis and my Pastors Bishop Gregory Dennis and Lady Tonya Dennis. Thank you for your love and revelation of righteousness.

A heartfelt thanks to Drs. Allen and Sylvia Bryant, Apostle James and Lady Gretta Tilghman, Dr. Phillip and Lauretta Halstead. Thank you for enhancing my life and being a tremendous blessing to me. Much love to my special flowers Claudia, Valerie, Kim, Sharon, April, Veronica, Lisa, and Sheila.

Continued thanks to those who helped me birth this project: Robin Kegler, Book Coach; Carolyn Friend, Editor; Brian Harding, Cover Design; Shanell Ringgold, Cover Photo; Marie Turner, Wigs; Andrea Garris Jackson, Financial Support; Dr. Michael Schultz

MD, FACS Cancer Director, University of Maryland St. Joseph Medical Group; Dr. Meera Rawtani, MD Obstetrics & Gynecology Towson, Maryland.

This book is in honor and memory of my family members who were affected by cancer and called to their eternal reward, Janice Powell, Maternal Grandmother; Audrey Sutton, Paternal Grandmother; Thomas Owens, Sr., Paternal Grandfather; Shirley Hall, Aunt; Theora Kellam, Aunt; Lenora Owens, Cousin; and Christina Sheppard, Cousin.

INTRODUCTION

"Although this world is full of suffering, it is also full of the overcoming of it (Helen Keller)." Regardless of age, ethnicity, race, or gender, sickness does not discriminate. While all sickness is not unto death, and often for God's glory, it is a part of life that many of us will encounter. God is the giver of life and only he knows the expiration date of it. Have you ever wondered why certain people die from their sickness and others survive? This book encourages us to use one of the most powerful tools ever given to man; our mouth. The bible states in Proverbs 18:21 that, "death and life are in the power of the tongue." Our words have creative ability. "For verily I say unto you, that whosoever shall say unto this mountain, be thou removed, and be thou cast into the sea; and shall not doubt in his heart, but shall believe that those things which he saith shall come to pass; he shall have whatsoever he saith" (Mark 11:23).

The words that we speak are powerful, and that power lies within us to speak to the mountain and say "be removed". We serve a mighty God who is faithful to deliver his people out of all troubles. The Lord is against every destroying mountain. Just as Jesus stood in the boat and spoke to the storm (Matthew 8:23-27), we too can speak in the midst of our storms and command calmness. For every storm we will encounter, God will always remain faithful and will not allow us to face anything beyond what we can stand. Through his strength, we can bear it. God desires to heal us, his word gives us life.

Could there be sin in our lives that could prevent our healing? Could unforgiveness be blocking our miracle? Refusing to forgive can keep us from receiving our healing. Christ can forgive all our sins and heal all our diseases (Psalm 103:3). There is a direct connection between confession and healing. Jesus Christ is the healer of every known sickness; yes, even that! Ask yourself, "Do I really want to get well?" God desires to heal us. His words are life and health to our whole body. He is our God and he will help us. This is our comfort in our affliction.

As I begin to pen my journey through sickness, I pray this book encourages all who read it. "You Still Roc" was birthed out of my personal battle with cancer in 2014. At that time, I was physically ill and even more so, emotionally challenged. I needed to know and feel that the Radiance of Christ (ROC) was still coursing through my being surpassing my state of feeling ugly and ashamed. It took weeks after the diagnosis before I could even look at myself in the mirror; before I could smile at myself and accept who I was and the challenge before me. It was then that I was able to life my head, encourage myself, and speak these words … "You Still ROC".

It is my endeavor to uplift all who may be going through any type of sickness, to trust God and to use the tool that he has given us for self-affirmation. This tool is our own words. I also pray that you will find the strength to look in the mirror again and become your own cheerleader by speaking the Word of God over yourself and remembering that "You Still ROC" no matter what you look like or what sickness is trying to dictate to you. Use your tool, its powerful!

Chapter One

GOD IS WITH ME

Fear thou not; for I am with thee: be not dismayed; for I am thy God: I will strengthen thee; yea, I will help thee; yea, I will uphold thee with the right hand of my righteousness" (Isaiah 41:10, KJV). Another translation of this same scripture says; "I've picked you, I haven't dropped you." Don't panic. I'm with you. There's no need to fear for I'm your God. I'll give you strength. I'll help you. I'll hold you steady, keep a firm grip on you (Isaiah 41:10, MSG). God has the whole world in His hands, including you! But, why do we sometimes feel like God has forgotten about us or seem so far away? In sickness, so many doubtful thoughts plague our minds because we feel as if God has forsaken us. We even question if it is His will to heal us on this side of eternity. Will I make it through this? How will my sickness affect my family? Will I still be able to work? What will I look like? How will I feel?

Have you ever felt this way at one point or another in your life? In fact, we should be asking God, "who am I that for are mindful of me?" (Psalm 139:13-16 NIV), states that "for you created my inmost being; you knit me together in my mother's womb. My frame was not hidden from you when I was made in the secret place. When I was woven together in the depths of the earth, your eyes saw my unformed body. All the days ordained for me were written in your book before one of them came to be". These scriptures encourage us to know that we are always on His mind and he knows right where we are and he loves us more than we can comprehend. Well, you may ask, if God is indeed with me, why would he let me go through a sickness such as this? God handcrafted us. The steps of a good man are ordered by the Lord (Psalm 37:23); do you think he made a mistake? Never!

My Storm

On July 24, 2014, I decided to schedule a "take care of me" day. This time of year was particularly unusual for me because I generally scheduled all of my appointments in January, which is my birthday month. I had scheduled all of my doctor's appointments which included a visit to the dentist who gave me a good teeth cleaning and a bi-annual checkup and he said, "See you in six months." My next stop was at my primary care physician's office. As we laughed and chatted about life, he checked me over and told me that my blood work was excellent and that he would see me next year. I had such a sigh of relief, as I always knew that if anything were ever wrong in my body it would definitely show up in the blood.

After leaving my second appointment at the primary care office and traveling to my third appointment to see my gynecologist, I called my mom to give her the good news about my lab results. When I arrived at the office, I checked in at the front desk as usual and updated some paperwork that the receptionist had given me. I waited about twenty minutes before being called back to see the doctor. After changing into my gown, I hopped on the table to be examined.

My gynecologist and I have a great relationship and we often talk about many things during my annual office visits, especially our children. As she examined my right breast, we continued to talk. I am nervous but praying that she would hurry up. She pulls the gown back up over the right breast and comes around the table to examine the left breast. Continuing to talk, she abruptly stops and says, "I feel a lump in your left breast". Flooded with emotions, I thought the worst. It had just been a year that I had lost my precious aunt and cousin five days apart, to breast cancer. The memories were ever so fresh as I was still processing and healing from those back-to-back losses. Breathless and faint, my thoughts were suspended in space. She took my hand and made me feel the lump. I immediately snatched my hand back as if I had just touched a hot stove because the lump was so hard and large. It measured 6 cm. I asked myself "how could I have missed that?" She asked me to get dressed as she made a phone call. I assumed she was making an emergency mammogram appointment for me. Instead, she was scheduling me an appointment to the Breast and Cancer Center, which was a block away. She handed me the script as I became instantly paralyzed.

Stuttering, I asked the doctor if I could walk to the center or did I need to drive. She said "you can walk its right at the end of the driveway." As I tried to approach the Center, my steps were like a baby just learning to walk. My knees were shaking and I felt helpless as I looked up to see the words "Breast and Cancer Center". I immediately turned around and got back in my car. "I can't do this I screamed! Oh God, not cancer!" With tears flowing down my face, I phoned my mother and then sent a text to my closest friends asking them to pray because at that time, I could not. I told them that I had just been sent to the Breast Cancer Center for testing. It took me about thirty minutes to reach the Center that was only a few steps away. Still crying, in shock, and speechless, I finally made it to the Center. I thought I was only going to get a routine mammogram, but my tests included two mammograms, an ultrasound, and a biopsy one right after the other. My God, what is going on I questioned?

Anxiously awaiting the biopsy results, the doctor asked me to get dressed and come into his office. While trying to unlock my knees, I finally made it into his office. He said, "I know you are upset right now and you may not be able to immediately process what I am about to tell you, so I will write everything down for you." With my thoughts still suspended in space, his first sentence was "it is likely malignant!" With fear I asked, "What do you mean likely?" he said, "Ma'am I have been a cancer doctor for over forty years and I know what I am talking about, however, let's wait to see what the pathology reports says on tomorrow." Before I knew it, I blurted out "I trust you," but as I was about to correct myself, he grabbed my hand and said, "No! You always put your trust in God first!" I believe God wanted me to know that he too was a believer.

My Pastor once preached a sermon on how storms were not designed to kill you, but to prove you. God is making your situation into a situation you can handle. Surely, there were many incidences during this storm of sickness where I felt like this was designed to take me out. I finally came to realize that storms often come from many directions, but it's how we maneuver through them that dictates our outcome. During my journey, I had to surround myself with positive people and emerge myself with quotes that impacted my life. My spirit had to be feed with words that could sustain me. Such quotes included:

"Life isn't about waiting for the storm to pass…its learning to dance in the rain (Author Unknown). I had to learn that the storms would pass and the rains would subside. However, they both are necessary ingredients to build character. There is purpose in every painful situation we must encounter. We must seek to find the good in it. We must realize that there is nothing that we will ever face that will catch God by surprise. Surely, he's the God of the storm, and in his own time and at his own command, the storm has to cease. "Nothing in life is to be feared, it is only to be understood, and now is the time to understand more, so that we may fear less" (Marie Curie). Although we may not truly understand God's plan for us, we must trust his path. "The ultimate measure of man is not where he stands in moments of comfort and convenience, but where he stands at times of challenge and controversy" (Dr. Martin Luther King Jr). Your greatest strength can be found in your weakest moment. Face the giant!

Scriptures remind us that God is with us because He declares in (Psalm 139:1-6 NIV) "You have searched me, and Lord You know me. You know when I sit and when I rise; you perceive my thoughts from afar. You discern my going out and my lying down; you are familiar with all my ways. Before a word is on my tongue you know it completely". We are never out of God's sight. Therefore, our sickness is not a surprise to him. Is there anywhere we can go to avoid him? Absolutely not! The Message Bible speaks of this passage as David describes God's presence this way; "If I climb to the sky, you're there! If I go underground, you're there! If I flew on morning's wings to the far western horizon, you'd find me in a minute-You're already there waiting! Then I said to myself, Oh, he even sees me in the dark! At night I'm immersed in the light!" It's a fact that darkness isn't dark to you; night and day, darkness and light, they're all the same to you." (Psalm 139:8-12) God is EVERYWHERE! Yes, even in sickness, he's sovereign and will bring good out of every bad situation. You see, although we cannot choose life's battles, God uses adversity to demonstrate His great power and love for us. He knows that we can handle them before we believe that we can. He knows our end from the beginning (Isaiah 46:10). Unfortunately, pain and suffering merely are a part of life.

How did I know God was with me in this storm? Various indicators proved that God was with me because first, I am writing this book to encourage others which says, that I'm still alive and have a sound mind. Secondly, I couldn't always trace him. but I could sense him nudging me on what to do next. The truth is I didn't always feel him, but I knew he was present. One significant act of him being with me was when he told me earlier in the year to obtain quality health care insurance. I had been without insurance for about eleven years because I was self-employed and could not afford it. At the same time, President Obama had implemented his Obama Care Act which forced Americans to obtain health insurance or pay a penalty. Once again, I launched out and tried to find an affordable policy that would meet my health needs as well as my monthly budget. To my excitement, there was a perfect policy tailor-made just for me. I applied and obtained that policy in April 2014 and to my surprise, I was diagnosed with triple negative, stage two breast cancer three months later. Whew, God is always on time! Had I not listened and obeyed His prompting of this very important matter, I would not have received the five-star cancer treatment that was available. It's the little things that help you through the big processes. I was blessed with a team of great doctors, nurses, and staff members that held my hand and genuinely hugged and treated me like I was part of their family and not just another sick patient. They reassured me that I could get through this nasty disease. We cried and laughed together often. I received phone calls not just from the staff, but from the doctors themselves on a regular basis, they really cared! If God wasn't with me, he wouldn't have shown His great love and care for me.

<u>God is Listening</u>

Father, in the name of Jesus, I confess your word concerning healing. You told me in Psalm 107:20, that you sent your word to heal me. Please breathe your healing presence upon me now. The life of God flows through me and brings healing to every fiber of my being. No weapon of disease or sickness shall prosper. In the name of Jesus, I declare that I have a blood brought right to answered prayers. I thank you Father because you hear my prayers and supplications. Exodus 15:26 tells me, "If I will diligently hearken to the voice of the Lord thy God, and wilt do that which is right in your sight, and wilt give ear to your commandments, and keep all your statures, you will put none of these diseases upon me, as you brought upon the Egyptians; for you are the Lord that healeth me". I come to you asking for forgiveness from anything that I may have done intentionally or unintentionally that was displeasing to you and toward others. As I forgive them, I forgive myself. Father, I also ask for forgiveness from every sin that I have brought against my body and against your word.

I thank you for your grace and mercy that are new to me every morning. It is because of your love and kindness that I am still here. Even on my worst days, you are still good. Help me to grow spiritually and physically as I walk through this journey of sickness. I will not die because you promised never to leave me. Though this storm is enormous, I pray that you will teach me what it is that I am to learn from it. You are the God of the storm and I am your property. I choose to remain stable and fixed under your shadow. No evil shall befall me. I thank you because your power is strong enough to attack my disease. I confess the word of God over my life now. In Jesus name, Amen

Chapter Two

MIRROR MEETINGS

Philip McCorkle

Did you feel ugly or ashamed after your diagnosis? Did you become angry or bitter with yourself or God? Did you pray or did you enter into a deep depression? Did you stop and encourage yourself, I sure didn't! Encouragement was the last thing on my mind. In fact, I became cynical, bitter, and angry with God and myself. I asked the questions, Why me? What did I do to deserve this? I even thought of my sickness as punishment. My faith was greatly tested as I distanced myself from God. One of my greatest desires is to be happily married and the very thought of cancer had abruptly invaded that thought. My heart was shattered and my dreams dimmed as I thought of being single forever. Who would want me because of my scars? Yes, I thought like this during this devastating time.

As each treatment wreaked havoc on my body, I prayed for a rescuing grace. I wanted him to do that quick, supernatural miracle in me and get me out of this storm. He did, in His own time, but it wasn't as expeditiously as I wanted. In fact, my treatment plan lasted for about eleven months. Surely, I knew I would be one of the ones exempt from having to go through all the treatment plans, but once again as devastating as it was, I had to fight till the very end. I fought extremely hard day after day to maintain my commitment of self-affirmation but too often, I failed as I didn't always believe in my own words.

I had to train and remind myself daily that "healing is a matter of time, but is sometimes also a matter of opportunities" (Hippocrates, 460 BC-370 BC). It was necessary for me to maximize each day as an opportunity to tackle my emotional healing before I could even deal with my physical healing. Encouragement had to come from within; no one could believe for me. I had to mix the ingredients of encouragement, faith, hope, patience, endurance, cheerfulness, gratefulness, thankfulness, self-worth and bake in the oven of my soul.

John C. Maxwell defines "encouragement as an essential nutrient of growing a positive attitude and improving life, and providing that encouragement benefits both the giver and the receiver(s)." Quite often it is easier to encourage someone else, rather than yourself. The most powerful warriors are patience and time (Leo Tolstoy). In many instances it seems easier to give up and believe the negative than to fight to believe the positive. "Each person comes into this world with a specific destiny; he has something to fulfill, some message has to be delivered, and some work to be completed. You are not here accidentally, you are here meaningfully. There is purpose behind you. The whole intends to do something through you" (Osho). I fought through layers of doubt and discouragement during my first few weeks of sickness. My mind was on the battlefield as I was confronted with both fear and faith. Truthfully, fear constantly knocked me down and won most of the time. There was very little fight left in me. It became the norm for me to go to my appointments only to want to come home and just lay in bed feeling sorry for myself. I felt that I was the only one going through such a devastating experience and became jealous of others that seemingly were going on living their lives happily ever after.

There were many people who showered me with love and kindness and many words of encouragements during my battle. I wanted so badly to believe them, but too often, I felt like they were just trying to make me feel better. My mind was saying, "but it's not you and unless you have walked in my shoes you can't feel my pain." I entertained bitterness, anger, depression, and thoughts of feeling ugly and ashamed. I was raised in church all of my life and it was customary for us to be taught to praise our way through every storm. We had to believe and thank God no matter what. I've been through some rough storms, but definitely this was a storm like no other. I remember mentally saying "God, please help me." Those were the only words I could say for the first few months. It seemed as though, I had forgotten how to pray. The words just wouldn't come out of my mouth. This journey for me was so personally devastating that I often could not articulate the pain. I had begun to harbor bitterness toward God and others and surely could not accept the fact that my life was so abruptly interrupted.

Quite often, I felt like I was being graded to see how and if I would pass this test. Generally, I was the one who would be the encourager. I knew God was able, but cancer had crippled my faith. I had many mental breakdowns and very few mental breakthroughs. I wanted to trust God again, but it seemed so far-fetched because I was still struggling with why he would let me go through such a terrible thing. Winston Churchill reminded me that, "If you're going through hell, keep going." While persistence and determination pushed me forward, that day finally came. The day that I opened my heart and mind and could receive from God again. I knew that he was the only one who could ultimately help and heal me. As Valentine's Day was approaching, I hesitated to visit the mirror because of the shame and embarrassment of being alone and bald. To my surprise, I heard these words, "You Still Roc"! Excuse me, what did you say, God? The Almighty had spoken directly to my spirit, and at that moment, I started to believe again. I was ecstatic as tears were flowing down my face. I could finally hear God for myself again. He encouraged me, gave me hope, and spoke His word right back to me, "Teresha, you are fearfully and wonderfully made in my image (Psalm 139:14)." Wow! What a Valentine's Day gift!

From that moment, I began to peel off my many layers of low self-esteem and decided I would no longer waddle in my own pity party. I gathered my thoughts with the little strength that I did have and came to my senses and began to realize who I really was and whose I was. For I belong to God and he belongs to me. After my soul was restored, we met in the mirror quite frequently. Now I was able to accept who I was becoming, hold my baldhead up, put a smile on my face, and believe everything would work out for my good. I named these visits "mirror meetings". My meetings with God in the mirror made me feel wanted and secure in who I was. They were special appointments because I could seemingly hear God clearer. However, there were still many days that I came to the mirror with tears flowing down my face. I cried; He wiped! I took lots of deep breaths while inhaling right into His presence.

I continued to push through chemotherapy, surgery, radiation, and all the nasty side effects that came with it. He constantly reminded me that he was always with me and he could feel my pain regardless of how I felt and what I looked like. He cares!

In his very presence was all the fullness of joy that I needed, but I had to fight to obtain and keep it. He sent me on a path that I didn't ever want to walk down however, his presence went with me and I had to walk in it daily. The word of God was life and medicine to my soul. The life of God flowed through my spirit and brought healing to every fiber of my being. I had to stand firm in faith and the full assurance that healing was mine; and that I was redeemed from the curse of sickness. Once I regained his presence, God gave me strength to move beyond my pain and find the purpose for it. For this battle was not about me, I was just a vehicle in which he wanted to use to help and encourage others who will walk down this path.

If you are sick, I challenge you to trust God, and find the strength to look in the mirror and encourage yourself. Even on your worst days, know that "You Still ROC" in the sight of God. He is perfect and even after the battle scars nothing he designs has to be altered or erased.

In this next chapter of our lives, it is imperative that we develop a reclining confidence in God, our father. We must rest and believe in him so that nothing can shake us. Life will surprise us, but it will never surprise God, for he is already in our future.

I had to repeatedly stand flatfooted and declare restoration from everything the enemy had stolen from me. I was determined to have miraculous breakthroughs not just in my body, but also in my mind. "Difficult times have helped me to understand better than before, how infinitely rich and beautiful life is in every way, and that so many things that one goes worrying about are of no importance whatsoever" (Isak Dinesen). I am redeemed from the curse of sickness and I refuse to tolerate its symptoms.

The enemy of our minds often come to make us doubt that we will make it through our storms of sickness. His job is to mentally wear us out by convincing us that we are the only one experiencing such hardship. As a result, no one attends our pity party. One of the hardest things for me during my struggle was to encourage myself. Quite often, I just didn't have the energy to believe that better days were ahead. I had to retrain my thoughts and search deep within my soul and find that inner peace and strength that I knew was there, but I had to fight for. Thich Nhat Hanh quoted, "sometimes your joy is the source of your smile, but sometimes your smile can be the source of your joy". Once we reach inside the depth of our soul and find that inner peace, we'll begin to understand, "when life happens, so does God" (Dr. Vikki Johnson). We can begin to smile again and know that this storm will pass. The joy is in knowing that we can turn our storm into an opportunity of greatness.

Meeting God in the mirror was vital in me picking up the pieces of my shattered life and believing in myself again. Surely, I had cancer, but cancer no longer had me. We must confess and believe that the word of God can heal us, and that the angel of the Lord encamps around us, and no evil work shall befall us. As we meditate on him, he gives us sound mind.

<u>**God is Listening**</u>

Father, in the name of Jesus, I ask you for strength to stand boldly before you as I look in the mirror no longer ashamed or embarrassed of my battle scars. 2 Kings 20:5, tells me that you heard my prayer and will heal me. It is in the mirror that I have come face to face with you, my creator accepting what you have allowed. I thank you that as I go from day to day you will heal me. I understand that healing is a process and I ask for your supernatural power to endow me. I declare restoration from everything the enemy has stolen from me. Please let me experience great victories and your miraculous healing power. I thank you, that I will win battles that I don't even have to fight. Give me the faith to believe that you will see me through this storm. This battle seems impossible, but with you, all things are possible. I pray that my cycle of pain and suffering are replaced with a cycle of joy and victory. Thank you because you have paid for my healing and I receive healing for my body. In Jesus name, Amen.

Chapter Three

SPEAK LIFE

Preparation for Victory

Our future is determined by God's unconditional love therefore, as we speak, God will create. God validates the words of heaven and positive words bring freedom and liberty. Since our mouth is a powerful tool that we use daily, we must formulate our words to catch up to what God has already said about us.

During my consultation with the cancer team, my treatment plan was mentally exhausting and overwhelming. My journey was about to become very intense with tests, treatments, and the agony of what was about to take place. One particular packet that crippled me was the "side effects" pamphlet. When the nurse was explaining the possible side effects to me, my mind became cloudy and I began to shut down as the tears flowed once again. I asked God repeatedly, "What did I do to deserve this?" I was in perfect health before and now I have to face this mountain of uncertainty.

When I was consciously able to open my mouth and realize that God was involved in each moment of my process, I took on a posture of strength and declared "this means war"! A war that only I could fight with God on my side. I was reminded of the scripture that I could decree a thing and it shall be done. However,

I needed to go back and grasp a better understanding on what it really meant to decree and declare. After a brief search, I came across a book entitled "Decree your Today" written by Brent Luck. He states that "decreeing and declaring is not just about reading out loud God's promises, but it is an instilling of His life and promise in us so deep that when we face a challenge or trial, the first thing that comes out of our mouths are the decrees, declarations, and promises that are in his heart for us". I sat down on the floor, crisscrossed like my children, opened my side effects pamphlet, and declared these words:

"Today, I accept what God has allowed. Father, you said by your stripes, I am healed (Isaiah 53:5). So today and every day I will trust and praise you. I opened my mouth and said:

- I decree and declare that the cancer cells in my body are gone, never to return to my temple.
- I decree and declare that my normal cells in my body will remain NORMAL and will not be affected by the chemotherapy or any other drug administered to me.
- I decree and declare that I will be able to walk in good health and strength.

- I decree and declare that the side effects of all treatments will be minimal and go away quickly.

- I decree and declare that I will lose only very little hair, but if you see fit for me to lose all my hair, it will grow back thicker, longer, and healthier.

- I decree and declare that I will not have to have a complete mastectomy.

- I decree and declare that my lungs, heart, kidneys, cells, or reproductive organs will not shut down or be affected by any treatments and will operate as they have been created to function. I plead the blood of Jesus over my entire body!

- I decree and declare that I will not develop anemia, shortness of breath, or weakness.

- I decree and declare that I will not experience any bruising, bad headaches, dizziness, joint pain or any discoloration of the skin.

- I speak to the red and white blood cells and command them to flow as normal.

- I decree and declare that chemo nor radiation will destroy any of my bone marrow or any drop in the levels that would lead to other problems. My platelet counts will remain in good standing.

- I decree and declare that any form of infection that would try to enter my body be blocked.
- I decree and declare that I will have no fevers, nausea, or vomiting.
- I decree and declare that my vision, speech, or mind will not be affected in any negative way by way of any medicines or any form of treatment administered.
- I decree and declare that I will not have to go through all that the doctors have scheduled for me. I am and will be the miracle for many to see.

Praying the Word

- Exodus 15:26 --
  Father, I thank you that as I listen to your voice and do what is right in your sight and obey all your commandments; you will put no diseases upon me.
- Exodus 23:25 --
  Father, I thank you for taking sickness away from me and giving me a full life span.
- Job 5:26 --
  Father, I thank you that I will not die until the proper time.

- Job 22:28 --

  Father, I thank you that as I declare a thing {my healing} it is done for me, I am healed
- Psalm 30:2 --

  Father, I thank you for restoring my health.
- Psalm 34:7 -- 10

  Father, I thank you that when I ask and need your help, you hear me and are waiting to help me. You are good and I trust in you. Because your angles encamp about me and deliver me and I will never lack any good thing.
- Psalm 34: 19 -- 20

  Father, thank you that you deliverer me from ever trouble and you hide me from harm. Therefore, my bones are strengthened and will not be broken.
- Psalm 42:11 --

  Father, I thank you that I can put my hope in you. I praise you my savior, for you are the health of my countenance.
- Psalm 91: 14 -- 16-

  Father, I thank you that I can pour my love upon you and you deliver me. Thank you because you know exactly who I am. When I call upon you, you answer me, you are with me in trouble, and

you deliver me and honor me. You satisfy me
with long life and show me your salvation all
the days of my life.

This prayer was a daily regimen for me as these
are typical side effects that come along with cancer
treatment. Nevertheless, I must be very transparent,
although I declared these daily, I went through most of
what I spoke against! Does that mean God didn't hear
me? Does it mean my prayer wasn't sincere? Did it
mean that I was doubting God? The fact of the matter is
that yes, he heard me, and yes, my prayer was sincere. I
doubted at times but it does not negate the fact that he
was able to do what I asked him to do. When faced with
these frustrations and abnormalities they only caused
me to continue to sharpen my on-going monologue with
the Father. Sometimes the answer is simply, "my grace
is sufficient for thee: for my strength is made perfect in
weakness. (II Corinthians 12:9). I found that the weaker
I got, the stronger I became.

You see, God orders some pain and suffering and
as a result it puts us on our knees and pushes us right
into the face of God. The test is generally two-fold. It
builds trust and confidence in who the Father really is
and then he turns around and gets glory out of it. That's

all he wants, just opportunities to show himself strong. Don't stop praying, don't stop declaring! When you are sick, learn to use your mouthpiece against your sickness and be healed.

<u>God is Listening</u>

Father, in the name of Jesus, as I am preparing for victory, I willingly open my mouth, stand firm on your word, and declare your goodness and faithfulness to me. I realize without you I am nothing and can do nothing. Therefore, I am already victorious. Please help me fight this sickness with confidence in you knowing that you control all sickness and disease. My body belongs to you and I choose life. On the days when I can't trace you, I vow to still trust you and give you praise. Father, when the battle becomes overwhelming for me, teach me how to rest completely in you. You are my help and it is my faith in you that brings my healing. In Jesus name, Amen.

Chapter Four

DON'T GIVE UP

Today, I do not feel like fighting. I don't feel as though I can make it through this horrible test. All the medicines I have to take are overwhelming and too much for me to absorb. My head is bald, my fingernails and my toenails are black, and my thumbnail is infected to the point that I had to skip chemotherapy today because of the infection. I have mouth sores along with an awful metallic mouth taste, extreme constipation, feelings of nausea, extremely fatigued, along with my emotions of fear, anxiety, doubt, worry, and hopelessness.

I know that fear, anger, and helplessness are common feelings and they intensify from day to day, but this is a bit much to handle at one time. My nights were extremely difficult as I wailed over and over in front of this mountain of forgetfulness, numbness, irritability and more anxiety. As my heartbeat raced and tightness gripped my chest, I felt more and more helpless. God, why all this emotional distress? I didn't know all this came with this package. There were no words left to describe the deep feelings of my aching heart. Unable, to fully express myself, I had to begin to rely on the inner man to cry out for me. Even though I had a tremendous support team waiting to carry out my next request, it seemingly was not enough.

Being newly diagnosed with cancer or any disease for that matter, cripples your very being. It is extremely emotional and very exhausting. I was so tired that the simplest task became complex. I was quickly becoming confused and had such a hard time of remembering things. I didn't realize at the time that memory loss was one of the side effects. This became frightening and embarrassing for me. I felt that people would really notice and begin to say, "She's really sick." My body became a target for infections. I had to train myself to become extra careful to stay away from germs and from people who were sick or had a cold. What a challenge this became because I am a daycare provider and constantly worked around children who quite often spread germs back and forth to each other, as well as myself. The nurses encouraged me to wear a face mask, which the kids thought was a cool game that I was playing and that I was trying to scare them. I wish that really was the case.

Just as I thought I could start to pick the pieces of my emotions off the ground, I was pushed right back down. I developed a blood clot. Wait a minute! God are you serious? I found myself back in the hospital for monitoring and now being put on an additional medicine; Coumadin. I had to insert needles in my stomach for weeks. My tears never really dried from the shock of this whole ordeal and now I have added uncertainty. Could it get any worse? Well, it did. A week later, I developed pneumonia. I felt like I was in the valley of the shadow of darkness where deep depression and despair lives and that my body had betrayed me. I had never really been sick in my whole life and to experience all of this at one time was way too much for me to comprehend. God, I know your Word says, "You won't put more on us than we can bear," but Dear God, you have to help me. I have just started chemotherapy and have ten more months of treatments to complete including surgery and radiation.

The very thought of the word "chemo" frightened me and made me sick for I was told that it would kill the bad, but also destroy the good. I began to battle in my mind with this because my healthy body was about to go through trauma to become healthy again. This part of my journey caused me to mentally shut down. I didn't see myself as a victor during this time. I knew I was not the first person in the world to walk down this road, nor would I be the last, but I sure did feel alone and that my life was in a downward spiral.

When you feel like you are in a boxing ring and you are down for the count, it's not over until you give up within yourself and you refuse to fight again. You may have physically lost that one particular battle, but because you stayed in the fight, you still won. "If you learn from defeat, you haven't really lost." (Zig Ziglar) The enemy will laugh in your face and tell you that you were not strong enough and because you did not win that battle, you will not win the next one. Stand flat-footed and face-to-face with him and declare, "greater is he that lives within me, than he who's in the world." The fact of the matter is that the enemy within is already defeated and no matter what we face in life, with Christ on our side, we always WIN. We can't lose because God gives us all the power we need. Our battles are customized. Our job is to show up to the practices. It is during our practices that we learn specific strategies to combat the enemy.

Well, what usually happens at practice? First, we must show up with a conquering attitude and train our heart and mind for the fight. A conquering attitude says, "I am equipped with everything I'll need to fight and win". Does saying this once or twice equip us? Absolutely, not! There must be a season of preparation. In our season of preparation, we must pray, and then pray some more, then after that, pray some more, and finally, pray again! When we intentionally take prayer to practice with us, it vertically aligns us with the God of the fight, and puts us in position to receive strategies to combat our enemy. Engaging prayer in practice also develops a personal relationship with God, the coach, for he made and knows the game.

I remember before I was diagnosed with cancer, I had that same dream for over a year. I dreamed that there was filth and darkness in a tight space around me and when I tried to escape from it, I couldn't. I paid attention to the dream because anytime I saw the same thing twice in a dream I knew God was trying to tell or show me something. Surely, because I saw this horrible site for over a year, I knew it wasn't anything good. In this case, I began to do a spiritual examination, but not a physical examination. I thought God was showing me that I was mean, or nasty and he wasn't pleased with something going on in my life. No, I'm not a sinner, but far from perfect. I only took prayer to practice occasionally. When I would have the dream, I would pray and then stop. After the diagnosis, it was revealed to me that this is what he was trying to show me. God was preparing me, but I wasn't prepared for him.

Secondly, we must fight with the reassurance and confidence that the Lord is on our side and embrace the fact that if we can face it, God can handle it, NO

MATTER HOW OVERWHELMING IT IS! Don't welcome the lie that our circumstances are bigger than God. Intimidation will knock strongly on your door, but keep the door dead bolted. It is natural to be apprehensive when the unexpected occurs, but we must cast down fear, and rely totally on God's guidance for he knows the plans he has for us. Each day we live contains new challenges, but it also contains new hope. New hope that today will be a better day; sometimes it will and sometimes it won't. He will empower us to turn our challenges into opportunities.

Finally, this is a great opportunity to develop a deep dependence on God. We must muster up the courage to trust him even in the roughest of times. We can't afford to let disappointments, devastation, or pain paralyze us. We must realize that some things are just an appointed occasion. Our lives are in God's hands and because he made us without mistake, He has numbered our days. I had allowed my diagnosis to paralyze me. It wasn't until I was able to recall His love for me that I realized my sickness wasn't designed to kill me. I had to approach each day remembering that God created that day for me and it was not a chance occurrence. It was designed to cause me to hope even more in him. I had to depend on him for my very being. My thoughts were so twisted, that on some days I didn't even know who I was. When I fell, he caught me; when I cried he bottled my tears and one day he will use them to make me smile again. When we fall, the safest place is right into God's presence, for he wants to give us inward glory.

<u>God is Listening</u>

Father, in the name of Jesus, I thank you that I will live and not die. I thank you for restoring my health and my faith in you. On the days to come, when I may feel like giving up, please hold me in your loving arms. I will make a conscious effort to rest in you, for you are my help. Please help me to better understand and accept the things that you have allowed. As you are healing my physical body, heal my mind as well. I refuse to tolerate the symptoms of this sickness and cast my cares and concerns back to you. I will take care of my body by eating the proper foods, resting in you, and following doctors' orders. Please forgive me whenever I may doubt you. I love you Jesus, and forever thank you for healing me. In Jesus name, Amen.

Chapter Five

EXPECT TO WIN

One of my biggest disappointments during this journey was that I didn't lose weight. I have been trying for years to lose thirty pounds and when life handed me this cancer punch I knew that at least the weight would come off as I went through my treatments. Unfortunately, it didn't and I only lost about fourteen pounds during my entire journey. The steroids in my chemotherapy fought against me. Although I couldn't taste most of my foods, my mind told me I was hungry, therefore, I ate and failed to take ownership of my health and weight. I found myself right back where I started and fell into depression. While others that I met at the treatment center lost quite a bit of weight, I was embarrassed and feeling a sense of failure because I couldn't. Week by week, one of the highlights of going to treatment was to hop on the scales to see how much weight I had lost. The numbers fluctuated only a pound or two generally on the higher side. Feeling defeated once again, I would go over to my chair to have my treatment administered to me with frustration in my heart because I blamed the medicine for taking over my health.

When life beats you down with sickness, and you feel ashamed or overwhelmed, look to God. He is forever in this fight with us. Better days are on the horizon. We may have experienced some bad days, but they only paid a visit to remind us to appreciate the good days ahead. If we live in dependence totally on God, we can rest assured that he has a brighter future for us. This test of sickness came to make us stronger. In recovery, we must rest, eat properly, exercise and follow our doctor's orders. Even on our worst days, we must pull ourselves together, stand in the mirror and remind ourselves that "I *Still* ROC"! Remind yourself that you wear the *Radiance Of Christ,* and the radiance of joy and peace, and you wear it with confidence. God gave you His radiance you cannot cover it up.

Let it shine even on your days of feeling ugly. Let it shine when you just want to lay in bed with the cover pulled over your head Don't be ashamed anymore to rock your baldness. Wear it and wear it well! When your fingers and toenails are darkening to the color of embarrassment, lift your hands up and say, "I am still here and I *Still* ROC!" When that chemotherapy and radiation is flowing through your blood stream, tell yourself; I *Still* ROC! When the organs and tissues of your body are compromised and infection tries to creep in, remind yourself, I *Still* ROC! When the cells arise that does not promote life and health in your body, simply say, but I *Still* ROC! When your joints are not functioning properly say, I *Still* ROC! When your immune system tries to break down, remind yourself, I *Still* ROC!

Speak the Word of God daily over your body! We only get one and our mental health is just as important as our physical health. Speak to your body and command it to function and operate the way it was designed to operate. Start today by encouraging yourself and resting in the confidence that God made you and whatever he does, he does it well! He handcrafted us just the way he wanted us to be and regardless of what we look like during our time of sickness, we ROC, because of God's glory. Wear it well!

<u>God is Listening</u>

Father, in Jesus name, I am HEALED! I confess you grace and mercy shown towards me. I put my hope and trust in you, and I praise you for you are my countenance. I declare and decree that this weapon of sickness will never return to my life again. I decree complete healing knowing that you do all things well. The blood of Jesus covers my mind, my body, and my spirit. Thank you because you have a great plan for my life and with your help, I will walk it out in perfect peace and perfect health because you are my God. I appreciate you love and care for me. I can never thank you enough. But, I will bless you with everything that is within me. Thank you for healing me forever! I love you Jesus, In Jesus name, Amen.

<u>Today Is Still A Good Day</u>

It is very important to journal our thoughts and our feelings. For the next thirty days begin to write down at least one GOOD thing per day that came out of your sickness. Think about what opportunities were created for you. This simple exercise will help to release what we may be feeling, but perhaps can't articulate. As we begin to look back over this journey, blessings will always outweigh defeat. Even though many bad days will appear, we are going to find the good in each day. Remember, even on a bad day, God is still good! The negative + the positive = POWER! We *Still* ROC! We Win!

Day One

Today, I feel . . .

_____

_____

_____

_____

_____

_____

_____

_____

_____

_____

_____

_____

_____

_____

_____

_____

_____

_____

_____

_____

_____

_____

It is still a good day because . . .

_____

_____

_____

_____

_____

_____

_____

_____

_____

_____

_____

_____

_____

_____

_____

_____

_____

_____

_____

_____

Day Two

Today, I feel . . .

_____

_____

_____

_____

_____

_____

_____

_____

_____

_____

_____

_____

_____

_____

_____

_____

_____

_____

_____

_____

_____

_____

_____

It is still a good day because . . .

_____

_____

_____

_____

_____

_____

_____

_____

_____

_____

_____

_____

_____

_____

_____

_____

_____

_____

_____

_____

Day Three

Today, I feel . . .

_____

_____

_____

_____

_____

_____

_____

_____

_____

_____

_____

_____

_____

_____

_____

_____

_____

_____

_____

_____

_____

It is still a good day because . . .

_____

_____

_____

_____

_____

_____

_____

_____

_____

_____

_____

_____

_____

_____

_____

_____

_____

_____

_____

_____

Day Four

Today, I feel . . .

_____

_____

_____

_____

_____

_____

_____

_____

_____

_____

_____

_____

_____

_____

_____

_____

_____

_____

_____

_____

_____

It is still a good day because . . .

_____

_____

_____

_____

_____

_____

_____

_____

_____

_____

_____

_____

_____

_____

_____

_____

_____

_____

_____

_____

_____

Day Five

Today, I feel . . .

_____

_____

_____

_____

_____

_____

_____

_____

_____

_____

_____

_____

_____

_____

_____

_____

_____

_____

_____

_____

_____

Teresha A. Sutton

It is still a good day because . . .

_____

_____

_____

_____

_____

_____

_____

_____

_____

_____

_____

_____

_____

_____

_____

_____

_____

_____

_____

_____

Day Six

Today, I feel . . .

_____

_____

_____

_____

_____

_____

_____

_____

_____

_____

_____

_____

_____

_____

_____

_____

_____

_____

_____

_____

_____

Teresha A. Sutton

It is still a good day because . . .

_____

_____

_____

_____

_____

_____

_____

_____

_____

_____

_____

_____

_____

_____

_____

_____

_____

_____

_____

_____

_____

_____

Day Seven

Today, I feel . . .

_____

_____

_____

_____

_____

_____

_____

_____

_____

_____

_____

_____

_____

_____

_____

_____

_____

_____

_____

_____

_____

_____

It is still a good day because . . .

_____

_____

_____

_____

_____

_____

_____

_____

_____

_____

_____

_____

_____

_____

_____

_____

_____

_____

Day Eight

Today, I feel . . .

_____

_____

_____

_____

_____

_____

_____

_____

_____

_____

_____

_____

_____

_____

_____

_____

_____

_____

_____

_____

_____

_____

_____

It is still a good day because . . .

_____

_____

_____

_____

_____

_____

_____

_____

_____

_____

_____

_____

_____

_____

_____

_____

_____

_____

_____

_____

_____

Day Nine

Today, I feel . . .

_____

_____

_____

_____

_____

_____

_____

_____

_____

_____

_____

_____

_____

_____

_____

_____

_____

_____

_____

_____

_____

_____

It is still a good day because . . .

_____

_____

_____

_____

_____

_____

_____

_____

_____

_____

_____

_____

_____

_____

_____

_____

_____

_____

_____

_____

Day Ten

Today, I feel . . .

_____

_____

_____

_____

_____

_____

_____

_____

_____

_____

_____

_____

_____

_____

_____

_____

_____

_____

_____

_____

_____

_____

_____

_____

It is still a good day because . . .

_____

_____

_____

_____

_____

_____

_____

_____

_____

_____

_____

_____

_____

_____

_____

_____

_____

_____

_____

_____

Day Eleven

Today, I feel . . .

_____

_____

_____

_____

_____

_____

_____

_____

_____

_____

_____

_____

_____

_____

_____

_____

_____

_____

_____

_____

_____

It is still a good day because . . .

_____

_____

_____

_____

_____

_____

_____

_____

_____

_____

_____

_____

_____

_____

_____

_____

_____

_____

_____

_____

Day Twelve

Today, I feel . . .

_____

_____

_____

_____

_____

_____

_____

_____

_____

_____

_____

_____

_____

_____

_____

_____

_____

_____

_____

_____

_____

It is still a good day because . . .

_____

_____

_____

_____

_____

_____

_____

_____

_____

_____

_____

_____

_____

_____

_____

_____

_____

_____

_____

_____

_____

_____

Day Thirteen

Today, I feel . . .

_____

_____

_____

_____

_____

_____

_____

_____

_____

_____

_____

_____

_____

_____

_____

_____

_____

_____

_____

_____

_____

_____

It is still a good day because . . .

_____

_____

_____

_____

_____

_____

_____

_____

_____

_____

_____

_____

_____

_____

_____

_____

_____

_____

_____

_____

_____

_____

Day Fourteen

Today, I feel . . .

_____

_____

_____

_____

_____

_____

_____

_____

_____

_____

_____

_____

_____

_____

_____

_____

_____

_____

_____

_____

_____

_____

_____

_____

It is still a good day because . . .

_____

_____

_____

_____

_____

_____

_____

_____

_____

_____

_____

_____

_____

_____

_____

_____

_____

_____

_____

_____

Day Fifteen

Today, I feel . . .

_____

_____

_____

_____

_____

_____

_____

_____

_____

_____

_____

_____

_____

_____

_____

_____

_____

_____

_____

_____

_____

_____

_____

It is still a good day because . . .

_____

_____

_____

_____

_____

_____

_____

_____

_____

_____

_____

_____

_____

_____

_____

_____

_____

_____

_____

_____

_____

_____

Day Sixteen

Today, I feel . . .

_____

_____

_____

_____

_____

_____

_____

_____

_____

_____

_____

_____

_____

_____

_____

_____

_____

_____

_____

_____

_____

_____

_____

_____

Teresha A. Sutton

It is still a good day because . . .

_____

_____

_____

_____

_____

_____

_____

_____

_____

_____

_____

_____

_____

_____

_____

_____

_____

_____

_____

_____

_____

Day Seventeen

Today, I feel…………..

_____

_____

_____

_____

_____

_____

_____

_____

_____

_____

_____

_____

_____

_____

_____

_____

_____

_____

_____

_____

_____

_____

It is still a good day because . . .

_____

_____

_____

_____

_____

_____

_____

_____

_____

_____

_____

_____

_____

_____

_____

_____

_____

_____

_____

_____

Day Eighteen

Today, I feel . . .

_____

_____

_____

_____

_____

_____

_____

_____

_____

_____

_____

_____

_____

_____

_____

_____

_____

_____

_____

_____

_____

_____

Teresha A. Sutton

It is still a good day because . . .

_____

_____

_____

_____

_____

_____

_____

_____

_____

_____

_____

_____

_____

_____

_____

_____

_____

_____

_____

_____

_____

Day Nineteen

Today, I feel . . .

_____

_____

_____

_____

_____

_____

_____

_____

_____

_____

_____

_____

_____

_____

_____

_____

_____

_____

_____

_____

_____

_____

_____

Teresha A. Sutton

It is still a good day because . . .

_____

_____

_____

_____

_____

_____

_____

_____

_____

_____

_____

_____

_____

_____

_____

_____

_____

_____

_____

_____

Day Twenty

Today, I feel . . .

_____

_____

_____

_____

_____

_____

_____

_____

_____

_____

_____

_____

_____

_____

_____

_____

_____

_____

_____

_____

_____

_____

_____

_____

It is still a good day because . . .

_____

_____

_____

_____

_____

_____

_____

_____

_____

_____

_____

_____

_____

_____

_____

_____

_____

_____

_____

_____

_____

Day Twenty-One

Today, I feel . . .

_____

_____

_____

_____

_____

_____

_____

_____

_____

_____

_____

_____

_____

_____

_____

_____

_____

_____

_____

_____

_____

_____

_____

_____

It is still a good day because . . .

_____

_____

_____

_____

_____

_____

_____

_____

_____

_____

_____

_____

_____

_____

_____

_____

_____

_____

_____

_____

_____

Day Twenty-Two

Today, I feel . . .

_____

_____

_____

_____

_____

_____

_____

_____

_____

_____

_____

_____

_____

_____

_____

_____

_____

_____

_____

_____

_____

_____

_____

It is still a good day because . . .

_____

_____

_____

_____

_____

_____

_____

_____

_____

_____

_____

_____

_____

_____

_____

_____

_____

_____

_____

_____

Day Twenty-Three

Today, I feel . . .

_____

_____

_____

_____

_____

_____

_____

_____

_____

_____

_____

_____

_____

_____

_____

_____

_____

_____

_____

_____

_____

_____

_____

It is still a good day because . . .

_____

_____

_____

_____

_____

_____

_____

_____

_____

_____

_____

_____

_____

_____

_____

_____

_____

_____

_____

_____

_____

Day Twenty-Four

Today, I feel . . .

_____

_____

_____

_____

_____

_____

_____

_____

_____

_____

_____

_____

_____

_____

_____

_____

_____

_____

_____

_____

_____

_____

It is still a good day because . . .

_____

_____

_____

_____

_____

_____

_____

_____

_____

_____

_____

_____

_____

_____

_____

_____

_____

_____

_____

_____

_____

Day Twenty-Five

Today, I feel . . .

_____

_____

_____

_____

_____

_____

_____

_____

_____

_____

_____

_____

_____

_____

_____

_____

_____

_____

_____

_____

_____

_____

It is still a good day because . . .

_____

_____

_____

_____

_____

_____

_____

_____

_____

_____

_____

_____

_____

_____

_____

_____

_____

_____

_____

_____

_____

_____

Day Twenty-Six

Today, I feel . . .

_____

_____

_____

_____

_____

_____

_____

_____

_____

_____

_____

_____

_____

_____

_____

_____

_____

_____

_____

_____

_____

_____

_____

It is still a good day because . . .

_____

_____

_____

_____

_____

_____

_____

_____

_____

_____

_____

_____

_____

_____

_____

_____

_____

_____

_____

_____

Day Twenty-Seven

Today, I feel . . .

_____

_____

_____

_____

_____

_____

_____

_____

_____

_____

_____

_____

_____

_____

_____

_____

_____

_____

_____

_____

_____

_____

It is still a good day because . . .

_____

_____

_____

_____

_____

_____

_____

_____

_____

_____

_____

_____

_____

_____

_____

_____

_____

_____

_____

_____

_____

Day Twenty-Eight

Today, I feel . . .

_____

_____

_____

_____

_____

_____

_____

_____

_____

_____

_____

_____

_____

_____

_____

_____

_____

_____

_____

_____

_____

_____

_____

_____

It is still a good day because . . .

_____

_____

_____

_____

_____

_____

_____

_____

_____

_____

_____

_____

_____

_____

_____

_____

_____

_____

_____

_____

_____

Day Twenty-Nine

Today, I feel . . .

_____

_____

_____

_____

_____

_____

_____

_____

_____

_____

_____

_____

_____

_____

_____

_____

_____

_____

_____

_____

_____

_____

It is still a good day because . . .

_____

_____

_____

_____

_____

_____

_____

_____

_____

_____

_____

_____

_____

_____

_____

_____

_____

_____

_____

_____

_____

_____

Day Thirty

Today, I feel . . .

_____

_____

_____

_____

_____

_____

_____

_____

_____

_____

_____

_____

_____

_____

_____

_____

_____

_____

_____

_____

_____

_____

_____

It is still a good day because . . .

_____

_____

_____

_____

_____

_____

_____

_____

_____

_____

_____

_____

_____

_____

_____

_____

_____

_____

_____

_____

"Nobody gets to live backward. Look ahead, there is where your future lies" (Ann Landers). Sometimes we can wear ourselves out by analyzing and planning our future. As a result, we operate on drained energy that takes our focus off of Christ. We must choose to follow him one step at a time and keep our mind on the present journey. He is with us and for us. Are we on the path of his choosing? Our assignment is to listen to him continually, as he has much to communicate to us. As we walk with him, we must trust that he will lead us into our divine destiny. In the end, "It is not the length of life, but the depth of life" (Ralph Emerson).

Life is worth living; therefore, we must not fail to embrace the present. Every minute and every breath is a gift from God. Every day is a miracle, and because God holds our future, we must daily seek his face and stay in his presence, for it's in his presence that we win. There are numerous things to worry about, but choose to trust God and let him carry the burden. "If you don't see yourself as a winner, you can't perform as a winner. You were born to win; but to be a winner, you must plan to win, prepare to win, and expect to win" (Zig Ziglar). Believe in God, hope in God, have faith in God, and find rest in God. By doing so, we gain confidence in knowing that we will never face anything alone. He has everything under control. When times are tough, keep going. We will not experience defeat, or crack under pressure, for the joy of the Lord is our strength. "When you come through it, you survive; when you grow because of it, you thrive; but when you can talk about it, you live" (Bishop Alan G. Porter). When God makes a declaration about us, things change!

__Healing Scriptures:__

These scriptures are the word of God. Read them and take action with your faith.

Psalm 107:20

Luke 17:12-14

Acts 3 2:8

Acts 9 32:34

Exodus 15:26

Matthew 20: 30-34

Acts 14:8-10

Matthew 5:10,13

Proverbs 3:5-8

Isaiah 53:5

Matthew 14:35

Psalm 103:1-3

Luke 13:10-13

Luke 4:18-19

3 John 1:2

Luke 18:27

Isaiah 58:6

Matthew 9:27-30

Proverbs 4:20-27

"When you die, it does not mean that you lose to cancer. You beat cancer by how you live, why you live, and in the manner in which you live"

(Stuart Scott).

Printed in the United States
By Bookmasters

ADVANCED HOLD'EM
Volume 2

ADVANCED HOLD'EM
Volume 2

More Advanced Concepts in No Limit Hold'em
& Example Hands from Both Volumes

Ryan Sleeper

ADVANCED HOLD'EM VOLUME 2

MORE ADVANCED CONCEPTS IN NO LIMIT HOLD'EM & EXAMPLE HANDS FROM BOTH VOLUMES

iUniverse books may be ordered through booksellers or by contacting:

iUniverse
1663 Liberty Drive
Bloomington, IN 47403
www.iuniverse.com
1-800-Authors (1-800-288-4677)

ISBN: 978-1-5320-4680-3 (sc)
ISBN: 978-1-5320-4681-0 (e)

Print information available on the last page.

iUniverse rev. date: 04/26/2018

CONTENTS

PART 4: ADDITIONAL STRATEGIES

SPECIAL THANKS ♣

I would like to give special thanks to everyone who has supported me in writing my first, second, third, and soon to be fourth, poker book. I would be remiss in mentioning all the online games and casino games that have helped me improve my game – and research for all my current and upcoming books.

THANK YOU: Mike Sleeper, Suzanne Sleeper (with Lila, Emily and the Ahwal family), James Sleeper, Shannon Sleeper, Shawn Sweat, Wyatt Sleeper, Tyler Sleeper, William Sleeper (and the rest of the Sleeper family), Brenda Moore, Patricia Olson Bono, RJ Bono (with baby RJ), The Kettlewell, Wieschowski and Jaskolski family, Oliver Smith & the rest of the Smith family (Becky, Nolan and Lenna), Shayna Bono (with Caleb and Cayden), Dylan Lelo, Alex Lelo, Ashley Kimberlin (with Cooper), Sara Moss, Blake Lelo, Chaz Robinson, Amber Kurtz (with Jacob and Brianna), Graylon J. & Jamie Prophet (and the rest of the Prophet family), Bobby and Kirstin Wallace (with Kenny), Sean & Meghan Pavliscak, Daysha Springer, Krista Maggard, Kristi Thompson, Jack Geer, Bonnie Brewer, Keven Johnson, Keve Manning, Jeff Berry, Dave Banwart (and the rest of the Puck's family), The Bradley family, James Quandahl, Jason Cloutier, John Domol, Sam and Anthony Zeer, Eli Ansara, Jordan Russell, Noah Garrett, Garrett Campbell, Ryan Gallagher, Marco

DiFazio, Brooke and Angelique Marshall, Andy and Allison Rybarczyk, Autumn Davis, Dan Walton, James Brooks, Matt Connelly, Eric Lichon, Fierra Harris, Gregory Lapham, Jordan Hayes, Lisa and Lindsay Wieczorek, Nick Pulford, Jeff Price, Sylvia Dao, Jaime Mascorro, Kyle Emmenegger, Josh Green, Brittany Peavy, Sherri Nafus, John Kistner, Keith Barje, Mihaela Mincu, Tom Rogala, Charlene Orlando, Jason Wick, Gwen Trice, Eric Folk and the rest of the Market Source family, and many others.

This book is dedicated to everyone who has supported me in my first venture as an author, and those who have purchased all my books (including this one). Thank you for your trust in my poker skills, my writing ability, and most importantly, me. Your support has encouraged me to continue writing poker books.

A SPECIAL DEDICATION TO
LOUISE BRADLEY (1968-2013).
THANK YOU FOR YOUR SUPPORT
AND ENCOURAGEMENT. YOU
ARE MISSED BY ALL YOUR
FRIENDS AND FAMILY.

AND A VERY SPECIAL THANKS TO
ALEXANDRIA BACON AND JOE
JACKSON FOR THEIR EDITING
AND STYLE TO MAKE THIS BOOK
EVEN SMOOTHER TO READ!

INTRODUCTION ♦

This introduction is not really needed, because I'm sure at this point, you know what to expect for every page you turn (new advanced concepts for no limit hold'em success), but let's just quickly explain what this book is all about.

If you have read Volume 1, then you know the "first installment" of advanced concepts and the basics behind their meanings. Here in Volume 2, I will explain most of them in greater detail. I will show you many examples of these instances in real life situations, so you can have a professional understanding with how these concepts are used correctly. I will also show you more advanced concepts to greater your skills at any poker table, on any level. I've also added some of the hands I played myself and some poker advice of all forms of poker, to complete this volume, as well as a quiz at the end.

Some players may say that these concepts are not advanced; failing to realize that poker is comprised of more average players than anything else. And these concepts are advanced to them. I've seen players play for years and not understand them. I've also seen players who have played for less than a year that understand them completely. All I have to say is that everyone is different. Everyone learns things at different speeds and levels. If you feel these concepts are not advanced, then you should be a well-known poker player making millions of dollars. If you're not, then maybe you're not understanding them correctly or using them at the wrong spot, in the wrong game, against the wrong opponent(s). Who knows? I mean, you're reading this book, which means you are looking for ways to improve your game. If you were a top-notch professional, I don't think this book would be in your hands, other than entertainment. Or maybe, you remember these concepts, but forget to use them at the right times – and against the right opponents. You've done well for yourself, maybe, but there are still some missing pieces of your game that's stopping you from playing at the highest levels.

Chances are you WILL learn something from my books; meaning I have done my job correctly. I have provided information that will help you become a better poker player, not just wasting paper with repetitive words. And that's the idea behind my writing. Not everyone will agree with the concepts, not everyone will learn everything they need to know to be successful, and not everyone will think this book is the greatest poker book in the world, but I can guarantee you this book will be forever thanked by millions of players all across the world, stating that the information found in this book or any of my books has improved their game on some level. Even the smallest improvement makes me proud that I did all this work and was able to share my strategies with you. Thank you!

I have read a lot of poker books by famous players, and some even advanced strategies, and I noticed that it's not really advanced to me, but most of the players today will see it as such. That's just like my books. There will be plenty of players who think my information is not advanced to them, but to the average player, it is. I can't count how many times and how many players fail to use the concepts correctly in live games and Internet games on all different skill levels. I have even seen players on television make mistakes that were covered in my books. True, it's easier when you see the cards, but these are mistakes that are obvious: tells, position strategy, and chip stack situations where a professional (or semi-professional) will continue to make easy mistakes. Maybe they should read my book.

All I'm saying is that all players, on all levels, should learn something from my books. If you feel these concepts are not advanced, then you're a better player than the average. Don't discount the books, just feel good about yourself that you are a good poker player and are considered by most, above average. Enjoy the book and the different situations that occurred in my poker career and see it, if anything, as an enjoyable read on a cold winter night.

PART 1

EXAMPLES FROM VOLUME 1

AFRAID TO FOLD EXAMPLE 1 ♥

We all know that newer players (even some older players) are afraid to fold big hands on any street. It seems like any time they see value, they must make the call, no matter what the price is. Here is an example of a player who is afraid to fold.

During the middle rounds of a tournament, you noticed a tight player sitting to your left. Every time she raises, she always has a big hand, so normally you fold almost any hand when she raises preflop, but this time you make a stand and call her raise with K♣-9♣ because her raise was weak, and you closed the action in the big blind.

Flop comes: K♥-10♦-3♣ and you call her big bet.

Turn comes a 9♦, giving you two pair and you call another big bet by her.

River is a blank and she says, "All-in." You call and lose to her set of tens.

If she is a tight player, then why are you calling her early position raise with K-9? From that position there is no way your hand is good. Then when the king hit on the flop, it just got you into more trouble. Then on the turn, comes a 9, making you virtually drawing dead, now you're in serious trouble. Of course, you fail to see that she is continuing to bet, meaning she has a big hand. She could have pocket Aces or A-K, but you're better off folding your hand preflop. Seeing the flop only got you into more trouble. Last, but not least, you call an all-in bet on the river, against this obviously tight player, and you end up losing a huge pot, and most of your stack. Shocker!

I don't care how your night is going in poker: When a tight player is raising and betting all the way down to the river, fold and save your money for a better spot, because you're obviously beat.

AFRAID TO FOLD EXAMPLE 2 ♠

You are in a one-table tournament (sit-n-go), and a player from middle position raises, he gets one caller before it gets to you. You are sitting on the button with A♦-A♥ and decide to 3-bet. Both players call.

Your preflop play was standard, whereas the original raisers call with mildly loose, but not as loose as the cold caller. Knowing the players, you can tell that the preflop raiser who called your 3-bet has a hand of value and is trying to hit the flop big. He probably puts you on a big ace or a decent pocket pair. He probably has A-Q, or a hand like pocket 10's or Jacks. The cold caller probably has a medium pair or an ace he can't get away from. Let's see how the flop plays out to narrow down their possible holdings.

The flop comes: K♣-Q♦-8♦.

The player in the first position decides to bet out about 2/3 the pot. The player next to act decides to raise. Now it's your turn to act. Knowing the players, the player betting probably has A-K or A-Q and is trying to keep the pot small. The player raising probably has two pair or better, knowing the 3-bettor (you) is still waiting to act. Most players with Aces will either call or raise to protect their hand or make a move to see where he stands. This situation happened to me, and I chose to fold. The hand played out with bets and calls all the way to the river and the player who made the original raise preflop ended up winning the hand with two pair (K-Q). The player who made the flop raise was trying to narrow the field with a straight and flush draw (J-10 of Diamonds.) He missed the turn, and river, and lost a large pot.

DON'T RAISE JUST BECAUSE YOU CAN EXAMPLE 1 ♣

Situations like this normally happen when you're having a bad run at the table and you're trying to get some action your way in attempts to take down some aggressive pots. Say for example, you're sitting at a $10-$20 no limit hold'em table and you keep catching second best. After your first rebuy you decide to start raising just because you can.

Your first hand in this spot, while sitting on the button is 3♦-3♣. A player in first position decides to raise. Mind you, this player is tight-aggressive, so his range is wide, but most likely a hand of real value. One player calls in middle position and you decide to 3-bet. The first position player decides to 4-bet and the middle position player folds. Now it's up to you. You flat call. The flop comes all big cards, and you end up check-folding. Even though you were on the button and making an aggressive play like this is not a bad idea in certain spots, in this situation it's a horrible mistake. The tight-aggressive player has a big hand. And whether you chose to make a squeeze play or not, you ignored his position. Ultimately it cost you more to see a flop then it should have.

If the flop was rags, 10♥-7♦-2♣, then a check-call may be correct if you feel your opponent doesn't have an over pair. Playing against a tight-aggressive player, you know his range can be A-K or a big pocket pair. A call on the flop may be correct, but if he fires a large bet on the turn, then a fold would be your best play. You may choose to raise on the flop to see where he stands, but your chip stack must be large to make such a play. If he calls, then play the turn and river cautiously. Of course, if he plays back at you, then quickly fold.

DON'T RAISE JUST BECAUSE YOU CAN EXAMPLE 2 ◆

A lot of situations explained in this book are for tournaments, so let's dip a little more in to cash games. Aggression is the key to being successful in any cash game, so raising and re-raising are key factors in winning. But all situations don't require raising. Understanding your opponents and how they play different hands in different situations, against different opponents, will determine which hands, of any value, are worth raising.... raising just because you can. Of course, in most situations, you are raising because you sense weakness, or you feel your opponent will fold, but in some spots, you will be raising just because you can. You may have a lot of chips in front of you and want to continue that trend.

Avoiding key spots and raising as your play could cost you more than you previously assumed. Some of these factors may include:

a. Misinterpreting a squeeze play. This is usually done against an opponent who is unaware of this play. You understand its' style, but you're up against an opponent who is legitimately calling with a hand of value and will most likely call your 3-bet.

b. Showing a few bluffs earlier in the game, so you feel you can raise to take down for uncontested pots. Better players will catch on and play back at you with marginal hands.

c. You feel you're playing too tight and your opponents know this, so you start raising without any rhyme or reason.

Here is an example of how you shouldn't raise just because you can.

You're sitting in a high stakes cash game and you've been playing well. Your big hands are being paid off and none of your bluffs are being called. You're sitting in late position with A♦-Q♥ and a player from middle position raises 4 times the big blind. You decide to 3-bet and make it large. You feel you're in control of the pot and the player making the original raise has a large raise and is capable of folding to a large 3-bet. Everyone else folds. When it comes back to the original raiser, he decides to 4-bet a large portion of his stack. You, being a smart player, notices that he is committed and decide to fold. You don't want to risk over half your stack with A-Q. Your opponent probably has A-K or a large pocket pair. Even though this is a cash game, and you should probably make more calls with less valuable hands than you would in a cash game, you feel you're beat and make the quick fold. After you fold, your opponent shows 2♣-3♣.

In all actuality, you chose to raise just because you didn't realize that your opponent knew you were going to make this raise, even though you were in position. He was hoping no one waiting after you would make a play, and that plan worked out. He decided to 4-bet with rags, knowing you couldn't commit yourself unless you had a monster hand. That's the kind of player you don't want to get involved with. He was studying your moves and understood that you like to use position to your advantage. Picking up more information on this opponent will help you make the right decision the next time you're involved in a hand with him. Maybe then you'll remember not to raise just because you can. You raised because you felt your opponent may fold, but you didn't realize that your opponent knew your game plan and was willing to risk it all to not only steal the pot, but to make a statement.

DON'T ACT ON REVENGE EXAMPLE ♥

Acting on revenge is a recipe for disaster. This situation usually happens after a tough lose against an opponent who probably shouldn't have been involved in the pot in the first place. I remember one time where I was playing, and this occurred. I felt like acting on revenge, but I held my play back and waited for a better spot.

I was playing at a $1/$2 no limit hold'em cash at MGM casino and I was in early position with

K♥-K♠.

The player next to me called as well as the player in the small blind. Everyone else folded. The player next to me was playing solidly, with the ability to mix things up, but in this situation, I felt his range was pretty high. He had position on me, but with me holding the second best possible starting hand, I knew my Kings were a huge favorite. The player in the small blind, on the other hand, was a typical newbie type player (even though he was old) and was capable of playing any hand of value. Hands that would include any ace, two face cards or any hand that would be a favorite against a random hand.

The flop came A♣-8♦-5♥.

The player in the small blind instantly came out firing a bet (2/3 the pot). I thought about it for about a second before mucking my hand. The player next to me called. They both checked the turn and the player in the small blind made a value bet on the river as the other guy mucks his hand face up (9♥-7♥).

The bettor shows A♠-4♦.

I was shocked to see what he flipped over. I angrily spoke under my breath, "How can you call an early position raise, out of position, with a weak ace." The player next to me shakes his head in agreement.

Now, my first instinct was to act on revenge against this player, but I knew that wasn't the best option. With the information given to me, I knew I could out play him in a bettor spot in a future hand and not only get my chips back that I lost to him, but the rest of his stack. Unfortunately, a few hands later, a player takes his entire bankroll on another similar situation. I was unable to get my chips back from him when he chose to not rebuy, but I wasn't surprised he lost his stack playing as bad as he did against me, against another player.

Now, every situation is not like this, for example I remember another time while playing at the same place at the same stakes, when a situation very similar to this came up (I was not involved in the pot). It was against two loose players where one lost a huge pot against the other on a bad beat, and he felt he wanted revenge on this player. He chose to ignore all the factors in that player's style and only focus on playing hands where he was involved in, which were very few. Here's how the hand played out:

Tight player: Q♥-Q♣
Revenge player: A♦-J♣

The revenge player raises preflop and the tight player decides to 3-bet. The revenge player calls in position. The flop rolls out:

A♣-Q♦-9♣.

The tight player checks and the revenge player bets pot. The tight player check-raises almost all his stack, and the revenge player flat calls (ignoring the tight image of the 3-bet preflop, the check raise postflop and the fact that he is practically committed in this pot). The turn is a blank and the tight player pushes all-in. The revenge player calls instantly. The river pairs the board and the tight player wins the pot with a full house.

You would think in most spots this may seem like a normal play, they just got outplayed, but if you think about it, there is no way the A-J was the best hand at any time. The 3-bet preflop raised some flags as well as the check-raise on the flop. The revenge player solely acted on trying to win his chips back and not the obvious factors that his hand is clearly beaten. When you focus on revenge or playing a hand while steaming after a tough beat, you tend to ignore the basic "tells" of your opponents. This usually results in losing more chips than you should have. Take some time to relieve any negative thoughts and focus on playing poker the right way; making correct decisions and adjustments based on your opponent's style.

ATTACK THE WEAK
PLAYER EXAMPLE ♠

Attacking the weak player sounds kind of obvious, but a lot of players ignore this cardinal rule of poker. Because when you try to out play a better player, you usually go home broke (unless you get really lucky). And, when you try to outplay and win chips from a weaker player, you usually walk away with more than just a story. You've established the fact the he's weak because you recognized his style of play and can make the proper plays against him. Here's a good example of attacking the weak player:

You've been playing at this current table for the past 3 hours and you've noticed that seats 4, 7 and 10 are weak. They seem to play only premium hands and will fold to large bets. During one hand, you decide to raise preflop (you're in seat 2 – in this hand you are in early position) with A♦-Q♦. Everyone folds except seat 7, 9 and 10. Lucky for you, two of the three are consider weak players. In your mind, you'll be able to outplay them if they miss the flop and the tight-aggressive player in seat 9 doesn't connect well.

The flop slowly rolls out as you look at the players involved and see how they react, showing:

Q♣-10♥-2♦.

The tight-aggressive player keeps staring at the flop as though he missed it but is acting kind of strong. He may have connected on some level, but he knows there are still 3 other players still involved in this pot.

The player in seat 10 is first to act and chooses to check (he missed the flop). The player next to act is me and with player 10 still waiting to act, I decide to check to see where I stand. The next player checks (definitely missed the flop), while the last player decides to bet a pot size bet (he hit something, but probably not better than my hand). The tight-aggressive player calls and so do I, while the last player folds.

The turn is a 7 of diamonds. This time the tight-aggressive player bets out (probably representing a middle pair and a diamond draw). With the weak player still waiting to act, I decide to raise to narrow the field and protect my hand. The weak player calls (no surprise), while the tight-aggressive player, knowing his position and the players action decides to fold. The river is a 9♥ and I make a large bet, knowing the player will most likely call, feeling he wasn't on a straight draw. I didn't bet too large to force him out, but enough to get full value for my hand. On the turn, I wanted to push out the stronger player and go heads up against just the weak player. In this situation, the weak player calls and shows K♥-Q♠ and I took down the pot.

This example shows a more advanced way to attack the weaker players. In most cases, attacking these types of players will involve seeing most flops when they are involved in the hand and you are in position. With strong players playing along, you'll be able to force them out when you feel you have a stronger hand and the weak players are check-calling the whole way. Be aggressive in these spots to assure your chances of winning those pots are most consistent. Of course, if it's just you and the weaker players seeing these flops, then it should be easy to know when you're beat and you when you have a chance to double up.

DON'T TAKE LONG SHOTS
EXAMPLE 1 ♣

When you take long shots, you're going against the odds of winning. Even though some factors may support your play to call a bet; instinct, position, implied odds, you're deciding to continue with a hand based on long shot odds. Here is an example of taking a long shot.

You're in a middle of a tournament and you have an average stack. Throughout the tournament you've been struggling and barely surviving with your chip stack. You finally win a big pot against a loose player by setting the trap. Now your average chip stack seems bigger than it is, and you decide to call on the cut off spot with 10-9 suited against an early position raise.

The player in early position is playing tight-aggressive but his plays of late seem predictable, so you feel you can out play him postflop. The flop comes:

6♣-8♠-A♦, giving you a gut-shot straight draw.

The preflop raiser decides to bet 2/3 the pot and you call chasing the straight draw. Everyone else folds. The turn is a 9♦, giving you middle pair and the draw. Now the preflop raiser bets pot and you go into a deep thought process... or are you? The turn gave you more outs to make you think you should stay in the hand. Not realizing that against his range, he probably has you dominated and the price is costs to see the river is not giving you the right price to call, but you call anyways thinking he has top pair with a big kicker.

Then river comes a 3♣.

This time the aggressor bets half the pot. What is your play as well as your thought process?

The bettor is showing strength on every street which indicates he is holding a strong hand. Even though you're only calling his bets, he put you on a draw or an ace with a weaker kicker. His half size pot bet on the river shows he wants some value. You decide to fold because you feel you're beat, and he flashes pocket Aces for a set. You just lost more than you should have. The best play would have been the fold on the turn, if not the preflop, based on all the information you've obtained prior to the hand in relation to his style and your recently accumulation of chips. Calling the bet on flop with only a gut-shot and then calling the pot size bet on the turn because it gave you more outs (in theory) cost you a lot of chips. Taking this long shot hurt you because you failed to see the information for what it actually was: a long shot that put a big dent in your chip stack. If you wanted to play this hand preflop then a quick fold on the flop would have been your best choice (see *future betting* for more information).

DON'T TAKE LONG SHOTS EXAMPLE 2 ♥

Like the previous example, taking long shots aren't always the best option even though in some cases I would say go for it and hope for the best, especially when the pot is larger than normal and it's a multi-way pot against opponents who play ABC.

Here is another example of where taking a long shot is not a good idea. This example is even more about odds, percentage wins and pot size.

You're playing in a cash game (blinds at $5-$10) and you're first to act with A♦-Q♦ and you decide to raise to $40. You get two callers before it hits the button (who folds) and the player in the small blinds calls as well. The big blind folds. Pot is $170.

The flop comes J♦-10♥-4♣. The small checks and you decide to bet $85. You get one caller in late position and the small blinds calls as well. Pot is now at $425.

The turn is an 8♦. Now you have a straight and flush draw with your over cards. The small blind checks again and you decide to bet $275. The late position player folds and the small blind shoves all-in for an additional $600. What is your play with the pot being at $1,300 and you having 15 outs (an ace or queen is most likely no good in this spot) for a positive winning hand?

It's costing you $600 to see a river with 15 outs giving you 3-1 odds on a pot price showing 2-1 ($600 to win $1,300). First of all, the odds are not in your favor and not including his range of hands that he would be making this play with.

If your opponent has Q-9, then your odds of winning are only 27% and if he has a set, then your odds only increase to 29.5%. And with other hands to factor in, your best odds of winning are around 32%+ if he has 2 pair (or a draw as well). Is calling the right play even though it's a cash game?

The odds don't seem to be in your favor and there's a lot of players who would call this bet and I wouldn't necessarily frown upon them, but I feel this is straight gambling against a player who obviously has a big hand. You decide to call, and the river is a blank. Your opponent shows a set of 10's, which decreased your odds if a diamond hit that paired the board.

This situation, I feel, is taking a long shot when the odds are not in your favor. The hand looked nice, but the price and the situation were a sign of a move that should have had your cards in the muck. The turn check-raise signaled that. You'll see more players make this call, in cash games more than you would in a tournament, but in poker, it's not about winning the most pots, it's about making the correct decision. More often than not, I would fold, but in some cases, if I wanted or needed to gamble, I would call his check-raise. It's a long shot, and usually not the right play, but there's always someone out there who strives on getting lucky.

PUTTING YOUR OPPONENT
ON A HAND EXAMPLE 1 ◆

Putting your opponent on hand is crucial in any poker game. If you only focus on what you're holding, then you'll never know if you're making the correct decision or not. You may be choosing to be aggressive when you should be slow-playing, or you decide to slow-play your hand when you should be playing it very aggressively.

Putting your opponent on hand will help you determine what the best play against them is. Of course, we know that when a player is very aggressive, and his range is unpredictable then we know to set traps more often against this player and let him/her do most of the betting. When a player is fearful and backs-off to aggression, then you know we must be aggressive and bet or raise more often. Here is an example of putting your opponent on a hand.

You're at a one-table tournament and you are sitting in the small blind with 10-8 suited (probably my favorite hand) when the player under the gun raises preflop 3x the big blind. There are a few callers before it gets to you and decide to call for implied odds as well as being in position (your chip stack can afford it, plus you know this opponent has a soft postflop game). The flop comes:

Q♦-J♥-3♣. Everyone checks.

The turn card comes an 8♦, and everyone checks again. The river is a 7♠ and the player who raises preflop bets half the pot. What do you think he has? While everyone else folded, it is now up to me. My instincts all along are with A-K or maybe a small pocket pair, but I'm leaning more towards a big ace. This hand actually happened to me and I called pretty quickly with a pair of 8's. I was right as he flipped over Ace-10.

Even though his raise came from an early position, I felt I could outplay him after the flop. I didn't feel he had a big pair because he would have made a bet on the flop or turn. I knew he didn't have Ace-Queen or Jack because he would have also made a bet prior to the river. I could only put him on a missed hand or a small pair. I was quite sure my pair of 8's was good, so my quick call paid off. If he would have made a bet on the flop, I would have folded. Once the turn hit and gave me my pair, then I put him on a hand that missed the board. Gladly enough, the river was a blank and I knew I had the best hand.

PUTTING YOUR OPPONENT
ON A HAND EXAMPLE 2 ♣

Another example of putting an opponent on a hand is when he plays out of ordinary preflop. Most players play preflop rather standard, but every once in a while, a player(s) will make a play that will make you scratch your head. Here's an example of this situation.

You're in a tournament and a player in early position raises 4x the big blind, and before it gets to you (on the button), another player (tight-aggressive) 3-bets.

You look down and see K♦-K♣.

You decide to call, hoping the original raiser doesn't 4-bet. There's no need to push because you may be beat by the original raiser, and if not him then the player who made the 3-bet. One of them could easily hold Aces. The big blind, who is sitting there with a big stack and plays very loose, decides to push all-in. Did not expect that from that type of player. The original raiser folds as well as the 3-bettor. Now it's up to you.

The original raise probably has a decent pair, while the 3-bettor had a similar hand, if not A-K. The loose player could be making a squeeze play, but from his past plays, this doesn't seem like his style. You're sitting there with the second best starting hand, but you feel your opponent could easily have Aces. He may be loose, but he is raising a tight early position raiser, a middle position re-raiser and a caller. Do you call?

In most situations, I think you should call. If he has Aces, then you'll just have to pay him off. Any other hand and you're a big favorite. If it was me in this spot, I would call. I'm not folding Kings preflop against this type of player. If his image and style was that of a tighter player, then a fold might be the best play. I really don't think he would show so much aggression against so many players with anything but Aces. So, with all the information you've gathered and the hands you put your opponents on, then push all your chips in middle and hope you don't run up against pocket Aces.

This reminds me of a hand I played in a cash game recently. This unexpected play took place on the river, but it was a play I never expected from this player.

During a cash game at MGM, I was first to act and limped with K♠-Q♠. The aggressive player at the table raised it to $10. The player in the big blind (an older rookie style of player) calls, and so do I.

The flop comes Q♦-9♠-3♣. We all checked. The turn comes a K♦ (giving me top 2 pair) and I bet $20. They both call. The river is an A♣. I checked hoping to induce a bluff from the aggressive player and he bets $55. The player in the big blind quickly calls, which I was not expecting at all. His play was totally shocking, and now it's up to me. I know I have the aggressive player beat, but I'm not sure what the player in the small blind is holding, so I go in my "tank" and start thinking of his range.

Before the Ace hit the river, there's no way he has me beat, so eliminate all the possible hands he could have, which includes a set. Once he calls on the river, I must think about which hands he could be holding that includes an ace.

1. A-K? No! He would have been more aggressive with it.
2. A-Q? No! Same as above.
3. A weaker two pair? Possibly. Maybe he thought I was weak on the river and called thinking his two pair was good.
4. A straight? No! He would have raised instead of just calling.
5. Does he have Ace-5 or Ace-3? No way! He called a bet on the turn with basically bottom pair, hoping to improve? That would be a horrible decision against 2 players of our caliber.

I decided to call based on all this information as well as what the pot was offering me. The original bettor mucks his hand and the player in the small blind flips over A-5. He called a $20 bet on the turn with a caller with second from bottom pair and he hits the river for the winning hand. Needless to say, I wasn't very happy!

BLUFFING IS OVERRATED
EXAMPLE 1 ♥

Bluffing is overrated when you play a hand and only focus on bluffing. This usually happens if the cards are not coming your way or you just lost a huge pot in a cash game and you're trying to get your money back too quickly. Sure, the pot may be large enough, and you may be able to pull off the bluff, but do you really have all the information needed to pull out a successful bluff when you're stuck?

Here is an example of when bluffing is overrated, or more simply put, when you're bluffing at the wrong pot.

You're playing at a casino during one of its local low buy-in tournaments and during the middle stages of it, you find yourself at the average stack.

On this particular hand you're sitting in the cut-off seat with 7♦-2♠.

A player in first position limps, while a player in middle position, whose range is larger than most, decides to raise 4x the big blind. It gets folded around to you. You know his range is usually weak, so you decide to 3-bet bluff to 13x the big blind. Your thinking is to push out the players and steal some blinds. If the player in first position had a big hand, then he would have more than likely raised first, and the middle position raiser is loose, and if we raise large enough, then he couldn't call, so we could take some quick blinds with the worst starting hand in hold'em.

The limper calls and the original raiser goes all-in. You only have 7-2, so this is an easy fold. While the original limper calls with pocket Kings.

The board runs dry against the all-in player who flips over A♥-Q♥.

And you just lost a chunk of your chips trying to bluff your way by stealing some blinds against players you thought were easy targets.

Let's dive into this hand a little more thoroughly.

A player is playing a hand in first position, which is a sign by itself that he probably has a playable hand, even to a raise. The loose player, who raises preflop, could hold any two cards and is trying to bully the table against possible weak blinds and a player (you) who is at average stack or below, and will only continue with a hand that's in the top 5% range. As long as the limper isn't holding pocket Aces or Kings (or even A-K), then he is in good shape. If the loose player knows about the limper in first position and puts him on a smaller pocket pair or a weaker ace, then his raise is being made based on information gathered throughout the tournament. He does have position on him postflop and could probably out play him if the board runs dry.

You're sitting there with nothing, and you're trying to steal the blinds, against opponents you feel are capable of folding in this spot. What you have failed to see is that both players are making the right moves to utilize their holdings and their preflop actions speak for themselves.

The limper knows that a loose player will raise, so when it gets back to him, he can either call and wait for the flop to push, or 4-bet and get all his chips in with the best hand. The raiser knows the limper has a decent hand and is trying to force him to make a decision for all his chips, by rising all-in. The raiser feels the limper could fold, but if he decides to call or push, then he has a hand of value. You, on the other hand, got involved when you shouldn't have, and it cost you some of your chips. You saw an opportunity but failed to see the proper information to proceed. You though you could steal the blinds against a first position player who is playing his hand weak and a loose player whose range is so weak, that he could be bluffing himself.

Next time you get involved, make sure position, player knowledge and proper adjustments are the primary reason for raising with a weak hand. Sometimes this play may work, but if the other players at the table are better than the average player, then trying to steal blinds against typical preflop plays, is a recipe for disaster.

BLUFFING IS OVERRATED
EXAMPLE 2 ♠

Here is another example where bluffing is overrated or a bluff that will surely fail more often than not.

You're playing in a $5-$10 cash game and you're on the button with K♠-Q♣. There are two players who limp, in late positon, before it gets to you and decide to raise to $45. The small blind decides to call, and only one limper calls.

The flop is A♥-6♣-6♦. The small blind checks and so does the player in late positon. Now is a good time to make a continuation bet, so you do with a bet of $90. Both players call.

The turn is a 10♣. Both players check again. You decide to make another bet, this time. $275. The small blind calls and now it's up to the player in late position. After some thought, he decides to push all-in, and you make the easy fold with only a gut-shot straight draw. The small blind quickly calls.

The river is a 3♥, and the small blind flips over 6♠-7♠, while the late position players mucks 7♥-7♦ face up. Trip 6's takes the large pot, while the late position player gets mad and walks away. My question is, "How did the player with pocket 7's not know the small blind had the better hand?"

To me, it was clear that the player in the small blind had a big hand, once he called on the turn. Of course, his call on the flop was a little suspicious too. In this particular hand, I could have easily put him on three 6's, especially with an ace on the board and against two players. He played the hand exactly like a rookie would play it; wait until the turn to extract more chips. I think a river raise would have been better, if he felt I also had a hand of value.

I guess the late position player thought he could steal the pot with a big raise. Did he even think about what we were holding? I mean, my raise preflop could have been a hand of strength, ignoring the fact that I raised on the button. The small blind calling preflop stated that he had a hand of value as well.

When the flop rolls out, I make the continuation bet and get a caller before it gets to him. With two players, you must think one of us has an ace and the other player is probably floating or chasing a long shot. True, I could be bluffing, but you must think the small blind has the ace, on a board like that, or at least a hand that has potential of improving.

When the turn hits and the same actions take place, then his raise makes no sense; we clearly have strong hands at this point. My continuation bet on the turn could still mean I'm trying to steal the pot, but when the small blind calls, you must believe he has a strong hand. By raising on the turn, you should know that I may fold, but it's unlikely that the small blind will fold as well. If he is willing to call two bets, then he is either holding an ace with a decent kicker or trip 6's. If he doesn't have trip 6's, then he could fold his ace, depending on what he puts his opponent on and how much it's going to cost him to see the river. If he folds, then you're in great shape, your bluff (semi-bluff) worked, but I've seen this type of situation many times before, I can almost always say that the player in the small blind, with this type of information, will call every time. Now you must hit one of your four outs to win.

Some players will call on the flop with nothing against a continuation bet to steal the pot on the turn, but when he failed to fire one with then 10 hit the turn, then you know he's not trying to steal the pot. He either has a missed hand opportunity or he is slowing playing a monster.

I put him on trip 6's once he called on flop. Most players wouldn't call preflop with a weak ace out of position in this type of game. If he had a bigger ace, then I would suspect him to 3-bet. The only reason why I feel the button made another bet on turn was to see for sure if the player in the small blind really did have three-of-a-kind. Once he called the turn bet, then it was clear he did. If he really did have an ace, then a check on the river would be the best play, if you didn't improve. How the player in late position missed all this information is beyond me. Bluffing can work, but not when it's obvious your opponent has a big hand.

TAKE RISKS EXAMPLE 1 ♦

Taking risks is crucial in any poker game. From time to time, you'll have to go against the odds, or your reads, and gamble by risking your hand (and chip stack) in a position where you know, or feel, you are behind. Here is a good example of taking a risk.

You're in a middle of a cash game and you decide to see a flop with K♥-J♥ after one raise and two callers. You were sitting in late position, where the raise came from a player with a wide range and felt you could outplay them postflop.

The flop comes: 6♥-9♦-10♣. The original raiser makes a small bet and both players call before it gets to you. You decide to call with a gut-shot and a backdoor flush draw.

The turn comes: 2♥. This time the original raiser makes an almost pot sized bet and gets one caller. Now it's up to you. With the weak flop bet and two callers, this is an easy call or catch a much-needed card. Now he decides to bet a large bet on the turn, while still getting one caller. The original raiser is playing like, either the turn gave him more outs, or he wanted action on a weak flop. The caller is playing his hand like he had top pair with a decent kicker or a strong draw with a pair.

It seems like this would be an easy call, but you must feel you are way behind, and your only out is hitting a heart for a flush. Even though the original raiser may have an over pair and the caller may have a hand that could outdraw you, I'd still take the risk and call the bet. Who knows, they may check the river card (if it's a blank) and you could steal the pot.

You decide to call, and the river is a blank. The original raiser bets pot and the other caller folds. You must make an easy fold now, since it's clear he has an over pair (probably Aces). A lot of players will make a small bet on the flop with a big hand to induce action. More people are more inclined to chase hands when there is a larger bet on the flop, than a small one. In many cases, on the turn the original bettor will check and give his opponents an unwilling chance to steal the pot.

The worst card would have been hitting a King or a Jack. If he makes the same large bet, then you'd have to decide if he really does have an over pair or he is trying to bluff the pot with a missed draw, assuming you missed as well. You definitely have to know your opponents game to understand his plays. You may think top pair is good, but I've seen a lot of players lose because they failed to make the obvious fold. I have no problem laying down top pair if I feel my opponent has me beat.

TAKE RISKS EXAMPLE 2 ♣

Here is another good example of taking a risk in a poker game. In this situation, we'll focus on a tournament.

You're playing in a satellite at the WSOP, and during the later stages of it, you find yourself holding pocket 8's in late position. There is a raise in early position from a player who plays straight forward but raises with any ace and any pair. The player in middle position decides to move all-in with a stack about even with you. Now it's up to you.

Your stack is clearly below average and you're trying anything you can to win this tournament to play in a bigger one. Against two players, pocket 8's, are not the best hand to go with, but it's a good opportunity to triple up. Do you take the risk? I've been in this spot twice in my life that I can remember. One time I folded and would have won, the other time called and lost to A-Q.

I think more often than not, in this situation (a satellite), you should take the risk and hope to triple up. Of course, if you feel one of your opponents has an over pair to your 8's, then it's a simple fold. Your gut instinct will tell which play to make. I went with my gut both times, and he was right, but unfortunately, the luck factor plays his role from time to time.

What other mediocre hands would be worth calling in this spot?

1. A lower pocket pair than 8's?
2. A medium ace?
3. Two face cards?
4. Suited connectors (i.e. 9-10 or J-10)

Whichever play you decide, make sure you have enough information on your opponents to make the right play. I honestly feel, even against two players, you should call with any pocket pair 8's or above or two face cards. Chances are one of your opponents has an ace, and with face cards, you could be a 3 to 2 underdog or ahead with your pocket pair. There's no way I would call with any ace, unless it's A-K or A-Q suited, and I definitely wouldn't call with a medium suited connector. If this was a cash game or a multi-table tournament, and I was short-stacked, then I would call with almost any of these possible hands described.

CALLING WITH NOTHING EXAMPLE ♥

Calling with nothing is not something you should do often, but in certain situations, it's a great way to steal pots from players who play postflop at a weak level.

Here is an example of calling with nothing... and it's the right move.

You're playing a multi-table tournament online and during the middle stages of it, you find yourself among the chip leaders, with control of the table at which you are currently sitting. The cards are dealt, and you have K♦-Q♦ in early position and decide to limp in because the table is playing soft and you want to see a cheap flop. Only this time a player on the button decides to make a standard raise. This player is a little loose, but plays postflop kind of weak, so you decide to call as well as two other players.

The flop comes: A♣-8♠-9♦.

You check and so do the other callers. The preflop raiser bets half the pot. Seems like a typical continuation bet and if you always fold to this type of play, then you'll never be successful. Of course, on the other hand, he could be trying to get some more chips by betting weak, hoping someone will call with a weak draw or ace. You decide to call to make a play on the turn. The other players fold.

The turn comes: J♦.

You decide to take a stab at the flop to see where you stand. The player on the button flat calls. Not what you wanted, but since he didn't raise, you feel he may have a weak hand himself, or at least some kind of draw. Most players who raise preflop, will continue to take the lead on all streets, but in this situation, he has given you the lead in the hand. The river is a blank and your only move is to make another bet (a large one) or check it and see what your opponent does.

If you check and he checks, then at least you have some showdown value. If you check and he bets, then you must decide if he has a made hand or is trying to take the pot away from you, since you gave up when the river hits. In this situation, it's best to make another bet, since you have control and hope he folds. The bet should be large enough or scare him, and an odd amount to make him think. If there is $1000 in the pot, then a bet around $765 should make him ponder his decision. If he has a hand, then he probably would have raised on the turn, unless he's the type of player to wait until the river to make this move. Some players may even call your large bet, on the river, with a mediocre hand if they feel their hand has some value. If he is that type of player, then I would check and hope he checks as well.

RAISE WHEN YOU SENSE WEAKNESS EXAMPLE 1 ♠

Knowing your opponent's game will help you make plays where you sense they are weak, and you can be aggressive and start raising pots, forcing them to fold. If you understand how they play certain hands in different situations, then you'll have a better understanding how to play against them; making the proper adjustments and forcing to lay down hands they are trying to steal.

Here is an example of raising when you sense weakness.

You're playing in a local tournament and the table you are currently at is playing a little tight, allowing you to steal blinds, play aggressive postflop and bluff more often than you're used to. During the later stages of this tournament you find yourself sitting with A♣-K♣ in early position, and you raise 3.5 the big blind. A player in the small blind (a tight-aggressive player), 3-bets you 9x the big blind. At this point, everyone else folds, and now it's up you. His style and playing after an early position raise indicates that he has a big hand. You decide to just call and see a flop.

The flop comes: J♠-3♥-6♣.

With this board, it doesn't seem like your opponent's range hit anything, unless he is sitting there with an over pair. Your opponent decides to check (which you didn't expect at all), assuming he missed the flop, and you make a bet to see where you stand. You bet slightly less than half the pot and your opponent quickly makes a min check-raise. He is raising with an over pair as you suspected?

You decide to call with over cards to see what the turn brings, because from your opponent's history, he doesn't play over pairs like this. The turn is flipped over and it's a 9♦. With a board of J♠-3♥-6♣-9♦, your opponent quickly checks. Hmm! It seems like he has given up the pot. You sense that he was just trying to make a play at the flop with nothing, so you called his check-raise. Now, he's checking again on the turn. Will he check-raise again? Probably not. You decide to make a bigger bet, and your opponent quickly calls. On the river, another blank hits, and this time your opponent makes a small bet. At this point, you're thinking:

> First, he: Flop check-raises,
> Then he: Turn check-call,
> And finally, he: River bets

This pattern of betting seems a little off and it's telling a story that doesn't add up. You're sensing weakness on his part with a dry board, since you didn't show too much aggression. You decide to push all-in, assuming he would only call with a monster hand, and your opponent quickly folds, flashing A♥-K♦.

RAISE WHEN YOU SENSE
WEAKNESS EXAMPLE 2 ♦

Here is another example of raising when you sense weakness, only this time we'll be discussing a hand during a cash game.

You're playing a small stakes cash game at your local casino. You've been playing really well, and your stack shows it. You feel you have a good understanding on how everyone is playing at your table, when a new player sits down a few seats to your right. He decides to play the first hand he is dealt. It's up to you, and you have A♥-Q♦, and decide to make a standard raise. You get two callers before it gets to the new player. He calls.

The flop comes: A♣-10♠-8♦.

The new player bets out half the pot and you call. Everyone else folds.

The turn comes: J♥.

Your opponent makes another small bet and this time you decide to raise to see if he really has a hand. He quickly 4-bets. What is he possibly holding?

When he sat down, he posted the big blind, so he could play the hand. With this action, he could be holding any two cards. He also called your raise preflop, which, hopefully, means he has a hand of value. He then bets into you on the flop and raises your bet on the turn. His demeanor displays a level of maniac, but maybe he is trying to take control of the table/pot.

With this information, and having top pair with a good kicker, you decide to 5-bet him enough to make a decision for almost all his chips. If he has you beat, which he could, since you don't have enough information on this guy, then it's a lesson learned. Your opponent ponders for a while, staring at you. Eventually he decides to fold face down, not knowing what he really had. My guess is he was trying to be aggressive and win as much as he could as early on as he could.

This actually happened at MGM where I was playing, and I wish I would have sat back or played the hand softer, so I could find out more about his style of player. Luckily, he folded, and I dragged in a nice pot. About an hour later he went broke. My assumption of him trying to bully the table early on seemed to be right. I never like to get involved in a hand with a player I don't know much about, but I sensed a little weakness on his part, so I had to do what I had to do.

3-BETTING WITH RAGS EXAMPLE ♣

3-betting with rags is a play that is more common is cash game, of course it's rare in any game, but you'll see less of this play in tournaments. Here is an example when 3-betting with rags is profitable in a tournament setting.

You're playing in a major tournament and you have an average stack during the later stages of it, and you're approaching the bubble. You've been playing at your table a while now, with the same opponents when you find yourself with:

J♥-5♥ in the big blind. The player in first position makes a standard 3x raise with one caller (the button) before it's to you. You decide to call, even though you are out of position with a weak hand, to see a flop at a good value. And based on your opponent's play postflop, you have good history of outplaying them.

The flop comes: K♥-3♦-6♣.

Everyone checks.

The turn is a 6♦.

The player in first position makes a small bet and the player on the button just flat calls. Now it's up you. Even though you have nothing, you decide to raise to see where your opponents stand. Unfortunately, they both call.

The river is a 2♥. The early position pauses for a while before making a half-size bet. The button decides to raise 3x his bet. What could they be holding?

The player in first positon, I feel, is betting on the river to steal the pot against two opponents who are showing weakness. He probably has a big ace or a weak pair. The player on the button probably has a hand with a weak king. The button could also be trying to steal the pot himself, giving the face that the early position raiser and I haven't shown any strength as well. And with a board like this, unless you have a big hand, everyone at the table is weak.

I decide to re-raise (3-bet) with my rags to see if my instincts were right. The player in early position folds, while button ponders for a few minutes. After about 3 minutes, the button folds flashing pocket 7's. I guess he assumed I have a king or hit a third 6 for trips. Knowing how my opponents play position and certain hands (along with my instincts), I was able to 3-bet with rags and take down a nice pot. Of course, making a play like this is rare, and usually only seen preflop, I knew I had a good chance of making my opponents fold, since they didn't show strength on any street, and even though the river wasn't a scare card, I knew they couldn't call unless they had a pair or Kings or better.

TAKE CONTROL OF THE TABLE EXAMPLE ♥

Taking control of the table is a sure way to take down more pots than the average player. Whether you're getting lucky or it just appears you're catching cards, taking control of the table can help you win pots early in the game to set the momentum during the later rounds. Of course, taking control of the pot in the later rounds, when blinds are high, is also a great way to assure yourself a successful session at a cash game or making the money in a tournament.

Here is an example of taking control of the table.

You're playing a tournament at your local casino and you want to start off being aggressive with low blinds to help you have a large stack early on (you are aware of going broke early, but you're willing to risk it at this caliber). During the first rounds of the tournament you find yourself catching nothing but rags, so you fold more often than you like. Finally, you find yourself in position to play a hand because everyone has folded before you and you're in the hijack seat.

You have 10♣-6♦ and raise 3.5 the blinds. You get one caller in the small blind and everyone else folds. The flop is dry, and you make a continuation bet. Your opponent folds. That's just one hand, but let's continue. The very next hand, you decide to make a similar play and it pays off. You fold a couple weak hands after that but continue to use position to make raises with weaker hand and large continuation bets to take down uncontested pots. Now your opponents are starting to see that when this hand comes up.

You have K♥-7♠ in the small blind and call a raise from a loose player in middle position. Even though you are out of position with a weak hand against a loose player, your "lucky of late" image may help you win this hand.

The flop is: A♦-10♣-4♠. You check to the preflop raiser and makes a standard size bet. You decide to call, floating to the turn. The turn is a 9♦. You check again, and your opponent makes a half size bet, only this time you choose to check-raise his bet 4x. He thinks for a while and decides to call. The river is a blank and your only choice is to make a large bet, so you do. You bet almost the size of the pot and he folds face up: A♣-5♣. You take down the pot with King high.

Did he make a good lay down based on the odds of him being beat or did he fold because you've been running well lately and felt he was beat? Your raise on the turn indicated that you probably hit two pair and was hoping to see an improvement on the river or at least hoping you would check it down. The fact that he was loose and folded a hand of value, my guess is that even though loose players watch the action throughout the tournament (not as well as tight-aggressive players), he knew you were catching cards (in theory) prior to this hand, and felt you are playing a rush with a hand that could beat his top pair.

Some occasions, for this to work, you'll have to show your hand to perceive the image of a player who is catching cards. So, when you're involved in a pot against a player who has a hand of value, they'll be able to lay it down if you play your hand right (and aggressive enough), to force them out of the pot, when it's not the right price to call.

This is almost labeled "table image." Whether you're playing tight or loose or even someone who appears be on one way or another, you can use that image to take control of the table, by make the proper plays to accurately defend that image to take pots down you wouldn't normally take down. I like to start a tournament a little tighter to see how my opponents are playing, and once I get a feel on the flow of the game and how they are playing, then my image will guide to more bluffed pots. When they see I'm starting to bluff more often, then I choose to make the same plays, only this time I have a strong hand to back it up.

RELY ON LUCK EXAMPLE ♠

Relying on luck is a strategy most players shouldn't rely on, but in certain situations, you must rely on luck. In case like this, you're either getting the right price to call or the best chance to double, or even triple up in a tournament, while you're sitting there with a short-stack. Here is an example of relying on luck.

You're playing in a multi-table tournament and you're nearing the bubble. Your goal in this tournament is to win, and not just cash. You've been playing well the entire tournament, but you're sitting at an average stack, when you find yourself with 5♠-5♣ on the button. There is a raise from an early position from a loose player whose range is unpredictable from any position, and you get two callers before it comes to you. Some players may choose to raise with this hand to force the callers out and hope to go one-on-one with the loose player. Others may even fold, and save their chips for a better spot, but you choose to flat call and see what the flop brings.

The flop is: 4♥-3♦-2♣. The loose player is first to act and makes a standard c-bet. One player calls and now it's up to you.

The loose player could be holding any two cards. He could have any over pair, or at least 2 over cards. The caller probably has a hand of value, but not a hand worth risking too many chips. You could flat call and see a turn, but in this situation, you decide to raise 3x the bet. The loose player thinks for a minute, then pushes all-in...he has you covered. The other player folds quickly. What is your move?

At the point, the loose player probably has you beat, but you've invested so much, and with the bubble approaching, you decide to call.

Your opponent flips over: 6♠-6♥. You have 6 outs.

The turn comes a K♣ and the river bring a 6♦, and you win with a straight.

Even though his raise came from an early position, and his range being larger than most, he actually had a hand of value. You were hoping he would have had a medium or strong ace, or even a similar hand like he had (medium pair), and with your raise, you could scare him off, but I guess he felt he had the best hand and chose to push all-in. Luckily, you hit one of your 6 outs to win the hand and surpass the bubble.

This is just one of many situations where you must rely on luck. True, you could have had the best hand, when you call his all-in, but in this spot, you were beat. On some occasions, you will have to call a large bet (sometimes an all-in bet) knowing you are beat. If the pot is too large and you feel you have plenty of outs to win the hand, or you feel it's time to make a move for a chance at some chips, then take a shot and rely on luck. Analyze all the possibly factors to make this unorthodox call. If everything is telling to take a shot, knowing you're behind, then by all means, gamble a little and hope for the best.

I rarely like to put my chips in the pot knowing I'm beat, but sometimes you must go against your instincts and take a chance at a pot with a high return. Pot odds, implied odds, and a straight gamble will determine if this is the right time to rely on luck and put your chips in the pot hoping for a long shot. With larger than normal size pots, many outs and the feel you may improve your hand, then relying on luck is not a bad play. If you only put your money in with the worst of it, then you should expect a lot of bad beats in your career.

MAKING NEW MOVES EXAMPLE ♦

Making new moves is the best way to keep your opponents guessing on how you play the game. It's a way of being unpredictable, but at the same time, making sure you are making these new moves when the factors line up. Here is an example of making a new move.

You're playing in a tournament at your local casino, and you've been playing really well without making any crazy plays, and you have a nice chip stack, when you find yourself with Q♣-10♠ in the small blind. There is a raise from middle position, from a loose player, and you decide to call. The player in the big blind calls as well.

The flop comes: A♦-Q♥-6♦.

You decide to check and so does the big blind. The preflop raiser makes a bet that is half the pot. You call, but the big blind folds.

The turn is a 9♠, and you quickly check again. This time the preflop raiser makes a pot size bet and how it's up to you. His bet on the flop could have been anything, and your middle pair could be good. When he makes a larger bet on the turn what is he trying to say?

1. Trying to protect his hand against a draw?
2. Trying to gain as much as he can, thinking you have a big hand as well?

3. He is bluffing and trying to force you out of the pot?

Any of these answers could be correct, but based on his style, you decide to make a new move against him and check-raise all-in, putting him to the test for all his chips (only a small dent in yours). He ponders for a while and decides to fold. Did he have you beat?

The answer is unclear, but at least you made a move that wouldn't normally make. Sometimes, you have to try new moves to see where you stand based on your image. Occasionally, you'll get called with a better hand, but at least you tried a new move. And believe me, the players at the table will notice that, and adjust their game accordingly. If they feel you are able to be aggressive with a hand less than valuable than most hands when aggression is normally show, then you'll be able to continue that trend and them, not only check big hands, but lay them down.

Try new moves with different hands, on different streets, against players you wouldn't normally make these moves against. Show them you are able to mix up your game and make moves that will make them think harder... and differently. You'll be surprised how often they lay down hands against you, and how much easier the game will come to you.

Learn to 3-bet preflop with weak hands, check-raise with draws, bet in early positions with middle pair, raise with the nuts against players who have big hands etc. Mixing up your game and making new moves will help you become a player against opponents who are capable of playing the same way. If they can't get a read on you, then expect to drag more pots your way.

ACT ON READS EXAMPLE ♣

In volume 1, I talked about how bluffing is overrated, and what I mean by this, was that a lot of players will strive on bluffing so much, that they will ignore all the factors it takes to pull off a successful bluff and focus solely on the bluff itself. They will ignore position, player knowledge, chip stacks, tells and the flow of the hand. Sure, bluffing is important but when is player bluffs too much for the joy of bluffing then this play is overrated (and of course, unsuccessful). Here is an example of a bluff that is overrated.

You're playing in a $1-$2 no limit hold'em cash game and you're in the big blind with A♦-A♠. There are 2 limpers before it gets to the small blind and he calls as well. You decide to raise it $10, to weed out the limpers, but hopefully can at least keep one caller to battle with. Everyone folds except for the small blind.

The flop comes: 2♣-9♥-9♠. The small blind checks and you make a continuation bet of $16. He calls.

The turn comes a 3♦, and the small checks again. What is your play?

The small blind calls your raise preflop and calls your continuation bet on a weak board. What could he be holding? You could put him on a small pocket pair and he's hoping you just have A-K, and decided to check on the turn, so he can take a stab at it on the river as long as no scare cards hit. He could be chasing for an over card, i.e. he's holding A-10, A-J or K-Q. He could have a big hand, say, pocket 2's or trip 9's. There are few possible hands he could be holding, but since this hand actually happened at a local casino I was at, and I was the one with pocket Aces, I felt he had big hand and I decided to check the turn. His style of player leads me to believe he had trip 9's.

The river comes with an A♥. The miracle card I wanted, if my read was correct. The small blind bets $25. A small value bet to either earn an extra bet from or he was afraid of the Ace, thinking I had pocket Aces or A-9. I thought about it for a few seconds to see how much of a raise I could win from him. I was sitting there with a big stack, so I wanted to win as much as I could, and if he really did have trip 9's, then there is no way he is folding to any size raise. I decided to push all-in for about $150. He ponders for a long time, but decides to fold face up, showing J♦-9♦, for three-of-a-kind. I muck my hand without showing him my rivered full house. Of course, many hands later I told him I had pocket Aces, and his response was that he put me on pocket Aces or A-9. And I told him, once he called on the flop I knew he had trip 9's, that's why I checked the turn. Most players will not check the turn in this situation, but I had a good read on how he played, and I knew he hit the flop hard. Luckily the river helped me, but unfortunately, he made a good fold. I wonder if I made a smaller raise, if he would have called?

LISTEN TO YOUR INSTINCTS EXAMPLE ♥

To an experienced player, listening to your instincts is extremely important when playing poker. I can't count how many times I've gone with my instincts and it was right. Even during weird hands, against players I don't really know, I've gone with my instincts and I was right. Of course, to have strong instincts, you must play a lot of players, while seeing a lot of hands. Study players around you and see how each player plays. After a while, your instincts will start telling you what to do. On some occasion, you may go against your instincts and you may be right, but in the long run, with enough experience, your instincts will almost always be right. Here is an example where I should have gone with my instincts... twice!!

During a tournament at Greektown, I got myself to the final table, and after a while we were down to 6 players.

I had the average stack when I was dealt 9♦-9♣ in middle position.

The shorter stack in first position, who plays like a rookie, decides to push all-in. The player to my right folds and now it's up to me. My though process was that he has a big pair or a big ace, but my instincts were telling me to call. After a few minutes, I decided to fold, so does everyone else.

He flips over 8♥-8♣.

I should have gone with my instincts on that one, but I felt he either had me beat, or two over cards, and I didn't want to gamble at that point in the tournament. I wanted to be the one showing aggression by pushing, not by calling.

A few hands later, with 5 players left, everyone folds to the small blind (me) and I'm holding K♦-8♠, and decide to limp in. The player in the big blind pushes all-in. When he pushed all-in, I felt he was just trying to leave and his range with wide, with a possibility of him holding a very weak hand. Of course, my instincts were telling me another story. After talking out loud for a few minutes, I decided to call, and he quickly flips over A♣-A♥. Not again! And of course, his hand held up and I was out of the tournament.

Twice during this tournament, and at such a short period of time, my instincts were telling me to do one thing, and both times, I went against it. I would have been right on both hands, and who knows how far I would have gone in the tournament. The way I was playing, it seemed like I had a real chance of winning the whole thing. That's why I can't stress enough to all those experienced players to go with your instincts. Even if it's a play you wouldn't normally make, your instincts know better. So, the next time it tells you to call a bet, you better make that call. You'll be surprised how often you are right.

DO THE OBVIOUS EXAMPLE ♠

Poker is not comprised of doing the obvious, but in some situations, you must, in order to protect your hand. Here is an example of doing the obvious at a poker table.

During a high stakes cash game, you've been playing really well, but not accumulating a lot of chips.

You are about even when you find yourself with A♠-10♣ in middle position.

Everyone folds to you and makes a standard size (3x) raise. You get two callers (one on the button and the big blind).

The flop is: A♥-9♣-2♠.

The big blind checks and you make a c-bet of just over half the pot. The button calls and the big blind folds.

The turn is a 10♠.

You make another equal size bet, in proportion to the pot, and the button raises your bet. He is not known for making obvious raises on the turn when he flops a big hand, so you rule out him having two pair or even a set. You feel he may be raising with a flush and/or straight draw, so to protect your hand, you decide to 3-bet him. Most players would fold in this spot if they have a draw, but this player is stubborn and decides to call (if your read is correct).

The river is a 3♣, and you push all-in, and he quickly folds. Was he really on a draw? It's possible he was, but he also could have had a pair and was trying to reach. Luckily for you, the river was a blank and you took down a large pot. I think your read was correct, but him having a draw. I'm shocked to see so many players still call on the turn to large bets with just a draw. They are obviously not getting the right price to call, but since they have out, they always want to see a river. Fortunately for you, you play your hand kind of obvious, in this spot, and was extra aggressive with it.

Since most players will fold to a 3-bet on the turn with a draw, and if he would have folded and you decided to rabbit hunt the river and it would have been another spade, completing the flush, then you would have hit yourself for not playing the hand more obvious and more aggressive. I know in a lot of cases, you'll choose not to play a hand obviously, but when you're playing well, or not, and you finally find a spot where you can earn some chips, sometimes it's best to play your hand obvious to protect it and assure an almost guaranteed victory of the pot.

PLUS: This situation is played more obvious in a tournament than a cash game, since in a cash game you're trying to extract more chips by keeping players in the pot and trying to force the weaker hands out. For example, if you had the same hand (A-10) in a tournament, and you flopped two pair and made the same bet, while your opponent raises you, then you can flat call and see a turn or do the obvious and raise him back.

If he flat calls, and the turn is a brick, then you must protect your hand be either betting out again or choose to check-raising for a large amount. You should only choose to check, if you know for sure he will bet into you. If he is capable of seeing a river for free, then do the obvious and make another bet, protecting your hand in case he has a draw, or a hand with a lot of outs. Make sure it's large enough for him to make a tough decision. If he raises you again, then you could be bet, but unless he has a set, you have the best hand and your only move is to push all your chips in the middle.

TAKING YOUR TIME EXAMPLE ♦

Taking your time to decide how to play a hand is very important when making the right decision. If you act too quickly, then you could be folding hands you should have been calling with. If you take too long when deciding, then you could start to think wrong. There's a saying in poker:

"If you think long, you think wrong."

If you think too long, you may overthink the hand and make the wrong decision. You must take your time when deciding, so you can assess the hand, and story, correctly, but you don't want to take too long when making a play. Here is an example of taking your time during a hand.

You're playing a mid-stakes tournament and you have just above the average stack when the bubble is slowly approaching. You look down and see 6♠-6♦, in late position and you decide to call a raise from a tight-aggressive player in early position. No other callers are involved in the hand.

The flop comes: Q♠-10♣-3♥. He is first to act and makes a standard size c-bet. Even though there are over cards, can your hand really be good? You make the call to see what he does on the turn.

The turn is a 3♣. Your opponent makes another standard size bet, in comparison to the size of the pot.

Is your hand still good? Most players will act quickly thinking there is no way your pocket 6's are good, but let's think for a second and see your opponents possible range could be.

He raised from an early position, which means he probably has a big pocket pair or a big ace.

1. Could he have pocket Aces or Kings? Maybe, but he isn't playing his hand strong enough to match what he is holding.
2. Could he have A-K? Possibly, with his weak bets.
3. Could he have A-Q? Again, possibly, but A-Q from early position isn't a typical preflop raising hand in this format.
4. Could he have a smaller pocket pair? Unlikely. His c-bet on the flop could indicate a smaller pocket pair, but with you calling, it's unlikely he would make another bet on the turn, so I would rule this hand out.

After taking your time, you decide to make another call, and the river is a brick. Your opponent checks, and you make a half pot size bet, and he folds quickly. My guess is he had A-K. If he would have made another bet on the river, I probably would have still called, thinking he is trying to 3-barrel his way to winning the pot.

Remember, just because you don't hit a set with your pocket pair, doesn't mean you're always beat when over cards hit the board. If you take your time and assess the situation, based on their style and how they play postflop, then you'll start to see their story clearer. A lot of times, their story will not add up, and it will obvious they don't have the hand they are trying to represent.

PLAY RAGS LIKE THE NUTS EXAMPLE ♣

Playing rags like the nuts is not an easy play to make, especially at a table with a mix of experienced players, novice players and rookies. From time to time, you will have to play a weak hand like you have the absolute best hand. If everything lines up to making this type of play, then let's hope it pays off in the end. Here is an example of playing rags like the nuts.

You're playing in a cash game at your local casino and you have a big chip stack. You've been playing really solid of late when you find yourself card dead (not catching any playable hands lately), until you are dealt 9♥-4♦ in first position and decided this is the time to make a move. The players in the blinds rarely defend them with a large raise and the table has slowed down their aggression. You raise 4x the big blind and only get two callers (a tight player in middle position and a rookie on the button).

The flop comes: A♥-J♣-8♣. You are first to act and make a bet 2/3 the size of the and only the player on the button calls.

The turn is a 2♣, and this time, you check because you are worried about the flush .... or are you pretending to be worried? The player on the button makes a bet half the size of the pot, and you think for a second before making a raise. He calls quickly.

The river is a 6♦ and make a large almost pot size bet and your opponent goes in to a deep-thinking mode. You're hoping he doesn't have the flush but based on loose range and style you probably put him on a weak ace or a missed draw. By check-raising the turn, you're trying to represent a big hand, possibly the nut flush.

After some thought your opponent folds face up, A♦-9♣, and you take down the pot with 9 high.

True, there are many situations where you can represent the nuts, but I wanted to show you a different way of playing this type of hand. Most players who make a bet on the flop with a draw, then hit in on the turn will most likely bet again, against a player who is loose, but in this spot, I wanted to show how some players used to play a flush. If I was holding 9-4, I would have probably played it more aggressively, and kept betting instead of check-raising, but against a loose player on the button I felt he would use that to his advantage and make a bet on the turn if I checked it, in hopes of stealing the pot if he was on a draw or hand a weaker hand of value. By check-raising I was able to tell my opponent I just improved my hand and I'm trying to extract more chips from you.

If you feel you can make the rags like the nuts in critical situations, then by all means, do it. If you feel you are card dead, or you need to gather some chips because the blinds are coming up or trying to alter the table flow at a cash game, then you'll need to bluff and play a weak hand strong. I know what you're thinking, that's obvious poker, and everyone does this, but most players do it wrong. They bluff to just bluff. They don't factor in flow, chips, player knowledge and self-image to successfully make a play like this. If you can get the flop short-handed against players you can easily read, then make a play, and play your rags like the nuts.

KNOWING WHEN YOU'RE
BEAT EXAMPLE 1 ♥

Knowing when you're beat is poker in a nutshell. You must always put your opponent(s) on hand to know whether you have the best hand, or you're beat. By doing so, you'll able to make the correct decision against them. If you only play your hand, then you will constantly make the wrong decision, and, you'll never be able to steal uncontested pots. Here is an example on knowing when you're beat.

You're playing at a one-table satellite table at the WSOP. You've been playing well, and there are only 5 players left in the tournament. You have the one of the large stacks. You look down, in late position, and find yourself holding, K♥-Q♦. A tight-aggressive player raises preflop in early position, he gets one caller before it gets to you. You call as well.

The flop comes: J♥-9♥-6♥.

You have a gut-shot straight draw and the second nut flush draw, and the preflop raiser checks. The player in middle position checks as well. Now it's up to you. Should you bet?

If you know the preflop raiser and his range, it seems like he may have a big hand, since he raised preflop, but didn't make a c-bet on the flop. The middle position player checks as well, meaning he probably missed the flop. You decide to see if your read is correct, and you make a small bet. The preflop raiser calls and the player in middle position folds.

The turn is a 3♣, and now, the preflop raiser makes a standard size bet. You have multiple outs to hits, if he doesn't already have the nuts, so you decide to call.

The river is a 10♠, and this time, the preflop makes a pot size bet. Are you beat with your straight? Yes, you are. His style of play and the fact that he check-called the flop and bet out on the turn and river indicates that he flopped a big hand, probably the nut flush. You decide to fold face up, and your opponent flashes the Ace of hearts. Did he really flop the nuts? My guess is yes, and you made a great laydown. A lot of players who raise preflop, then slow-play their hand postflop, usually have a big hand and are trying to extract more chips by letting his opponents bet. If he would have made a c-bet, you have been more inclined to call the river bet. By slow-playing his hand, you missed out on an opportunity to take more chips from you. You knew you were beat, so you made the easy down.

You should almost always c-bet when you raise preflop. It puts the control in your hands, and the only way your opponents can call is if they have a big hand themselves; pairs and big draws. The only time that you should not make a c-bet after raising preflop, is when the pot is multi-way, you're in early position, and the board is wet with potential hands your opponents' range could call with. If the board is dry, even if it's multi-way, you should still make a c-bet. Even if the bet is small, it's still, more than likely, going to force out the weaker hands.

KNOWING WHEN YOU'RE BEAT EXAMPLE 2 ♠

Here is another example of knowing when you're beat. This time we will focus on a cash game, where the stakes, and hands, are of high value.

You're playing at a high stakes cash game in between tournaments at the WSOP. You've been playing kind of tight and the players at the table are aware of this. But, they know you are capable of mixing it, so they don't try to get too out of line against you. You're sitting on the button with A♣-J♣. A player in middle position makes a raise preflop and you decide to make a large 3-bet. Everyone else folds and he makes the call.

The flop is: Q♣-8♥-6♣.

The player in middle position checks and you make a standard c-bet with your nut flush draw. He calls.

The turn is a 6♦.

This time your opponent bets half the pot. You decide to call with your draw and over card, suspecting he doesn't have the range that would include a 6.

The river is a 10♣.

You have the nut flush and your opponent checks quickly. You feel your flush is good, so you make a value bet. Your opponent ponders for a moment before making a large raise. Now it's up to you.

You have the nut flush, and he just check-raised you on the river. What is he trying to represent?

1. Would he check-raise with a weaker flush?
2. Would he check-raise with a bluff?
3. Does he have a better hand with a full house?
4. Would he check-raise with any valuable hand?

This type of play only reminds me of players who would make this move with a full house or better. You can think all you want, but I would be surprised if he had a hand that was worse than yours. He is trying to get more chips from you, knowing you would make a river bet "representing" a flush, even though you do have the nuts, and by checking on the river bet, he feels you'll call with it, so he makes a large enough raise to gain the most value. If you've played long enough, you should know to make this fold. I wouldn't show him I have the flush, but know in the back of your mind, you just made an amazing lay down.

Pretty much any check-raise on the river will mean the nuts. If they feel you have a good hand, a hand worth betting, then most players will check the river with nuts to extract more chips. Most players will call this river bet thinking you are trying to steal the pot, since most players that don't have show-down value, will bet the river. On occasion, you will see a player check-raising on the river with a bluff. This is usually done against tight players who are capable of folding big hands or large raises.

A player tried that on me while I was holding king high, but I decided to raise him back, and he folded quickly. I knew he was trying to make a move, based on his style, so I felt it was an easy play to make. I would rarely make this move, but if you know your opponent's well enough, you can take a stab at the pot and push him out. I don't suggest you do this very often, but when your instincts tell you, you have to listen to them.

DO THEY REALLY HAVE IT? EXAMPLE 1 ◆

Can you tell if an opponent really has what they are representing or not? If you know your opponent well enough, you should be able to put the pieces together, and see if the story adds up. Here is an example of: "Do they really have it?"

You're playing at your local casino, and you decide to play in one of their weekend tournaments. After a few hours, you find yourself as the chip leader, while the player two seats to your right is on tilt. The cards are dealt and the player in first position makes a large preflop raise, the tilt player calls and the player to your immediate right makes a 3-bet, and you fold your hand. The player in first position calls and the tilt players decides to push all; massive over raise. Does he really have a big hand, or is he trying to push everyone else out?

First, the player in first position raises preflop, which is a clear indication of a big hand. The tilt player calls. The player in late position decides to 3-bet. A very clear, and obvious sign of pocket Aces, maybe Kings. The first position player calls, which shows he has A-K or a good pocket pair. Now it's up to the tilt player, who pushes all-in. Do you think he really has what he is trying to represent? Would he play Aces or Kings this way? My guess is probably not. Unless he knows for sure the player to his left is about to raise, there is no way he has a strong hand. He is probably trying to, "go big or go home" type of play.

Here is what each player had:

1. The player in first position had A♥-K♦.
2. The late position 3-better had A♠-A♦.
3. The tilt player had 2♠-2♣.

Not the worse hand to have to try and force your opponents out, but it was clear that both players had a strong hand. If you are going to make a play like this, then you should be the one 3-betting, not calling and then pushing all-in with your opponent re-raises the preflop raiser in first position. True, the tilt player was beat, but he didn't know that until it was too late. Both, the first position raiser and the 3-better, made obvious plays to protect their hand. Why the tilt player didn't see that is shocking. I know going on tilt messes with your thought process, but both players made obvious plays, and he should have known his pocket pair was no good. Even by pushing all-in, he should have known he was going to get at least one caller.

Even though this section seems like it should more geared towards, "When a player tilts", it gives a good, and different, perspective, on when your opponent displays a title of:

"Do they really have it?"

The next example, with the same title, will focus on a hand that is played postflop. That example will give you an even better understanding on knowing if your opponent really has the hand he is trying to represent, or he is just trying to bluff his way to the pot. Many examples and concepts in this book, will help you determine what your opponent has in his hand. Player knowledge is so crucial in the game of poker, and by studying your opponent's game, you soon realize that most stories they are trying to tell are obvious ones. The more experienced players are capable of making up a story no one understands. That's why they are more successful. You can be successful too, if you study the game and the players well enough and once you see the story they are trying to tell, you'll be able to determine which ones are real and which ones are fake.

"Do they really have it?" You can answer that question the next time you're involved in a pot with them.

DO THEY REALLY HAVE IT? EXAMPLE 2 ♣

Here is a better example for when a situation comes up, and you must ponder, if your opponent has the hand he is trying to represent, or he is just telling a false story.

You're playing on an online poker tournament and half the field has already been eliminated. You have a good chip stack when you find yourself with A♠-K♥ in middle position. A player in early position limps, and you make the easy raise. Two players call before it gets back to the early position limper. He calls.

The flop comes: A♣-10♥-J♦.

The first position player checks, and the early position player bets half the pot. You decide to call just flat call. Everyone else folds.

The turn is a 7♥.

The early position player checks this time, and you make a large bet, protecting your top pair, top kicker, with a gut-shot straight draw. Your opponent quickly check-raises 3x your bet. What could he have?

1. Two pair?
2. Flopped the straight?
3. A bluff?
4. A set?
5. A pair and a draw?

With your raise preflop and call on the flop, you must have a pretty good hand. When you bet the turn, you're still showing you have a hand of value, but he chooses to raise your bet. Could be possibly have a hand less valuable than yours? No! The way he played his hand, he clearly has a strong hand. But how strong?

The river is K♣. Your opponent makes, what seems to be, a value bet. You go in to the "tank" and think about his range could possibly be. You have two pair and you're really not worried about a set, since he limped-called preflop. Your only option is that he flopped the nuts with K-Q or he is playing two pair really strong. I mean, he could have a lone Queen, but when he limped preflop, what hand could he call with that included a Queen?

1. K-Q?
2. A-Q?
3. Q-10?
4. Q-Q?
5. Q-J?

None of these hands really make sense, unless he called with suited cards. A lot of players will limp with such a hand, and even call a raise with it, but depending on his style, he could just be trying to represent the straight. Even his value bet looks suspicious. It's tough to say what your opponent is holding. He could be betting with a worse hand than yours, but at the same time, with you playing a long to the river, he must know you have a good hand as well. Maybe he is putting on you on a dry Ace.

If it were me in this spot, I would probably fold. There are too many hands that could have you beat. Even though you have a strong hand with two pair, the story he is trying to tell is that of a hand that beats you. If the player is known to bluff more often than most, than a call might be correct. Your gut instincts will tell you what the best choice is.

And, if you're playing in a tournament, I would fold 40% of the time. If you're in a cash game, I would call 60% of the time with this hand. Use your best judgment, but think to yourself, "Does he really have it?"

PART 2

MORE ADVANCED
CONCEPTS

CONTROLLING THE POT SIZE ♥

Controlling the pot size, in any poker game, is crucial for success. By controlling the pot size, you'll be able to win more pots and have more showdowns than normal for a minimal cost. And how do you control the pot size? It's easy. The best time to take control of the pot size is on the most vulnerable spot postflop: ON THE TURN.

On the turn, you must take control of the betting. Understanding that the best way, and the probably the only way to control the pot size, is when you are first to act, and you check, letting your opponent bet. Of course, you must call on the flop to see a turn card. When you hit the turn, you choose to bet out, by making a small bet in hopes of your opponent not raising, so you can see a river card for a minimum price or forcing him to fold. Examples of this may vary.

> *Don't just think playing Fourth Street is the best way to control the pot size. The flop can be used for control as well, when you choose to bet into a preflop raiser, on a dry board that, you feel, doesn't include holdings of his range.*

The reason you're betting out on the turn is to control the pot size, because you most likely have a draw (or some other mediocre hand and you feel your opponent may be weak) and if your opponent makes a big bet on the turn, you won't have enough pot odds to call; meaning you are being priced out of the pot. You also know the odds of catching your draw are now slim, so by betting out, you'll get to see the river card cheaper than expected.

Another situation where controlling the pot size is when you feel your opponent is bluffing and you want to see what he is holding. If he doesn't raise – or call – then you know he was just trying to make a move at the flop. This information will you help you in future situations with this particular opponent. If he raised preflop, then you know he is known for making continuation bets postflop. So, the next time you're involved in a pot with him, assuming others have fold or are weak, then you can start raising him out of the pot. On some occasions, you may choose to call on the flop, then raise on the turn or river.

Here is a quick example of controlling the pot size. Say, you hold

J♦-10♠

in the small blind. A player in middle position raises preflop and decide to call, for reasons of your own. Of course, calling a raise out of position is not the best play, but let's assume you have your reasons. The flop comes:

8♣-9♦-K♥.

You check and your opponent bets 2/3 the pot. You decide to call with your open-ended straight draw.

The turn is a 3♥.

Now, it's time to control the pot size. If you check, your opponent may make another big bet and force you to fold. You only have 8 outs (most likely – but maybe more) and a big bet might be too much to call with. You made a sizeable bet and let's see what your opponent does. If he calls, hopefully you hit your hand on the river. If you don't, you may choose to check it down, unless you feel you can steal the pot with another bet on the river. If he folds, then you know he was weak and you'll win the pot with a semi-bluff, which is a great way to win the pot – because you choose to control the pot size. If he raises, then you know he has a big hand and you can safely fold at a minimum cost. He decides to fold, and you take down the pot. Chances are he was making a continuation bet with a bluff. By controlling the pot size, you were able to steal the pot with a weak hand.

YOU HAVE 1 OUT

TURN = 4.3%
RIVER = 2.2%
TURN AND RIVER = 4.3%
ODDS = 22.3 TO 1

YOU'LL NEED TREMENDOUS POT ODDS TO CONTINUE WITH THIS HAND – LARGER THAN NORMAL SIZE POT.

PLAYABLE: A♥-K♥ - BOARD: 10♥-J♥-2♣-2♦ (AGAINST POCKET 2'S) IN A MULTIWAY POT THAT SHOWN AGGRESSION.

PROBABLE: J♣-J♠ - BOARD: J♦-6♠-6♣ (AGAINST POCKET 6'S) IN A SHORT-HANDED POT WHERE THE HAND IDICATES A PLAYER HAS AT LEAST ONE 6.

FOLDABLE: 7♦-8♦ - BOARD: 4♦-6♦-A♦ IN A MUL-TIWAY POT THAT SHOWS A LOT OF AGGRESSION BEFORE IT GETS TO YOU.

GAMBLING WHEN YOU'RE UNSURE ♠

In some situations, you will have to gamble when you are unsure of what your opponent is holding. In these situations, you have put yourself in a spot where luck is the only factor. You may have put your opponent on a few hands, but none of them are clear, the pot is large and you're willing to gamble for a high reward, so you decide to call or push all-in. Sometimes you lose, sometimes you win, but at least you have gained some information on that particular opponent, so the next time you are involved in a hand with him/her you will be able to make a more correct decision.

When you gamble preflop, you are deciding that you are in position, the pot is too large to fold or you know your opponent's game well enough to possibly out play them postflop. Even when one of these reasons is applied, you still must factor in other aspects before making a call. First, if you know you are beat, or dominated, and then you should fold no matter who is in the pot or what the pot is offering you in return. For example, say you hold A♠-Q♦ and you're in middle position. The player in first position, a tight-aggressive player with a large stack and has been playing kind of tight, limps in and gets another caller before it comes to you. You decide to just limp as well, incase the limpers are setting a trap. The button decides to raise, probably because he has position, and the small blind folds. The big blind who is known for making a squeeze play decides to 3-bet it. The first limper 4-bets it, and the second limper makes a quick fold. Now it's up to you. Even though you have a hand of value, and the chances of the big blind actually making a squeeze play against the more-than-likely, button raise with a wide range, you still can't take a chance and you opt to fold. The early position limper clearly has a strong hand and is willing to 4-bet and big blind raise. Everyone folds, and he takes down the pot. He flashes a King, so chances are he either had A-K or pocket Kings. My guess would be pocket Kings.

Even when you can out play your opponent more often than most, you still should realize that in some situations, your opponent may hit the flop hard or is in a state of mind that he is not folding. I remember many times where a board is showing concern for a straight or a flush and an opponent (or I) is trying to represent the hand, my opponent will refuse to fold big pocket pairs, two pair or even a set.

When you gamble postflop, you are deciding in similar reasons that took place in your preflop action, only this time, you know you have more possibilities: straight draws, flush draws and backdoor draws. Position, player knowledge and chip stacks all factor in, when making a decision. If they all add up, then it's a simple call no matter what. If they all add up, except actually putting your opponent on a hand, then sometimes you will have to gamble and call his bet.

A lot of players feel if you have 13 outs or more, then you should be calling every bet or being aggressive by pushing all-in (when your chip stack is lower than normal). On some level, I do agree, but just because you have a good number of outs, it doesn't always mean you should be aggressive with it. Sometimes you should play your hand slower to extract more callers. But if you feel you must gamble and be aggressive with it, then push all-in.

Every time you play poker, you know that you should always try to put your opponent on a few hands, to decide what the best play against him/her is. On those rare occasions you can't, then gambling when you're unsure is probably the best play. Folding is a close second. Just make sure all the factors add up to earning more than you'll ultimately lose, while deciding to make this play against the right opponent at the right time. In cash games, gambling is more affective, while in tournaments, it's always better to take the safe route, unless the blinds are increasing quicker than your chips stack. So, the next time you're in a spot where you don't know what your opponent is holding, and you feel your outs, and the pot is too large to fold, then simply be aggressive and play it to the end. And let's hope the result is positive.

YOU HAVE 2 OUTS

TURN = 8%
RIVER = 4%
TURN AND RIVER = 8.4%
ODDS = 10.9 TO 1

YOU'LL NEED SOLID POT ODDS TO CONTINUE WITH THIS HAND – MAKING SURE THE POT IS OFFERING A LARGE RETURN IF YOU HIT IT.

PLAYABLE: Q♣-Q♥ - BOARD: PREFLOP - AND BOTH PLAYERS ARE ALL-IN, AND THE OTHER PLAYER HAS A HIGHER PAIR.

PROBABLE: 10♦-10♠ - BOARD: PREFLOP - AND MUTILPLE PLAYERS ARE IN THE POT AND YOU'RE SHORT-STACKED.

FOLDABLE: 4♦-4♣ - BOARD: PREFLOP – THERE ARE MORE THAN ONE ALL-IN BEFORE IT GETS TO YOU.

PUSHING WITH DRAWS ♣

Pushing with draws is a play I am not fond of. It pretty much shows you, that you are risking all your chips knowing you're behind. Of course, in some situations, it may be your only choice. Say, for example, the pot is large and there are only a few players involved in the pot. The player in first position makes a small bet and he gets two callers. You are sitting there with middle pair and a flush draw. Now, you know you're behind; showing a good chance that someone has at least top pair, but if your chip stack is dwindling, then you might want to push all-in. Some players may even fold their top pair, while others will call instantly. You know you have an out, so let's hope the turn or river improves your hand for the win.

To push with a draw, you must know your opponents well enough to make the move, as well as the pot being large enough for a profitable return. I feel if the pot is twice your chip, then it's an easy play, but if the pot is less than what you have in front of you, then it might not always be the best play. Occasionally, you may choose to push with a small pot, but you're better off pushing all with a draw, when the pot is larger than normal.

Now, what kind of draws should you really be pushing with? Straight draws? Flush Draws? Backdoor draws? Over cards? Gut-shots? The best draw to push with when you have a pair is a flush or straight draw. Any other kind of draw should not be played when you know you're beat, if not dominated. I've seen too many players go broke chasing for over cards, gut-shots and back door draws. Stick to what has the best chance of improving: straight and flush draws.

For example, you hold A♥-9♥ and the flop is: 9♠-J♥-4♥. Someone betting in early position may have a Jack, but you have a pair, an over card and the lock flush draw, so you potentially have 14 outs. If the flop consisted of a straight draw instead, then you're looking at least 13 outs. Like I've mentioned before, a lot of people love to be aggressive and raise or 3-bet all-in when they have at least 13 outs.

Of course, pushing with a draw (and a pair) is not always the best play. I remember one, I chose to slow play A♣-Q♣ in the small blind, by just limping in after one person had limped in before me.

The flop was K♣-6♦-3♣,

giving me, an over card and the lock flush draw. I checked, with the idea of check-raising, the big blind bet pot and the player who limped in raised. I felt the only hand he could have was a set, so my only choice was to raise all-in or fold, since my chip stack was short. I decided to fold, because I truly felt the raiser has a set. The original bettor decided to push all-in. The raiser called. The big blind shows top pair with a weak kicker and the raiser (who I suspected to have a set) shows a set of sixes. The turn and river were blanks and trip sixes won the pot. I told them, after the hand was over, that I folded the lock flush draw. They were shocked to hear that, but I told them that I felt the raiser had a set and I wasn't interested in risking my tournament life with a flush draw, when I felt I was dominated.

Pushing with draws is only valuable when you know your opponents hand and the pot is offering you a huge return. If anything adds up that doesn't feel right to risk it all on a draw, then simply fold and wait for the next hand. Draws are only draws, just like A-K, so any time you feel it's not right to push with it, then your only choice is to fold, especially if you feel your opponent is holding a made hand.

YOU HAVE 3 OUTS

TURN = 12%
RIVER = 6%
TURN AND RIVER = 12.5%
ODDS = 7 TO 1

YOU'LL NEED SOLID POT ODDS TO CONTINUE WITH THIS HAND – POTS WITH A LARGER RETURN IN RATIO TO A SMALLER SIZED BET.

PLAYABLE: K♣-7♠ - BOARD: 10♦-6♣-4♣-Q♦ AND YOUR OPPONENT HAS Q♥-7♥.

PROBABLE: A♣-10♥ - BOARD: K♠-8♦-4♥-9♣ AND YOU SUSPECT MIGHT HAVE TOP PAIR, BUT THERE WAS NO RAISE PREFLOP, AND HE WOULDN'T LIMP WITH A WEAK KING.

FOLDABLE: Q♠-J♦ - BOARD: 6-7-8-9 – (A BURNED 10 FLIPPED OVER ON THE FLOP) AND YOUR OPPONENT CHECK-RAISES ON THE TURN. DOES HE HAVE THE STRAIGHT ALREADY?

SLOW PLAYING ◆

Most of poker, at least at a successful level, is being aggressive with every hand possible. Anytime you have a strong starting hand or flop a made hand, you should come out betting no matter what. Even if you raised and re-raised preflop, you still should come out betting to show aggression to assure yourself the pot. But is this how you should always play your hand? I mean, what if you continue to be aggressive and your opponents are too scared to call and end up folding most of the time? Then you're not getting full value for your big hands. On occasion, you must slow play your hand to assure yourself the absolute full value for your never-seem-to-get strong hands. Defining when to slow play is determined by your position and the players still involved in the hand.

When you raise preflop, and are first to act, you should bet out virtually every time, even if you hit the nuts. The rare occasion would be to slow play, if you feel your opponent has also hit the flop and you know he will bet out. Of course, if you raised preflop, and are last to act, then you should come out betting virtually every time. If a player bet into you, then you must decide the type of player he is and how he plays hands in those spots. A lot of tight players and newbies will bet out against a preflop raiser when they hit top or better. Some may even bet out with middle pair or a draw. Determining what your opponent is holding will be decided on his/her previous plays. Betting patterns, tells and the strength or weakness of the board will help you make the correct decision. Most of the time you should be raising to show aggression, representing an even stronger hand. If you feel this person only bets with strong hands and will not fold, then you simply must fold and save your money for a better spot.

3-bets preflop should always follow up with aggression postflop. If you are the re-raiser preflop, then your opponent knows you most likely have a very strong hand and will continue to show aggression to the river. No matter what hits the flop, you should come out betting and raising to the end. If you feel your opponent may have you beat (out drawing you), then you need to slow down and either call his bets or check it down. You may have been aggressive preflop by 3-betting, but there are still a lot of players who call with weaker hands, like, small pairs and weak Aces. It's very possible that your opponent has either hit two pair or a set. If that's what the case shows, then never be afraid to slow things down or even fold. Most players respect 3-bets preflop, especially at higher levels, but you will always find players who love to gamble with weak hands, in and out of position, hoping to catch a big flop. If your reads are correct, then you'll either save yourself a lot of money or with the biggest pot of the night, by being even more aggressive. Either or, the decision is up to you, by all the angles and their sum.

Slow playing on the flop is extremely valuable when you know your opponent is loose or you feel he hit the flop almost as hard as you did. By checking, you'll be able to induce a bet and you can decide from there whether to just flat call and raise on the turn or river or come out raising on the flop (check-raising). You may not want to check-raise every time you hit the flop hard, especially in early positions. Sometimes you'll want to bet out to confuse your opponents. Choosing to slow play or bet out is determined by the players still in the pot. You know against looser players you'll earn more by checking, while against tighter players it's better to just bet out. Check- raising a tight player is only valuable when you have the nuts or close to it. Since you know they will only bet with stronger hands, you know you'll need a stronger hand to compete with. But against looser players, you'll need to mix it up; depending on what you feel he/she is holding. Check-calling or check-raising is the best play against the looser players. Loose players love to bet and gamble with almost any hand, so do what you can to earn more money from then. Will you check and call on the flop? Will you check and raise on the flop, or will you check-call to the river, then raise? The choice is yours based on the information you gathered from the players around you.

Slow playing is great for short-handed pots, in an unraised pot, while making the same play at full table, raised or not, can cost you a lot. Your opponent could easily out draw you, so choose wisely when making the daring play. On some very rare occasions, you'll want to slow play in late position at any table, when you feel you have a monster hand and you sense great weakness from your opponent(s). For example, say you flop a set and two or three players in front of you check quickly, and you know this is a sign of weakness. You may want to check, to see if they can catch a hand on the turn. Who knows, they may even try and bluff on the turn since everyone checked on the flop. Then you can decide to raise then or wait until the river. More often than most, you should raise to force weak draws out. Player with top pair or middle pair may call you down, so we don't want to raise too much and force them out too.

All-in-all, slow playing should be used on occasion in different positions, when you know your opponents are weak and you want to catch a little piece, or you know your opponent will bet out with weaker hands. You don't always want to bet out with your strong hands, choose carefully when it's time to slow play... and earn a little extra.

Now for a more professional approach. Professionals are capable of slow playing at the right time, against the right opponent all the way down to the river. Believe me; I have had my fair share of slow plays, and some even to the river. If you know your opponents game well enough, you can slow play your hand to the river, then choose to raise. For example, you know he has top pair, and you have a set, you can slow play all the way to the river, then raise for maximum value. Even if there are draws out, you can still make this play based on the information you have on your opponent. Of course, if this opponent is capable of betting or raising with draws, then you slow playing your hand may not be the best play, and that's why studying your opponent's game is so important. It can really help you out in making the best decisions for all it's worth.

YOU HAVE 4 OUTS

TURN = 16%
RIVER = 8%
TURN AND RIVER = 16.5%
ODDS = 5 TO 1

YOU'LL NEED AN ABOVE AVERAGE SIZED POT TO CONTINUE WITH THIS HAND – NORMAL MUTLI-WAY POTS CAN CONSISTENT OF THIS SIZE AND MAKING THE CORRECT CALL.

PLAYABLE: A♣-J♠ - BOARD: A♦-J♥-2♣ (AGAINST A SET OF 2'S).

PROBABLE: 10♦-8♦ - BOARD: 6♠-7♦-3♣ IN A MULTI-WAY POT WITH A GUT-SHOT AND OVERCARDS (AS-SUMING A PLAYER MAY HAVE AN OVER PAIR WITH PREFLOP AGGRESSION.

FOLDABLE: 4♥-5♥ - BOARD: A♦-2♥-K♣ IN A SHORT-HANDED OR MULTIWAY POT WITH AGGRESSION.

SETTING TRAPS ♥

Setting traps is an important key for success, when playing the highest levels. Sure, it's very similar to slow play, but this section truly deserves its own "separate" explanation. Slow playing requires to play a strong hand weak for potential maximum value, while setting traps is slow playing a hand for a guaranteed level of maximum value, because you are always checking your monster hand. When you choose to slow play a hand, you don't know for sure if your opponent will bet. Even if he does, and you choose to check-raise, he may fold. When you set the trap, you know for sure your opponent will bet and even if you raise, he will most likely call you down, because you know for a fact your opponent has a valuable hand.

For example, say you raised preflop with 9♣-9♦ and your opponent, who is labeled "very tight," decides to 3-bet. You know he has a big pocket pair, but you have a huge chip stack and decide to make the call, even though you are out of position (which is a great spot for setting traps).

The flop is 9♠-3♥-2♦.

With this flop, your opponent will bet out, so you obviously check. And as long as no big cards come out, you should have no problem just calling him down to the river, then deciding to raise. In this situation it is best to just check-call and the way down. You know he has a big hand, so no need to raise, unless his bets are small. If that's the case, then make small raises (usually a little more than twice the original bet).

Slow playing and setting traps are extremely useful when playing poker against the top players (mixing it up is almost important). The reason for that is that you can't always play the same way with the same hands against the same opponents. After a while, the professionals will see that and adjust their game to assure themselves to making the right decisions against you. By occasionally slow playing and setting traps (and mixing it up), you'll be able to keep your "professional" opponents confused about your plays. They won't have a read on your and you'll be able to win more pots, sessions and tournaments, because ultimately, they will start making the wrong decisions. Times you are bluffing, they will fold, while times you have the nuts, they will call.

When you set a trap, you must know for a fact that your opponent has a strong hand, but not quite stronger than yours. Early positions are better for setting traps, but you can also set traps in later positions. Calling your opponents bet, and not raising, can induce bets on every round and it displays an image of your style of play. For me, a lot of players know I love to set traps, so every time I check; they are hesitant to bet, because they are afraid to get check-raised, which enables to be to steal a lot of pots. But if you feel they have a hand and are capable of slow playing or setting traps themselves, then I won't think twice about trying to steal pot. On some occasions, I have stolen the pot with a bluff, whether I bet, raised, 3-bet, check-raised or even raised a 3- or 4-bet. If I feel I can steal the pot, I will make the attempt. Since I'm known for setting traps, I can make aggressive plays with my opponents thinking I have the nuts.

BUT WAIT - Let's not forget about setting traps preflop. Most of the time you should be 2-betting and 3-betting with big hands preflop, but occasionally you must slow play for set the trap, by just calling. For example, a player raises preflop and you know he has a good hand, you could 3-bet, but you choose to just call with your pocket Aces. You are in position and you know you can out play him/her. The flop is weak, and you choose to set the trap by making him think you have a smaller pair or draw. The turn (or river) comes and you choose to either bet out or raise. At this point, your opponent has no idea what you have, and will most likely call you with any decent hand. You just got paid for setting the perfect trap. I'll bet anything he had no clue you had pocket Aces. But beware, playing a strong hand softly preflop and to continue that postflop could cost you a lot. You opponent may out draw you, so make sure when you choose to make this play, that you know your opponent game so well, that it's almost like you can see what he is holding.

YOU HAVE 5 OUTS

TURN = 20%
RIVER = 10%
TURN AND RIVER = 20.3%
ODDS = 3.9 TO 1

YOU'LL NEED AN ABOVE AVERAGE SIZED POT TO CONTINUE WITH THIS HAND – NORMAL MUTLI-WAY POTS CAN CONSISTENT OF THIS SIZE AND MAKING THE CORRECT CALL.

PLAYABLE: K♥-J♣ - BOARD: J♠-8♥-4♣ (AGAINST POCKET ACES OR QUEENS).

PROBABLE: 9♥-10♥ - BOARD: 9♠-A♦-A♣ AGAINST NO AGGRESSION – NO RAISES OR BIG BETS.

FOLDABLE: 6♠-7♦ - BOARD: 7♥-A♣-K♠-Q♦ IN A MULTIWAY POT WITH AGGRESSION.

MAKING UNUSUAL PLAYS ♠

At the highest levels, we know that poker is all about correct decisions based on your opponent's information displayed throughout the game. We also know that occasionally we must gamble when we know we are beat. And on those rare occasions you decide to make plays that have no true meaning but to be aggressive and to (hopefully) force your opponents to fold. Of course, making plays with no reason is not the best way to be successful; it's still something you'll need to learn to make in order to compete with the professionals. These plays are ones where position, tells and previous information on your opponent ignored and you proceed by making a play opposite of what you should be doing more often.

For example, you know that an opponent will only raise preflop with monster hands, yet this time you choose to play a weaker hand hoping to outdraw them. Sometimes it pays off, but occasionally you will get paid. On those times that it doesn't work, hopefully you only lose a minimum amount. On those times you do get paid, hopefully you were able to extract as much as you could.

In order to make an unusual play, you must know your opponent's game as well as each of their chips stacks and how they play different positions. When you break down the different types of players, you'll see that the tighter players may ignore position and chip stacks and just play their hands. To make an unusual play against them is rare but can be done when you feel his bets are somewhat weak. If he is betting in an early position (even though he may not realize that), then you know he has at least top or better. If he is betting in a middle or late position, then his beats vary on the number of players waiting to act after him. If there were no raise preflop, then he could be sitting there with a weak top pair, middle pair and an over card or a draw. This would be a good time to raise if there are only a few (or less) players still waiting for act. In this spot, a tight player may feel his hand is best and will bet. If you show aggression he may back down.

When you play against looser players, then making an unusual play against them is - and should be – more common. Of course, setting traps and slow playing is the best method for looser players, because you still from time to time must make an unusual play against them. Since looser players won't fold as often as a tight player, you must make your play at the perfect spot. Position raises will be your best play. In order to make an unusual play work against a looser player, you must use your "late" position to maneuver the act. Loose players love to bet no matter what position they are and will continue with playing their hand even if they have a weak pair or draw. To make this play against them, start raising with mediocre hands when acting after him. Occasionally you should check-raise when you sense weakness. Now, I know what you're thinking and that is these are normal plays against looser players, but here is the kicker. When you raise and check-raise, be even more aggressive then you should when you actually do have a hand. Raise more than you normally would. Sometimes just pushing all-in (if on the shorter stack – with a weak hand), is the play to make. Normally you would raise and check-raise a loose player to extract more money, this time you are raising to force him out of the pot. You must learn to raise and 3-bet with weaker hands than normal against looser players. They are capable of doing it, so you should be as well.

Against better players and professionals, you must make the unusual play when other factors have caught their eyes. For example, a professional bet in middle position postflop and a tight player calls. This is your chance to raise with any hand possible. A professional knows that a tight is sitting to his left and will only call with good hands. If you raise, you are telling the professional that your hand is better than the tight player's hand. A professional may see that as strength and fold almost any big hand; even top pair, top kicker. You are making an unusual play knowing you are beat and knowing the tight player is along for the ride. If you show aggression, a better player will see that and fold more often. Let's hope the tight player folds as well.

These are the kinds of plays you need to make against the better players at the table. A better player – or professional – sees it all and will adjust his game accordingly. But before you make this play, factor in all the angles: chip stacks (must be high for all players remaining), position (always better to act last – though sometimes in early position when you sense weakness in your opponents), flow the game (making sure the table is not being more aggressive than more) and the player still involved (professionals and rookies). If the table is all tight players, loose players or professionals, then making an unusual play may not be your best move. Sometimes, just sitting back is enough to provide you with a win.

YOU HAVE 6 OUTS

TURN = 24%
RIVER = 12%
TURN AND RIVER = 24.1%
ODDS = 3.15 TO 1

YOU'LL NEED AN AVERAGE SIZED POT TO CONTINUE WITH THIS HAND.

PLAYABLE: A♣-K♠ - BOARD: 3♦-6♠-9♥ WITH AGGRESSION PREFLOP.

PROBABLE: K♦-9♦ - BOARD: Q♠-8♣-A♦-2♠ IN A MULTIWAY POT WITH NO BETS ON THE FLOP.

FOLDABLE: A♦-Q♠ - BOARD: 8♥-9♦-10♣ IN A MULTIWAY POT WITH EVEN SOME AGGRESSION.

OPPONENTS MAKING
UNUSUAL PLAYS ♣

When an opponent makes an unusual play, and ends up winning the pot, you may scratch your head in disbelief - surprised by his play. Then, you look at the plays made leading up to that point, and you see a "tell" of strength by his opponent. Yet the winner of the pot decided to be aggressive and risk most or all his chips, relying on luck and ended up winning. This type of play happens all the time, but you can't let it affect your play against either of the previous opponents. Yes, he may have gotten lucky, by outdrawing his opponent, but his unusual play was a fluke and he'll most likely lose the next time he makes that same play, so don't try and make the same move he did. Play your game and adjust your game properly to your opponents. A lot of players will slope to an opponent's level because they seen them get lucky many times, not realizing that the luck he has obtained today, is not the luck that happens to him all the time. Today may be his day, but tomorrow will be the opposite.

Now, what if the player who made the unusual play won the pot against you? Would that affect your game? Of course, it would, but try not to let it affect future hands against him or any other player at the table. His unusual play may have been a sign of "tilt" or a level of "giving up." A lot of players make plays; even when they are unaware of its correctness. They might not understand all the angles of successful poker playing, and on those rare occasions, they seem to get lucky. I'll guarantee you that over their poker career, unless they improve their skills, they will go broke.

To play against unusual players and unusual plays, you must not let it alter your game. You should know in time that this type of player is inexperienced and will most likely go broke. Just give it time. You made the correct play, it's just your opponent got lucky. I doubt the next time he makes that same play against you, he'll win. Of course, if a player is known to make unusual plays, then the best way to help it to your advantage is to avoid pots with them, until you have a monster hand yourself. Once you have them right where you want them to be, then make the proper adjustments for full value... and the win.

Professional players are capable of making unusual plays, but they have legitimate reasons behind it. They may feel you are capable of folding a big hand, so they raise your bets; forcing you to fold too often. They may have found a "tell" or information that has leaked that shows weakness; making you fold all your bluffs. In these spots, you can't be successful against the better players, then you can do the same as they do. And if you think about it, it's not that hard to do. Just make similar plays they do. Learn to raise and 3-bet with weaker hands, in and out of position. But before you do that, you must learn on which opponents this will work best. All I have to say is, the better the player, the more likely he will fold. Professionals have no problem folding if they feel they are beat. Weaker players have a hard folding with a hand of any value, so try and ignore plays like that against them. Let the better players make the unusual plays, because you know you can do the same to that player. Spot out those players who are capable of making unusual plays and start doing what they do, when the situation calls for it.

YOU HAVE 7 OUTS

TURN = 28%
RIVER = 14%
TURN AND RIVER = 27.8%
ODDS = 2.6 TO 1

YOU'LL NEED A STANDARD SIZE POT ODDS TO CONTINUE WITH THIS HAND.

PLAYABLE: A♥-9♣ - BOARD: 6♦-7♠-10♣-3♥ WITH CHECKS ON THE FLOP AND TURN IN A MUTLWAY POT. ACE COULD STILL BE LIVE.

PROBABLE: J♠-8♠ - BOARD: Q♣-10♦-7♥-2♠ WITH LITTLE AGGRESSION OR SMALL BETS. YOUR JACK COULD STILL BE LIVE.

FOLDABLE: Q♦-5♦ - BOARD: 3♠-10♦-A♥-K♣ WITH ANY KIND OF STANDARD BETTING. SIMILAR TO THE PLAYABLE HAND BUT WITH LESS ODDS OF WINNING. YOUR QUEEN IS AN OUT, BUT WE KNOW IT'S NO GOOD.

FORCING YOUR OPPONENT
TO FOLD ♦

Forcing your opponent to fold is crucial when you either have a weak hand yourself and the pot is large, or you feel your opponent will fold because of the strength you are representing. You're playing to win the most money, and to do that, you'll either must have a slightly stronger hand than your opponent when pushed al in or you must force your opponent to fold.

To get your opponent to fold, you must evaluate his skills prior to playing a big pot/hand with him or her. In my first book, and remembered in the second book, I talked about putting your opponents into categories. Understanding what kind of player, he is and how he plays hands in different situations. At any time, you feel he is in that particular situation and is showing weakness by the instincts you have obtained throughout the game, then this is the perfect time to be aggressive, forcing your opponent to fold.

The best players, who will fold more often, are the better players. Most rookies or players newer to the game will call almost anything of value. Professionals will find every reason not to fold, and most likely force you to fold, when they choose to 3-bet you... or flat call you on early streets to steal the pot on later streets. While calling stations and looser players will call just about anything, either thinking you are bluffing or thinking they have the best of it. Players like these love action, so they will do anything it takes to be in the middle of it. They fail to see other aspects of your game and focus more on ammunition (chips) and aggressive plays. Professionals can do the same, but they will adjust their game to yours to assure themselves they are making the correct play. More often than most, a professional will make the right play against you, but from time to time I have seen many top players – even well-known professionals – make countless mistakes against an opponent making an obvious play. I know it's easier when you see the hands, on television, but the display of weakness or strength by an opponent should be obvious, when that player is making an obvious move.

To make an opponent fold, do this:

1. Figure out what kind of player is he/she.
2. Is he loose, tight or professional-like?
3. What position are all the players in, and who are still involved in the hand?
4. What was the action preflop?
5. Any information displaying strength or weakness?
6. Hand values of everyone at the table.

Answer these questions simply by putting the story together. First, what kind of player is he? Let's say for example, he is tight-aggressive. Then what are the positions everyone is in? The tight-aggressive player is sitting in early position and you are in late position with a weak-tight opponent is in the middle position. You can out the weak opponent as long as he is not showing signs of strength, so let's just focus on the better player. Next, what was the action preflop? Say, the tight-aggressive player raised four times the big blind, so he probably has a big ace or a middle pocket pair. His position should narrow the hands he is most likely raising with. In early position, I'll give him either A-K or A-Q; maybe even pocket 10's or Jacks. He could have a bigger hand, because any raise from first position is 99% likely a big pocket pair or A-K. Let's see how he plays his hand postflop to determine his holdings. Now, remember, I never told you what you're holding, because it doesn't matter when you're forcing your opponent to fold, but knowing his position and the type of player he is, you have a strong hand yourself. If you had a weak hand, like, A-10, A-J or a small pocket pair, you would have folded preflop; easy fold against that type of player and his position.

The flop was all low cards and the tight-aggressive player checks. The weak player checks, and you decide to make a move and bet half the pot to see where you stand. Plus, you have a good hand yourself. It's not wise to bet into a player who has raised preflop but checks on the flop without a quality hand. A lot of players of his caliber will raise preflop but check the flop when he hits it hard. In this situation, the tight-aggressive player check-raises. Now we know he has a big hand. The weak player folds and it's up to you. We know at this point, based player knowledge and position that he has you beat, and a fold is the easy choice, but let's say the pot is too large to fold and you feel you can outplay him on the next street, so you decide to call. You have a good hand and you feel your outs are live. The turn is a scare card and your opponent checks. This sign for me would mean he was trying to make a move on the flop, thinking you'll fold to a check-raise, but oddly enough you called. This would be a great time to make a big bet. Chances are he will fold. You decide to make a large bet and your opponent folds instantly. You may not have had the best hand, but you were able to force him to fold. Your call on the flop confused him and made him lay down a possible better hand.

More often than most, you should have folded. He made a play that standard tight-aggressive players make postflop when they hit the flop hard. Fortunate enough for you, you were able to take the pot down. Not a player you should normally make, but luckily it worked this time. Now, this is just one of the situations where you need to force your opponent to fold.

Others would include:

1. When you sense weakness and raise with a less than valuable hand.
2. When your opponent checks the flop, and you are last to act. Betting out may force your opponent to fold hands better than yours.

3. When the pot is large, and you want to protect your hand with larger than normal bets/raises.

4. When the blinds are increasing, and you risk a large portion of your chips to last longer in the tournament.

5. Making unusual plays to confuse your opponent to make them make abnormal lay-downs.

6. Just to win pots in cash games. All pots are extremely important in cash games, so any time you can win a pot, is a bonus.

7. When you feel your opponent will fold to a big bet or raise. A lot of players may feel aggressive betting means strength, so they may fold more often.

8. When you feel they "may" be bluffing, and you know you can't win the hand if you check it down, so you play above your level and raise an unusual amount.

9. You found a "tell" of weakness and you act on it. I can't count how many times I have seen an obvious tell of weakness and my opponent folds. If I were in the hand, I would have raised instantly.

10. Playing a hand overly aggressively to force other opponents to fold draws and weaker pairs. You want to narrow the field down to protect your hand, or to steal the pot later, since we all know that the fewer the players involved, the easier it is to steal the pot.

YOU HAVE 8 OUTS

TURN = 32%
RIVER = 16%
TURN AND RIVER = 31.5%
ODDS = 2.17 TO 1

YOU'LL NEED ALMOST ANY SIZE POT TO CONTINUE WITH THIS HAND – ESPECIALLY IN MULTI-WAY POTS.

PLAYABLE: ANY OPEN-ENDED STRAIGHT DRAW IN A MULTIWAY POT.

PROBABLE: AN OPEN-ENDED STRAIGHT AGAINST AGGRESSION – BIG BETS AND RAISES – IN A MULTIWAY POT.

FOLDABLE: AN OPEN-ENDED STRAIGHT DRAW WITH BIG BETS, RAISES AND/OR ALL-IN'S BEFORE IT GETS TO YOU. ESPECIALLY IN A SHORT-HANDED TOURNAMENT.

PATIENCE ♥

Patience is the key to successful poker. It allows you to play accurate hands under accurate circumstances, which results in more positive outcomes, when your reads are correct. Failing to have patience will result in playing abnormal poker and ultimately losing more than you expect. Reasons for this is that you'll unconsciously play outside your limits and play a style your mental level of skills is not used to. You'll start playing hands you don't normally play and end up making calls you shouldn't be making, and the result would be going broke.

I've seen many times in a poker game where player has chosen to play way too many hands. Sure, he may get lucky early on, but his result will be a negative. This player is simply relying on luck and failing to see the true value of his starting hands and the players around him. Tells, player knowledge and position are ignored every time this person plays a hand. When he looks down he sees potential value stating that the flop could be anything, not realizing that the odds are not in his favor. If he is sitting at the same table as many experienced players, his chances of being successful are slim. The more experienced players will simply out play him and take all his chips.

To be successful in any poker game you must have patience; and choose your battles on which starting hands to play and which opponents to play them against. I feel, early on in a tournament you must be patient and play only stronger starting hands. With this, you'll be able to see how your opponents are playing. Once you have a good understanding on how each player plays, then you open your game up more. If you're not catching good cards early on, then you may choose to start playing hands outside your limits. Occasionally steal blinds and be aggressive by 2-betting and 3-betting hands less valuable than your normal requirements. Having patience is great for gathering information on all your opponents. Without information, you'll be playing blind poker and relying solely on luck. We all know that luck doesn't last forever, so quality information on your opponents can help you last longer in tournaments and provide great decision-making plays for optimal value.

Patience in cash games are a little different. I feel by being less patient in cash games you can help keep your image undetermined and you'll be able to keep your opponents guessing, which can result in more traps and full value for all powerful starting hands. Of course, this may not always work in every cash game. Sometimes, you'll need to be patient. For example, cards are not going your way, too many calling stations at your table, other opponents are playing too loose – or too tight. In games like this, just sit back and let the cards come your way. Once they do, make sure you are making the right adjustments for a full return.

Ultimately, don't feel that the flop will always be favorable. Even though it could, it doesn't mean you should be playing every hand. Assess the player and the situation at hand before playing your hand. Folding can save you from going broke, and when you use the information you've gathered on your opponent you are displaying strength. True odds of flopping anything, and the price it's going to cost in ratio to the return, is very important when playing a hand. Know the math, the position of all your opponents and the expectancy of the implied odd, will factor the whether folding or calling is the best option.

YOU HAVE 9 OUTS

TURN = 36%
RIVER = 18%
TURN AND RIVER = 35%
ODDS = 1.86 TO 1

YOU'LL NEED ALMOST ANY SIZE POT TO CONTINUE WITH THIS HAND – ESPECIALLY IN MULTI-WAY POTS.

PLAYABLE: THE NUT FLUSH DRAW IN A MUTIWAY POT. ANY FLUSH DRAW WHEN IT'S SHORT-HANDED.

PROBABLE: ANY FLUSH DRAW IN A MULTIWAY POT WITH SOME AGGRESSION.

FOLDABLE: A WEAK FLUSH DRAW IN A MUTIWAY POT WITH AGGRESSION.

BEING AGGRESSIVE ♠

Being aggressive in most cases can be very rewarding at the poker table. By being aggressive, you'll have control of the table and most likely win most of the pots. You'll even make opponents fold hands of some value. Even some hands they wouldn't normally fold in that spot. They're simply afraid of playing with you or back at you, so they would rather fold then get involved in a pot where it could cost them their entire bankroll.

But in some cases, being aggressive might not always be the best play. Occasionally you'll have to slow things down and let someone else be more aggressive. Reasons for this vary.

If someone is starting to slow play hands or set traps against you, then this is the time you'll have to slow things down. Most professionals can spot when a player is playing a different style than they are used to. For the first stages of any tournament or cash game you see them play pretty standard, while you are being aggressive, betting, 2-betting and 3-betting almost every pot. Now, you're being a maniac when you do this, but you noticed how soft everyone else is playing, so you make the proper adjustments by playing faster than them. Then, after a while you start seeing player limps and call big bets postflop, which catches your attention. They seem to know that you'll most bet or raise on the next street, so they decide to set the trap. Low-and-behold, when the next street comes, they choose to check-raise. Now it's time to slow things down and re-start your style.

Once you re-start your style, then you'll know when to be aggressive and when to slow things down. Of course, in cash games, being aggressive more often pays off than any tournament. In tournaments, usually patience is the key to a successful win. Once you've established a decent chip stack, then varying your pay from tight or aggressive in proper spots is the best way to make a final table and ultimately a first-place win.

If you choose to play tight, that's fine. If you choose to be aggressive, that's fine, too. Just remember, sometimes you'll have to make the proper adjustments to a winner. Don't believe me? Just ask any professional online or in live games. You must change the speed of your game to be successful in poker. If you play the same way throughout the duration of any poker game, you'll soon discover quick exits and empty pocket. I feel the best way to play is to be aggressive when you have a good hand and slow things down when you feel your opponent has a stronger hand.

For example, I remember one time during an online poker tournament, it got down to the final table, and during the later stages of it, I noticed the player to my right will always raise on the button when everyone else has folded to him. During this one hand, he chooses to just limp. I thought to myself, "This is a

rather odd play by him", so I just call in the small blind
with

A♥-J♣.

The big blind checks.
The flop comes A♠-5♣-8♦.
I check and so does the player in the big blind. The
limper on the button bets about 2/3 the pot. I instantly
fold, while the big blind calls all the way down losing to

A♦-Q♠.

What a sick lay down by me, but I knew I was beat.
He was raising on the button virtually every time,
which is the right thing to do in that spot, but I noticed
his limp, which was unusual for his style. I truly felt he
had a big hand, so folding top pair to an unraised pot
was as easy as they come. A lot of players will ignore
when a player makes an unusual play. You must watch
your opponents and learn how they play, so you, too,
can make the proper adjustments.

Overall, I really feel aggression is the way to go,
but I also feel patience and picking your spots is a
successful way to play. Whichever way you choose
to play, just make sure you know when to slow down
because you never know when the player next to you
is a setting a trap.

Here are some aggressive moves against different
opponents in different situations:

1. When a player is aggressive, but often folds to a 3-bet, learn to 3-bet more often with almost any two cards.

2. When a player is loose and considered a "donkey", try not to bluff, and make sure you make big bets with strong hands.

3. When a player is known to make continuation bets almost 100% percent of the time, learn to call more often withy marginal hands and strong hands. Always check the flop, especially when you flop a big hand.

4. When a player is considered tight, realize that he won't often fold to a 3-bet, since his range is fairly tight to start with. Only 3-bet with big hands, never with a bluff. If he is the type of player who checks when he misses the flop and bets when he hits it, then you can check behind him and bet the turn no matter what hits.

5. When a player is hyper loose aggressive, be careful when you 3-bet. He could easily 4-bet with any two cards. Only time a 3-bet would be correct is if you the bet puts you all-in, in this case, your play might work, since it has fold equity. Sometimes you may choose to 3-bet this opponent with big hands, knowing he will most likely 4-bet, giving you a chance to gain full value for your hand on the current street or on the next round.

6. When playing against a professional, you don't want to play postflop poker when you're out of

position. Rarely flat-call and make large 3-bets, out of position, in efforts to take down the pot right there. A professional has no problem folding big hands, if they feel your 3-bets are hands in your range of big pocket pairs and A-K, while on occasion A-Q or medium pocket pairs.

Those are just some of the ideas behind being aggressive against particular types of players. Now, here some concepts with aggressive moves when an opponent 3-bets and your response to them, when both stacks are large. The next section will include the same concepts, but both stacks will be small.

1. When the size of your opponents 3-bet is small, make a small 4-bet with A-A. If the pot is large, then make a large 4-bet (possibly all-in).

2. No matter what size your opponents 3-bet was, only call with K-K through 10-10 and don't push for a 4-bet. Play the hand postflop and see how he plays it out. If you are first to act and the board is weak, a bet might be the correct play to see where you stand. Make the bet sizeable to let your opponent, that you have a hand of value and are willing to call an all-in.

3. If you have pocket 9's through pocket 6's, then simply call the 3-bet and the play the flop accordingly. If the 3-bet is too large, then simply fold and wait for a better spot.

4. A-K through A-J suited are good hands to call a 3-bet with when in position. If you have A-K suited, then call any 3-bet, even if it's an all-in bet, unless it's clear your opponent has Aces or Kings. If you have A-Q or A-J suited, then only call if the 3-bet is small or you sense weakness. If it's too large or you sense strength, then fold and play on to the next hand.

5. If you have medium to weak Ace suited, then folding might be your only option no matter what size the 3-bet was. Occasionally you may want to 4-bet with these hands if your opponent is loose and is known to make aggressive plays with weak hands. If he is capable of reading an opponent for being weak, then a 4-bet may push him off the pot.

6. Other hands like off suited Aces and face cards, all the way down to rags, should be folded, unless you feel your opponent is making a move and your 4-bet would push him off, stating the price being too high.

Here are some concepts with aggressive moves when an opponent 3-bets, and your response to them, when both stacks are small.

1. Big pocket pairs should be 4-betted into any size 3-bet from your opponent. As well as A-K, A-Q and A-J Suited.

2. If your opponent is capable of pushing the short stacks around (even if he is short-stacked), then start 4-bettng with medium pocket pairs, medium suited Aces, K-Q and K-J.

3. Weak suited Aces, and off suit connectors below K-10, should be folded to any size 3-bet.

4. All other hands including A-10, small pocket pairs and other marginal hands, should be folded to any size 3-bet, unless the pot is multi-way and you feel your opponents are holding similar hands. This play is only good when most of your chips are already in the pot sitting in one of the blinds and it's your best chance, to at least, triple up.

These are great concepts in being aggressive in tournament poker, but I think we need to talk a little more about position when it comes to aggression. Most people associate aggression when a player makes a preflop raise from the button, but what about other spots, like the hi-jack seat or the cut-off? As players understand the standard button raise, they tend to start raising preflop from these two other spots in order to take away the buttons aggression. Since this is an advanced book, we should talk about making plays from the cut-off and the hi-jack seats, which we will, and for those who can't wait, here is the simple play to make against these types of plays:

1. If you're on the button, then simply 4-bet with all hands of strong value. This would include big pocket pairs, A-K suited or unsuited, A-Q suited or unsuited, A-J suited and most medium pocket pairs.

2. If you're on the cut-off seat and face a raise from the hi-jack seat, then simply make the same play as previously stated, but on some occasions, you may want to just call with big pocket pairs to trap the player who is sitting on the button. If that opponent is capable of 4-betting with advanced knowledge the hi-jackers play, then set the trap by flat-call with your monster hand and let the button 4-bet. Once it gets around to you, you may jam and push all-in.

3. If you have a medium valued hand, then simply call and play postflop accordingly. You will have position in most cases, so you'll be able to see how your opponent plays the flop. If his bet is weak, then you may choose to flat-call the flop, and raise on the turn. If the board shows concern for draws and the players in the blinds have called preflop, then you might want to raise on the flop to force them out.

We talk about hi-jack and cut-off defense plays. Now, here are some plays you need to make when a button raises preflop:

1. Always 3-bet when holding pocket Aces, Kings and Queens.

2. Make small 3-bets when holding pocket Jacks, tens or nines. By making a small 3-bet, you'll be able to get away from it if your opponent pushes all-in.

3. If you have medium pocket pairs like, pocket 5's through 8's, then I would make are large 3-bet to force your opponent to fold. He has position on you if he calls your 3-bet, so try and take down the pot preflop. Only call his 4-bet all-in if the price is right.

4. If you have big suited Aces like, A-K, A-Q A-J or even A-10, then make a sizeable 3-bet. Force your opponent to make a tough decision. If he 4-bets all-in, then only call if you feel you have the best hand or at best a coin flip and the price is right.

5. Other suited Aces, like, A-9 through A-8, are also hands you can make a sizeable 3-bet with, but always fold to a 4-bet (especially if it's an all-in move). Even though the button raised preflop, it's still a standard play, and you don't want to call an all-in bet with medium Aces.

6. Off suited Aces and Kings, you should just flat-call the buttons raise and play the flop. Play it cautiously when the pot is multi-way, but aggressive if it's short-handed. Learn to check-raise with hands of value.

7. Other hands like, suited face cards, suited and unsuited connectors, you should just call and play the flop accordingly.

8. Of course, if you have rags, then you can choose to make a large 3-bet against loose players, but fold to any player who is playing tight, or is not known for making the standard button raise. And of course, if you choose to 3-bet, and your opponent 4-bets, then the only clear choice is to fold.

YOU HAVE 10 OUTS

TURN = 40%
RIVER = 20%
TURN AND RIVER = 38.4%
ODDS = 1.6 TO 1

YOU'LL NEED ANY STANDARD NON-AGGRESSIVE SIZED POT TO CONTINUE WITH THIS HAND.

PLAYABLE: Q♣-J♣ - BOARD: 9♦-10♠-Q♥ IN ANY VALAUBLE SITUATION.

PROBABLE: MIDDLE PAIR WITH AN OPEN-ENDED STRAIGHT DRAW WITH STANDARD BETTING.

FOLDABLE: BOTTOM PAIR WITH AN OPEN-ENDED STRAIGHT DRAW WITH AGGRESSION.

PLAYING TIGHT ♣

Playing tight is a great way to play when you are either first starting to play poker or your table is playing loose. Whether you're playing a cash game or a tournament, if you notice your table is filled with loose players or maniacs, then tightening up your style might be the best play. Let them do all the betting and raising, while you set the traps and slow play big hands. Of course, if you're new to the game, then playing tight is a great way to learn the game and the style of players sitting around you. But this is advanced hold'em, so I'm sure none of you are just starting out in this game. All of you, I assume, are looking for advanced strategies behind playing tight.

When you choose to play tight, for one reason or another, you must learn that you can't always play tight if you want to be successful. You must learn how to loosen things up and play a looser style; a style that will keep your opponents guessing. Sure, I agree that playing tight early in any game is a good way to see how the table is flowing as well as how the players at your table and decides to play against it, but as time goes on as well as the hands playing at your table, you must learn to change it up from time to time.

By starting out tight you've given the impression, by the other players, that you're only playing big cards and will only continue with them if you have a strong holding. Normally two pair or better. When they see you bet or raise, they know you got the goods and will fold most hands. Also, by playing tight you'll avoid being out played and being outdrawn. Most tight players will only continue when they know for sure they have the best hand, so when looser players are involved in a pot with them, they will most likely be drawing slim or dead.

Once you've established an image of a tight player, now it's time to loosen things up. Don't start right off the bat, playing weak hands in and out of position or betting and raising with less valuable hands than what your opponents are putting you on. Choose your spots. Analyze the situation and adjust accordingly.

When the players at your table see you're only playing big cards. They will most likely slow down on the turn and river when you're involved in the pot; unless they have a monster hand themselves. If you can pin-point the spots where they are acknowledging this, then this is the time to start bluffing by betting in early position with less than one pair and raising on the turn or river with less than the nuts. They are going to assume that your bets in early position represent a very strong hand and their hands mean the nuts. From the time a loose player will play outside his normal style and know you're going to make this play, so they choose to bet out with the nuts or any hand of high value, waiting for you to raise. This usually happens when the board shows cards that may have helped a player of your stature; big cards, flush draws, open-ended straight draws and so on. If you notice the other players catching on to you, then you'll need to return to stage one and start playing tight again. This is what professionals call, "shifting gears." A lot of players today don't shift gears. They play one style and hope it's successful until the game is over. But most often, playing one style may lead you to cash, but it won't always lead you to that 1st place finish or walking away with a double buy-in during the most important cash game you have ever played.

The saying, "Playing tight is right" is true for the most part, but you'll also have to play loose from time to time. Keep your opponents guessing until you have complete control of table. Instincts and unusual plays by your opponents should help determine when to be tight and when to be loose.

Play tight when:

1. Your table is playing loose.
2. Multiple opponents have a read on you for bluffing in certain situations. Button raises, last to act bets and checked down river bets.
3. When you're not catching any cards of value for a long period of time.
4. To mix up your image.
5. To fool the blinds when you're on the button, and tight-aggressive players are in the blinds.

6. When your opponents are playing their "A" game and your reads are off.
7. If you're happy just to make it in the money. This usually happens in a tournament when you're running bad, but barely hanging on.

YOU HAVE 11 OUTS

TURN = 44%
RIVER = 22%
TURN AND RIVER = 41.7%
ODDS = 1.4 TO 1

YOU'LL NEED ANY STANDARD NON-AGGRESSIVE SIZED POT TO CONTINUE WITH THIS HAND.

PLAYABLE: A♥-J♥ - BOARD: A♦-10♥-6♥ WITH ANY NUMBER OF PLAYERS.

PROBABLE: TOP PAIR WITH AN OPEN-ENDED STRAIGHT DRAW IN A MULTIWAY POT WITH AGGRESSION.

FOLDABLE: MIDDLE OR BOTTOM PAIR WITH A STRAIGHT DRAW IN A SHORT-HANDED POT.

PLAYING LOOSE ♦

Playing loose is a great way to keep your opponents guessing on the type of hands you play and how you play them to the river. By playing all kinds of hands, your opponent will never be able to put you on a hand. But be careful, playing too loose too often or against the wrong opponents could cost you more than you bargained for. Some players like to play loose early on in tournaments to either establish an early chip lead, to become the bully, or get knocked out to join other tournaments or side games. They don't feel like sitting around in the early stages of it and get knocked out somewhere in the middle and not get paid. They'd rather set the flow in the beginning to make a strong run when it gets down to the bubble and to the final table. One of the best players in poker, Stu Ungar, played this style of poker. But one thing you must remember is Stu knew how to slow things down and switch his style to tight. Since he could read his opponents better than anyone I ever saw, he knew when his opponents had a stronger hand and are not in the mood to fold.

For myself, I like to play rather tight in the beginning to study how the players around me are choosing to play. Once I have a good understand on the flow of each players game, then I'll make the proper adjustments for accurate plays. As a cash game or tournament would proceed, and as long as I had a comfortable chip stack, then I would play a little looser; take more chances with draws and make abnormal plays with check-raises and 3-bets with hand of minimal value.

Playing loose is a great form of action and a good way to obtain chips. Of course, we all know not to be too loose when a tight player is providing all the action. At time we will have to fold when the price is wrong, or your gut is telling you you're beat, and folding is the only option.

Playing loose in a tournament is a good style when you have a good chip stack and can bully the table. Don't believe me; just ask 2010 WSOP main event winner, Jonathan Duhamel. Once he had the chip lead, he continued to be aggressive and play loose. He tried to bully the table with his stack to have a tremendous chance of winning the whole thing. Luckily for him, he accomplished that goal. Even when he got to the final table he was still playing loose; 2-betting and 3-betting almost any hand of value. But there was a time when he started losing his stack, so he decided to slow things down and play a little tighter. He even folded A-K against Michael Mizrachi's 3-bet. He felt he wasn't in control of table (or he felt he was beat badly) and didn't want a confrontation of that magnitude. Once he got some of his chips back, he started to play loose again, especially heads up after he took a huge stack off Joseph Cheong.

Playing loose worked for him (and Jamie Gold), but it doesn't always work out like that. Sometimes playing tighter or tight-aggressive the whole time is the best way to win a tournament, while occasionally mixing it up and playing loose when tight players are playing soft or a loose player is being semi-aggressive. You should almost always know when a player is playing a hand that you feel he is uncomfortable with. When this action is being displayed, then it's up to you play loose and steal those pots. And most importantly, watch out for those players who are capable of folding hands when scare cards hit the board. These people are the best players to play against loose to gain control of a large pot. But don't forget, this style doesn't always work in all poker games. In a cash game, normally the loose players will prevail victorious. With players being able to re-buy at anytime (but still capable of folding to save a bet), the loose players have the advantage of being the most unpredictable (and successful) players at any poker table. Loose players will choose to play more hands in and out of position and make daring raises against players who are more likely to protect their stack. To be a successful cash game player, you must be able to take chances. Tournaments are structured to a certain style of strategy to have players protect their stack to move a spot, where as in cash games it's an all-out war for chips with no risk of being blinded out.

Play loose when:

1. Your table is playing tight.
2. When your opponents are reading you as a tight player.

3. When you're getting short-stacked and the blinds are increasing quickly.

4. When you're playing in a cash-game, and the players around you are protective of their stack.

5. When you're in a tournament and the players in the blind are considered "tight" players.

6. When you've established an image of a "bully", you should continue to be aggressive, until someone makes an unusual play against you. Like limping in early position, when they know you're going to raise preflop, based on your previous plays.

7. When you read your opponents as being weak postflop players. You can outplay them once the flop hits, which gives you an opportunity to play loose the entire hand.

8. To keep your opponents guessing, by playing a loose hand that even you're not used to making in that spot. Sometimes making a play that you've never made before can keep your opponents off the pot you're trying to win. Large pots, when your opponent is weak or is playing abnormally in that particular situation, is the best time to make unusual plays yourself.

YOU HAVE 12 OUTS

TURN = 48%
RIVER = 24%
TURN AND RIVER = 45.2%
ODDS = 1.22 TO 1

YOU'LL NEED ANY SIZE POT TO CONTINUE WITH THIS HAND – I'D EVEN PLAY THIS IN AGGRESSIVE GAMES.

PLAYABLE: TOP PAIR WITH A FLUSH DRAW IN ANY SITUATION.

PROBABLE: N/A. READ BELOW.

FOLDABLE: BOTTOM 2 PAIR WITH AN OPEN-ENDED STRAIGHT DRAW IN A MULTIWAY POT WITH HYPER AGGRESSION PLAYS AND ALLIN'S. THOUGH IN SOME GAMES, I WOULD PUT THIS UNDER THE PROBABLE CATEGORY.

ON THE BUBBLE ♥

There's no real solid strategy for playing when the bubble approaches. In any tournament, you need to make the correct decisions during and away from the actual poker hands. You also need to make the correct decision on which games you choose to play as well as what stakes. But one of the easiest decisions in poker, besides having the nuts, is when the bubble is coming up quick and when the bubble actually is upon you.

When you're in a tournament and the bubble is creeping up to you, you need to decide how you're going to play your game prior and beyond that level. In most poker books they tell you play aggressively, especially against opponents who are playing tight and are just happy making the money. In some cases, I agree with this. But don't you think other people are thinking on the same level as you? They might be setting traps, letting donk off your chips when they decide to check-raise you. Being aggressive is the best way to approach the game if leading up to that, you have been catching cards and have established a level of being luck or bullying the table. But if the cards are not going your way, or you're only in that spot because of a sick outdraw, then playing tight might be your best option. You're lucky enough to make it that far, why blow it on playing too loose before making the money.

There's no set strategy on playing the bubble. If you're playing your "A" game and you have a big chip stack, then you should be aggressive; more aggressive than anyone at your table, except for the biggest stack (unless that's you). If your chip stack is average, then play your position and your cards accordingly. If you can't believe you're still in it, then play tight until the bubble spot has passed, then choose to be overly aggressive.

Tournaments should be all about winning, but in some cases, just making some money is most profitable. If you're known not to win too many tournaments, but you are a successful poker player, then people wonder how you do it. You simply tell them that you are a master of survival and can make the money virtually every time. You can choose to play tournaments where the buy-in ranges from $50-$1000, and no matter how many people enter the tournament you almost always seem to make the money. You're playing a tight survival mode, but you're still making money. You're leaving the game with more money than you entered with. This is a great tool to obtain when you're just starting out in poker or you only have a few years under your belt. It's a part-time job for you and you can continue to make money until you start playing bigger tournaments and you start playing outside the box and play a more aggressive style of poker. You may not make the money as often, but when you do, you'll have a huge payout.

The bubble can be a scary spot for anyone. Whether you're playing for an hour or seven days, you'd like to walk away with some money. But don't let it affect your game too much. Play tight if you're happy to take some money home. Play aggressive to bully the table for more chips if only first place matters. First place should always matter, but making money is the most important thing in poker. Sometimes going with home with a few hundred dollars in your pocket can make you feel the same way as going home with the 1st place prize pool.

Whatever strategy you decide to play, make sure you do it against the right opponents. See who is playing tight and who is playing loose, sometimes you'll mix it up to take advantage of every pot that is possible. Understand on each of your opponents are playing, and then decide to make the right moves against them. Watch out for odd limpers and abnormal cold calls. It could be a trap. Which player(s) is changing their style because of the bubble and who is playing the same style hours ago, while ignoring the bubble? After a few minutes, it should be easy to find out who is trying to make the money and who only has their eye on that 1st place prize.

HERE IS THE BUBBLE FACTOR WHEN DETERMINED ON YOUR CHIP STACK:

Your Stack	0%	5%	10%	20%	30%	40%	50%
0%	1.00	1.00	1.00	1.00	1.00	1.00	1.00
5%	1.00	1.10	1.10	1.20	1.20	1.30	1.40
10%	1.00	1.10	1.30	1.40	1.40	1.60	1.80
20%	1.00	1.10	1.20	1.60	1.80	2.10	2.50
30%	1.00	1.10	1.20	1.60	1.80	2.10	2.50
40%	1.00	1.00	1.10	1.30	1.60	3.00	3.70
50%	1.00	1.00	1.20	1.30	1.40	1.50	4.00

For example, four players are left in a tournament where the payouts are 50/30/20 and you have 20% (left side) of the chips going against an opponent who has 40% (top row). With this chart, you'll be able to see that your bubble factor is 2.1, if the other players have the remaining 40% (20% each) of the chips. And the close you get to the prize bubble, the higher the average bubble factor becomes. If the other players remaining do not have about 20% of chips left each, then the higher the bubble factor number is. We all know that the more chips you have, the better chance you have, to win the tournament, but knowing the factors behind the bubble will help you better understand the odds of it.

YOU HAVE 13 OUTS

TURN = 52%
RIVER = 26%
TURN AND RIVER = 48.1%
ODDS = 1.08 TO 1

YOU'LL NEED ANY SIZED POT TO CONTINUE WITH THIS HAND – PLAY THIS ONE AGGRESSIVELY YOURSELF.

PLAYABLE: FLUSH OR STRAIGHT DRAWS WITH OVER CARDS – AND HITTING PAIRS.

PROBABLE: N/A

FOLDABLE: N/A

TOURNAMENT OR CASH GAME SPECIALIST ♠

Are you a tournament or cash game specialist? Or are you the rare case where you can be successful in both fields? My guess is that you're either one or the other. Very few players can be successful in both tournaments and cash games. A lot of players today think they can bring the same strategy in to both games and be successful. Well they're wrong. If you play a cash game like a tournament buy-in, you'll ultimately go broke. You'll be too worried about protecting your bankroll that you'll slowly lose your stack. And if you play a tournament like a cash-game, then you'll play too loose and get knocked out of tournaments more quickly than you can count.

When you play a tournament, you use your chip stack as ammunition, while at the same time you're protecting it. You'll force yourself to fold more marginal hands so that you won't make a daring call and lose most, if not all, your stack, when the blinds are increasing faster than your ability to increase your stack in tells. Where as in a cash game, you won't be afraid to make daring calls with marginal hands, because if you lose, you can always buy back in. Also, in tournaments, you choose to play certain hands cautiously or wisely, knowing the blinds are going to increase and the bubble is approaching rapidly. So, at times you may sit back, or you may fold hands you wouldn't normally fold earlier in the tournament.

In cash games you ignore the blinds and focus only on winning pots. What you win in a pot or a session is what you keep for the night. So, you're playing to win as much as you can before the night is over. While playing a cash-game you focus on reads, pot odds, implied odds and so on. Since the blinds don't go up and there is no bubble, your only focus is like a final table. You're going to win money no matter what, but exactly how much can you earn? Of course, in some cases, you will go broke, but you can either buy back in, in hope to win your money back, plus more. Or you can walk away and chalk it up to a losing session and return the next night for revenge. Hopefully the next night is better for you. In a tournament, you win what you win. And in most cases, you'll win more cash game sessions than tournaments. More luck is involved in tournaments because of the level of players involved as well as the structure of it (blinds increasing). In cash games, you only focus on accurate reads and winning pots, no matter how big or small they are. You don't have to worry about the blinds or the payouts. Just your game in each hand you play.

Being a cash game specialist, is a great way to make a lot of money. Most professionals make their money from side games, not tournaments they play in. It's very hard to be a cash-game specialist and it's extremely hard to be a cash-game and tournament specialist in equal value, but if you can adjust properly, like, caliber players of Phil Ivey or Doyle Brunson, then you too can be a very rich poker player. As for tournaments, it's a great way to earn some money, while gaining great experience. It may take you a while to win a tournament, but when you do, it will be like nothing else. It's the best feeling in the world and it also gives you an opportunity to play more poker, higher stakes and it allows you to play in cash games with a bankroll to fall back on.

For myself, I'm a tournament specialist. I have geared my game for tournaments of any kind: re-buys, add-ons, shoot-outs, sit n' go's, multi-tables etc. I'm trying to learn more on the proper strategy to play in cash-games, but my lack of emotional attachment to money still has a hold on me. When I'm able to ignore the money in front of me and focus only on the game at hand, then I'll become a better cash-game player. But for now, I'm doing quite well in tournaments with my fair share of wins. Maybe one day I'll have the skills to be successful in both cash-games and tournaments, but until then, I'll play more tournaments than cash-games.

YOU HAVE 14 OUTS

TURN = 56%
RIVER = 28%
TURN AND RIVER = 51.2%
ODDS = 0.95 TO 1

YOU'LL NEED CHIPS IN FRONT OF YOU TO CONTINUE WITH THIS HAND – PLAY IT STRONG.

PLAYABLE: FLUSH AND STRAIGHT DRAWS WITH PAIRS, BUT USUALLY WHEN YOU HAVE THESE MANY OUTS, YOU'RE AHEAD OF MOST OPPONENTS.

PROBABLE: N/A

FOLDABLE: N/A

IS BLUFFING UNDERRATED? ♣

In *Advanced Hold'em Vol. 1*, I talked about bluffing being overrated, which states how many players today strive more on bluffing than actually reading their opponents and making correct plays. In this section I want to talk about bluffing being underrated. Stating how a lot of players focus more on their cards than position, chip stacks, player knowledge and situation at hand.

I think most players today are capable of bluffing, as well as playing weaker hands in and out of position, but at the same time, I'm not sure they are always doing this at the right time, or against the right opponents. I feel they are making this play because they feel it is time to make a move their opponents are not aware of. Not realizing that when you play against stronger opponents, they are able to see right through your move and counteract with either calling your preflop raise, then betting out, while occasionally check-raising or they choose to 3-bet preflop in knowing you were going to make that particular move. If they see you folding a lot and decide to themselves that you are only play big hands, yet this time you choose to make a rare raise preflop in a position where it's known to make a standard bluff play, then they may choose to play with or back at you, forcing you to fold your hand. This is usually done when the player making this play ignores the players in the blinds. If the players in the blinds are tight-aggressive players or even loose players with vast experience, then you just may be setting yourself up for a lost pot and inevitably future pots with a hint of tilt.

You can't just sit back at just play your cards, unless your table is filled with maniacs. You must learn how to bluff in abnormal situations. Prior to making this play, you must understand the players still waiting to act (especially the blinds) and the image you feel the players have on you. Learn to bluff in proper spots against all types of players. If your image is tight, then bluffing may work in the beginning, but later in the game, players will choose to play with you or take chances with 3-bets. If you're loose, then your bluffing may rarely work. It might work the first few times, but once they understand your style, then they'll be happy to play a hand with of almost any value.

So, is bluffing really underrated? In some cases, yes, it is. Players who ignore all the factors before playing a hand are players who need to learn how to bluff more. I remember playing a tournament where not one of my bluffs was called. The table I was playing at was filled with loose players watching me playing very few hands. Once I understood the image they bestowed on me, then I started to bluff more. When it got down to heads up, I mixed things up and was able to take down the win. Very rare for a player to not have one of his bluffs called all night. I'm sure I've pulled off at least 10 bluffs prior to heads up, then when it got down to myself and my opponent I knew exactly how he was going to play this match and was able to make the proper adjustments for ultimate success.

Sometimes you'll need to sit back and wait for hands, while other times, you'll need to get in there and mix things up. All-in-all, bluffing is both over and underrated. It all depends on the player you are and the players you play against. Establish an image and once you feel your opponents have that read, then mix things up and start making odd plays against them. Beware of players who understand this move, so you don't get caught up and trapped for most, if not all, of your chips. Bluffing may be easy, but it's hard to perform successfully at high levels, when you're not sure who's watching you and who's watching their cards. Factor in all the important aspects of the game before making a decision. Is it time to bluff or wait for premium hands? Ultimately, you should focus more on your reads and gut instincts, but you will have to bluff from time to time. If you can't bluff correctly, then you need to do your homework on the game and wait for optimal circumstances.

Here are some bluffing opportunities when it's correct to do so:

1. Check-raising on the flop. Check-raising on the flop is effective when against tight players and loose players who act in later positions on a dry board. You can learn to check-raise when

anything from top pair all the way to down to a draw or air.

2. Floating the flop, and raising on the turn. Most players understand that a raise on the turn means strength. Against player who truly understand this, you make bluff with almost any two cards, especially if the flop was checked. Position in this spot is crucial. Make sure you are in late position against players who are not known slow-playing big hands on the flop.

3. Check, then min raising the turn, and moving all-in on the river. If you sense weakness from an opponent on the turn, then making an all-in bet on the river should take down the pot. A lot of players will check the flop and bet the turn with marginal hands, just trying to take down the pot. If you make a small raise on the turn, they will most likely call the raise, but check the river. Now, is the best time to bluff, and push all-in on the river. But before making this play, make sure your opponent has fold equity and is not priced in. Assure yourself that both of your stacks are large enough not to be called.

4. River bluffs. River bluffs are great to take down a sizeable pot, when you have a weak hand, and your opponent(s) follow suit. Bluffing on the river is effective, when your opponent likes to make a thin value bet, just trying to win the pot with their marginal hand. By raising their soft

bet, you'll be able to take down a lot of pots. As long as no one is known for slow-playing all the way to the river, you should have no problem taking down the pot with a large river bet bluff.

YOU HAVE 15 OUTS

TURN = 60%
RIVER = 30%
TURN AND RIVER = 54.1%
ODDS = 0.85 TO 1

YOU'LL NEED CHIPS IN FRONT OF YOU TO CONTINUE WITH THIS HAND – PLAY IT STRONG.

PLAYABLE: FLUSH AND STRAIGHT DRAWS WITH PAIRS OR SETS, BUT USUALLY WHEN YOU HAVE THESE MANY OUTS, YOU'RE AHEAD OF MOST OPPONENTS.

PROBABLE: N/A

FOLDABLE: N/A

BLIND POKER ◆

Blind Poker is the ability to play poker in a way where your cards don't matter, only the opponents involved in the hand. To be able to play at this level, you must have an advanced take on how all your opponent's play in different positions, different stakes, as well as in different spots; full table, short-handed tables, heads up, playable hands as the chip leader, playable hands as the shorter stack and playable hands when they are the short stack and have less than 10 big blinds.

Blind poker also factors in how they've been playing prior to a particular hand in which you are deciding to be aggressively almost card blind and relying solely on your read and the actions of which your opponent(s) will most likely respond with. But since we are in advanced stages of this conversation, we can ignore the basics factors and focus only on the things most people may not know about.

We all know that blind poker is playing a hand without even looking at your cards, not to be confused with blind luck, which is the amount of luck a player receives when they get their first 2 cards. If a player catches A-A on the hand, then is dealt K-K on the very next hand, then that's just blind luck. Blind poker is not knowing what you have, even if you looked at them, but playing your opponents to the fullest.

When playing blind poker, look at the factors needed for this play to be successful. First understand the players at your table. Loose players tend to make loose calls no matter what their chip stack is, while tighter players will sit back and wait. So, making a play against a tighter player may not be the best play unless they are in early positions or in the blinds Tight-aggressive players will mix it up, but tend to play a little tighter when they receive a large pot earlier in the game. These types of players you can bluff with blind poker, since the odds of them playing back at you are slim. They may be able to play the best poker at the table, and are geniuses at mixing it up, but a lot of them will back off if they are playing well but are getting very unlucky. And if they just won a large pot, you can bet they will slow their game down to assure themselves they won't lose what they just won. After a while, the will loosen up, but before that time comes, learn to play blind poker against them.

Cash games are a little different (and more effective) than tournaments when playing blind poker. Since cash games are more about playing the opponent than your cards, blind poker is played much more often. Aggression with 3- and 4-bets is more common. Players playing in a cash game tend to be more aggressive and will risk more chips if the pot is large and the player playing back at them are playing tighter than normal or they sense they are weak by the style they've been playing prior.

In tournaments, blind poker is only effective when the right factors fall into one of many lines:

1. Tight players in the blinds.
2. A player making the action before you are not running too well and is out of position.
3. Your image has been tight, and the blinds are about to increase.
4. Mixing it up to keep your opponents guessing when the table flow is running slow.
5. No one at the table is paying attention to the actions before or after them.
6. Your opponents are mixing it up too much without proper information, which gives you an opportunity to 3-bet with marginal hands.
7. When you're short-stacked and your only move is to push all-in, when you know the opponents acting after you, will only call with premium hands.
8. The players luck level varies drastically, so they are capable of folding hands of value in optimal situations.

Blind poker is a great way to learn how your opponents play by ignoring your own cards. When the factors are lined up correctly, you can win easy pots without even really knowing what you have. Blind poker is best played against tight players or tight-aggressive players when in position. Against loose players, playing blind poker is not always the best play unless you sense weakness, and/or they are out of position (even sometimes in position when they are on a rush), by which 3- and 4-betting would be the correct play. Loose players are capable of 3- and 4 betting against you with rags to put pressure on you, but if you feel they are just making a play, then being more aggressive than then should take down the pot. The only time I wouldn't make this play is if the loose player is on tilt and you are pricing them in. Make sure when you make this play your chips stack towers over their chip stack. Same rule applies for any player who is raising your bets. If they know you or their opponents are priced in, and they are 2 and 3-betting, or even sometimes 4-betting, then they know a call will most likely be made. In cases like this all players should know that a monster hand is held by one of the players and the chances of forcing him/her to fold is unlikely.

YOU HAVE 16 OUTS

TURN = 64%
RIVER = 32%
TURN AND RIVER = 57%
ODDS = 0.75 TO 1

YOU'LL NEED AGGRESSION TO CONTINUE WITH THIS HAND – I'D RISK MY STACK ON THESE ODDS.

PLAYABLE: ALL HANDS

PROBABLE: ALL HANDS

FOLDABLE: NO HANDS SHOULD YOU BE FOLDING WITH THESE MANY OUTS. MY GUESS IS, YOU DON'T NEED OUTS TO WIN THIS HAND.

ADVANCED POKER TELLS ♥

Agree or not, poker tells are still a part of successful poker. I know you've noticed a lot of players on television playing poker and not really staring at the players across the table looking for tells. They're just looking down trying to figure out what the next, and best, move is. When a player is looking down pondering their next move, they already know what it is. They are just delaying it. They've already put their opponent on a hand and know they have the best hand. Rarely will they have the nuts, but they feel through other information that their hand will hold up. Tells are not going to help them in this situation but in a lot of other hands, they will. When your opponent is highly skilled at mixing up their game and you're sitting there with a tough situation with a hand that is mediocre, a "tell," along with your instincts, will help you make the best decision. Personally, I think tells are displayed before any action or play is being processed. This usually happens right as the cards are being dealt, the flop is being rolled and the turn and river cards being flipped over. Don't misinterpret that tells are not important as chips stacks, instincts, player knowledge and position, because they are. As the years pass you'll see more and more people rely less on tells and more on player style and situation at hand, simply because tells are easily hidden, especially with high stakes players and players who play in a statuesque manner. Right, Patrik Antonius?

Tells are important no matter who you play against. And I'm going to give you some advanced tells that will definitely help you make easier, and more profitable, decisions. Most will not just be about facial and body movements.

1. During preflop action, and the size of a player's raise. Betting patterns preflop are a huge factor on the strength or weakness of a player's hand. Minimum raises in early position usually means a strong hand that is trying to get callers for maximum value. A standard 3 times blind raise usually means any hand of normal strength; a pocket pair or big ace. A raise that is more than 3 times the big blind can vary of the strength of that hand, depending on the player making the raise and the position he/she is in. An early position over raise usually means a strong hand that is trying to be protected. This is usually done from a weaker player. A strong player who makes this type of raise is making this play based on the players in the blinds (they're considered tight) and the flow the game in ratio to the strength of his hand. In this situation he is most likely holding any hand of strength: any ace, any pocket pair or two face cards. Only 3-bet this player if they have been doing this on fair occasion. If this is

a rare play, then simply fold, unless you have a strong hand as well. You will have position on him, so seeing a flop might not be a bad play.

2. The percentage a player sees the flop and how he/she plays it. How often do they see a flop, make a continuation bet or try to steal pots with check-raises or 3-bets with any two cards? For the most part we know how much a tight player or loose player sees the flop and how often they make continuation bets and aggressive raises, but let's break down the percentages in more detail. The looser the player, the most flops he will see, and the more c-bets and raises will occur. A loose player will see about 85% of the time in a short-handed game, and about 65% at a full table. If a loose player raises preflop, he will most likely make a c-bet about 100% percent of the time. Most of the time you will fold against, but occasionally you'll need to play back at him and either call to make a play on the turn or raise on the flop or value. If he plays back at you, then you'll need to decide what the best play is. Most of the time, you should call him down to the river to assure yourself a bigger payout and protect yourself from being forced out. A tight player will rarely see a flop unless it is cheap and will only c-bet with a big hand. Sometimes he will c-bet if they table or pot is short-handed. Since the player is tight a check-raise or 3-bet is correct when the

flop is weak. A tighter player will see a flop at about 25% at a short-handed table and about 45% at a full table. A tight player would love to see flops, while in the blind, and no one has raised. It's easier to play back at a tighter player since he feels he is probably beat. He will only continue if they have a strong hand or you are known for making plays like this. Even tight players have the ability to understand when a player is making a move.

3. How a player plays while in the blinds. If multiple players have limped in, and the player in the small or big blind raises, then he most likely has a big hand. His holding consists of no less than a pocket pair 9's or higher and an ace that is stronger than A-10. A looser player may choose to raise in the blinds with smaller pairs or weaker Aces, depending on the limpers. If the players who have limped are capable of folding to a raise, then a looser player may raise with a weaker than yours. First, your choice to limp is based on the slow flow on the game hoping to see a cheap flop with a hand of some value, and in most cases, this is the wrong play. If you can't stand a raise then don't limp in the first place, but occasionally this play is correct, because not all players will raise in later positions with weaker hands, in understanding that he will be out of position postflop and will most likely get multiple callers.

4. Standard raises preflop form the cut-off seat or the button. Most players know to 3-bet a position button raise, but this same play must be done as well against a player who raises from the cut-off seat. If you don't know, the cut-off seat is the seat just before the button. When a player raises from either position, you must learn to 3- and 4-bet against them when the situation calls for it. Play back at them when the player on the button is known for making standard button raises, you're in the blinds and your chip stack is substantially higher than the player making the raise. Don't be afraid to risk your chips against a looser player making an obvious play.

5. Another betting tell is when a player bets using smaller denomination chips, when larger chips of value would be easier and more obvious, is a sign of a bluff. Choose to call or raise when a player makes this type of play.

6. When a player takes longer than normal to raise, this usually means a bluff. A quick raise would indicate a bluff as well unless it's coming from a weaker/newer player. When a player makes a normal amount of time to raise then he most likely has a strong hand. To determine the length of a player's action simply see how he plays his strong holdings. When a player is taking a large number of minutes to make a decision, then he is pondering whether to

fold or to raise. The only time a player may have a strong hand in this spot is when he is displaying a sign of weakness but sighing or acting confused.

7. When a player is check-calling all the way down, and then chooses to go all-in on the river after a rag has hit, then this person is most likely bluffing. He/she has missed the chance to improve his hand, so he is trying to steal the pot with a large bet. Of course, making this play, you must know your opponent is not that strong and is capable of folding hands of value. Most people don't slow-play until the river, so often they are bluffing. Only tight-aggressive players will slow-play to the river if the bets are weak and his opponent is known for firing bets on every round no matter what hits.

8. Comfortable betting is usually a bluff, where uncomfortable betting usually means a hand of high value. More people are more comfortable bluffing versus having a strong hand. How they move, handle chips, bet and act after the move has been made will determine his level of comfort.

9. Heavy breathing usually means a strong hand. Just like the previous statement it's all about comfort. If a player is breathing heavy, you can tell by the vein in his neck, and chest/neck movements after he/she has made a bet or raise.

10. Most people who announce their bet or raise are bluffing. The only time where his hand may have a strong value is when he is making this play against a loose player. He knows a loose player will play back at him, so acting weak by verbally announcing their large bet or raise, will most likely get them full value for their hand.

11. Noticing a player's movements just before making your bet is a good tell to watch for. He will indirectly show whether he is interested in the hand or not. He may hold his cards in a folding manner or look at his chips to see how much he wants to raise.

12. Any time a player is showing a style of reserved (locked fingers, crossed arms or legs) status is usually displaying a sign of weakness. If a player is showing a level of openness (open arms and fingers, legs relaxed and spread out, chin up, open eyes or close to the table in full interest), then he most likely has a good hand.

13. When a player touches his face or neck, he is usually weak. He feels uncomfortable and is trying to hide his face from giving away information.

14. Double checking their cards when a board has all the same suit is a sign that they have not hit the flush. Some will check to see if they even have a card of the same suit displayed on the board.

15. When a player grabs for chips before it's his turn to bet or call is usually holding a weak hand. Always bet into a player who is acting in this manner.
16. Minimum raises on the river are rarely bluffs.
17. Check-raises with multiple players still waiting to act are hands of real strength.
18. Check-raises then checks on the turn or river are signs of weakness. He tried to steal the hand on the previous street, but you called, so he is shutting down on the next street. If he chooses to check call the turn, but check-raise the river, then he is bluffing again, trying to make another attempt at stealing the pot. This play is normally done only by loose players.
19. Acting weak with verbal phrases are signs of strength. Saying things like:

    i. "What do you have?"
    ii. "Do you really have it?"
    iii. "Bluffing again?"
    iv. "Trying to steal the pot?"
    v. "This is so sick!"

These saying are usually followed by a raise. When a player does this, he has a strong hand. Don't be fooled by the act of weakness. Players may do this against players who have an advanced understanding on tells. Don't do this against players like Mike Caro. He may know this tell too well and know you are trying to play reverses psychology.

YOU HAVE 17 OUTS

TURN = 68%
RIVER = 34%
TURN AND RIVER = 59.8%
ODDS = 0.67 TO 1

JUST GO ALL-IN - OF COURSE, THEY SAY THE MORE OUTS YOU HAVE, THE MORE UNLIKELY YOU'LL HIT ONE OF THEM.

PLAYABLE: ALL HANDS

PROBABLE: ALL HANDS

FOLDABLE: NONE!!! I'M PRETTY SURE YOU'LL WIN THIS HAND.

NOW YOU'RE A PRO ♠

Not a lot of people will utter the phrase that they are a professional poker player. It's not an easy job to get into. Even with a major win under your belt, it's still not something a normal person should pursue. Playing poker recreationally is the best way to handle the business, but there players out there that are determined to become a full time professional and once you're at that level, do whatever it takes to maintain that status.

You've been grinding it out for years and you've just won a major tournament and you've decided to become a professional poker player. You've made this decision not on a whim, but through hard work and determination. Years of experience and doing your homework and now it's time to call yourself a true full time professional poker player. Now it's time to begin a journey of that greatest job ever.

There are many different factors you must consider when becoming a professional poker player. Things like:

1. Bankroll Management
2. Travel Expenses
3. Taxes
4. Separating House Hold Bills from Poker Money
5. Works Hours with Mental and Physical Stress
6. Keeping Records

7. Dealing with Bad Beats and Losing Sessions
8. Getting Staked
9. Game Selection
10. Family and Social Life
11. AND SO MUCH MORE!!!!

Should you really quit your day job? The best answer is no, but for a lot of players, they want to leave their "9 to 5" and make money playing poker. Their experience and recent success have parlayed themselves to obtain a position amongst the ranks: Phil Ivey, Doyle Brunson, Phil Hellmuth, Daniel Negreanu and so many more. Of course, these players have been playing for years. They would never let one single tournament or successful cash game session make that decision for them. I hope you're not doing the same. Before becoming a professional poker player, have years of experience under your belt, a bankroll you can handle swings and all the rest of the list stated above (1-10).

BANKROLL MANAGEMENT:

Bankroll management is one of the most important factors in becoming a professional poker player. It's the ability to manage your money in ratio to earning more. Stating not to play in games outside your limit, below your limit for lengthy parts of time and playing games, you can afford (tournaments). Bankroll management is also knowing when to stay and when to leave a game (cash game). Since cash games differ from tournaments, you should set a separate amount aside for each structure. Tournaments focus on time it takes to complete it as well as the correct portion of your tournament bankroll. A good percentage of your stack tournament buy-ins is determined on how many tournaments you plan to play that year. If you only plan to play during the WSOP, then decide how many tournaments you plan to play.

For example, let's say:

> 12 tournaments and your bankroll is: $200,000.
> $200,000 / 12 = $1,666 per tournament buy-in.

Of course, some tournaments cost more, so you'll have to break it down individually by each one, and never add any amount if you cash or win in one in your original tournament schedule. Calculate a percentage of that best suits your time frame and the max you are willing to buy-in for. With a $200,000 bankroll your tournament schedule should probably look like this (in any order):

Tournament 1: $1000
Tournament 2: $1500
Tournament 3: $1500
Tournament 4: $2000
Tournament 5: $2000
Tournament 6: $2500
Tournament 7: $2500

Tournament 8: $5000
Tournament 9: $5000
Tournament 10: $10,000
Tournament 11: $50,000
Tournament 12: $10,000 (Main Event)

As you can see you still have about $107,000 left in your bankroll. You can choose to play more tournaments or add it to next years bankroll. Never use the remaining money for cash games, stage shows or loose spending. That would result in improper bankroll management, unless you take money away from your cash game expenses and replace with the same amount used during your tournament run.

Cash games are determined on the number of big blind buy-ins you can afford and the right level game you are more comfortable and most successful at. You normally want to have at least 100 big blinds to enter a game with over 2000 big blinds still in your bankroll. As long as you stick to levels you are comfortable at and gradually learn to move up, you should be all right. Your current rate of wins ($ amount) will help determine your accurate level of success.

Here are some expected win rates per hour for games of different (expert) levels:

> $2/$4 = $7 to $9
> $3/$6 = $10 to $12
> $4/$8 = $12 to $14
> $5/$10 = $14 to $16

$6/$12 = $16 to $18
$10/$20 = $24 to $26
$15/$30 = $32 to $36
$20/$40 = $42 to $48
$25/$50 = $52 to $60
$30/$60 = $58 to $66
$40/$80 = $65 to $75
$50/$100 = $70 to $80
$100/$200 = $120 to $140

The rate per hour decreased and you move up in blinds. The smaller games also have weaker players that stronger players can prey on. In most situations, it's better to play a lower level for maximum return. You will eventually have to increase your skill level in comparison to the blinds, but most of your games should be at where you win the most. Even if it's a level you continue to play for years and years. You know you can win at the level, so why not keep playing there? If it ever gets boring or you start making bad decisions based on its flow, then it's time to move up and play bigger blinds and better players for a while.

TRAVEL EXPENSES:

All your travel expenses should be separate from everything else; poker money, food, souvenirs etc. After all your expenses have been divided, you should have extra for travel. This should also be your smallest amount. Basic traveling is the best way to go unless you are a multi-millionaire and can afford extra spending.

Travel expenses are just normally:

1. Airfare
2. Gas Money
3. Bus/Taxi Rides
4. Food.

Quick but healthy meals and drinks are most sufficient when playing poker. Celebrate with fancy meals and high-end gourmets after you have a successful day at the tables.

TAXES:

Taxes should be investigated before starting a career in poker. Even though the IRS can't detect the small wins, they can, however, find out about larger payouts. Even tournament wins over $500, can be detected, because in those situations you must fill out a W2-G form. Bigger payouts over $10,000 are obviously noticed by the IRS and its transaction from the cashier.

Just because it's not a "real" job, try not to ignore the IRS and their taxes. Be smart about it and just pay it like a normal employer would. No need to getting in trouble over small amounts of paid taxes. It's not worth the hassle when failing to pay them. The cost of ignoring it could be larger than paying them.

SEPARATING HOUSE HOLD BILLS
FROM POKER MONEY:

This section is obvious in referring to bankroll management. Simply separate the money you are willing to play poker with from the money that your bills will acquire over a certain period; normally a year. First is to figure out on average all your bills. Example, rent or mortgage, electricity, heat, water, car, insurance and so on. Then the remaining should be divided into other expenses that are necessary to survive on. Then take the rest and use it towards poker. Try not to dip into your bill money and use it for poker or any other expense.

WORK HOURS WITH MENTAL
AND PHYSICAL STRESS:

You must treat poker like a real job, even though poker may include working more hours in a day then a real job. The stress and mental swings can be ruthless, but it must be handled professionally. Any time you feel your work is over bearing or an overload, simply take a break and start fresh. Unlike a real job, vacation time and time off are more common. Take as much time as you need before returning to work, so assure yourself a clear mind when playing poker again. There are a lot of mental abilities when playing poker, so always make sure your mind is at the greatest form before sitting down at a poker table. Away from the poker table, you should form a habit of eating right and exercising regularly. Physical health can help provide the mental health a stronger state of mind.

KEEPING RECORDS:

Keeping records is vital when playing poker professionally. Knowing how you do and where you do well at is essential when choosing the right games, the right stakes and the right place and time. Not keeping track of records can leave a negative mark on your poker bankroll and leave your mental stability in a blur. Knowing where you do best at and the stakes you continually win at, can help any player improve your stack and provide a financial security for years to come.

Each record book should include:

1.   The places you play at. Focus on the places you win the most.
2.   The time you play. Figure out what time is most profitable.
3.   How much you bring to the table and the wins and loses you obtain.
4.   The type of game you're playing. Is it a cash game or a tournament? Keep separate records of each with the same information provided above.

**DEALING WITH BAD BEATS
AND LOSING SESSIONS:**

Bad beats and losing sessions will happen all the time. Dealing with is not easy, but it's necessary to be successful. All professional poker players, maybe not Phil Hellmuth Jr, can deal with ups and downs of poker. They understand that you can't win them all, so why let it affect your game. Whether you're lucky or unlucky, a talented poker player knows that the numbers will even out, and you should end your career in the positive.

Good ways to prevent yourself from going on tilt or from buying back in, into a game you can't win are:

1. Walk away from the table and take a break.
2. Listen to some music. Preferably your favorite song.
3. If you go broke, and you know you can't win at this particular table then leave the game and find one of smaller stakes.
4. Get something to eat and return in a better state of mind.
5. Take a break from poker for a few days to re-gather your thoughts.
6. Put everything you lost at the roulette wheel and bet on red. You can't lose. I'M JUST KIDDING ABOUT THIS ONE.

GETTING STAKED:

Getting stakes when a player decides to pay for some or all your buy-in, in hopes you'll cash, so he can take a portion of it. Deals like this are made all the time. Even the top professionals do this. It affords then to enter a large event at a smaller price. It saved them money and in return helps the person win money doing nothing.

Getting someone to stake you is not easy. It's done though connections. Knowing someone with money and the understanding of your level in the poker world is key one is getting someone to take such a high risk. They must know that you're a solid, talented and experienced poker player with great odds to win. Exceptions are the WSOP Main Event, but they know if they do cash (or win), the return is extremely profitable.

GAME SELECTION:

Game selection is just like the section on "Keeping Records". Understanding which game best suits your style and your bankroll. Never play outside your limits until your bankroll can afford it and your have learned the flow of that new table. Also, if you're a cash game specialist, then primarily play cash games, with the occasional tournament. Tournament specialist should do the same, while playing cash games on occasion. It's not easy to successful in both games, but it is possible. Focus on one as your main source of income and the other as bonus money. If you lose in a game you're not as experienced in, then start playing lower stakes to get the hang of it.

FAMILY AND SOCIAL LIFE:

Family and social life was described more in Volume 1, so you should know the basics of this section. Poker is your job, not your life. Be social and spend with your family. They are just as important as anything else in your life. Spread quality time around for an overall success and happy life. Their acceptance, love, support should provide you with a positive outlook when playing at the poker table. When you're happy, you're winning!! Bad beats don't occur in that department.

All these factors will play a role when choosing to be a professional poker player. Keep in mind that being a professional poker player is a hard way to make a good living. Most players who become professionals decide after winning a major event with little experience behind their belts. In situations like this, they will hire a financial manager to handle all their expenses. Some even hire poker coaches; players who have a greater experience in the poker business. These players are usually well-known and very experienced, as well as successful. But for those who choose not to take this route end up playing by ear and using their bankroll and play in various tournaments and cash games with no direction. These players usually go broke before their tenure is up. So, before becoming a professional poker player you must take the proper steps in assuring that your status will remaining as years pass.

YOU HAVE 18 OUTS

TURN = 72%
RIVER = 36%
TURN AND RIVER = 62.4%
ODDS = 0.60 TO 1

LIKE THE PREVIOUS ODDS – JUST GO ALL-IN – ESPECIALLY IN MULTI-WAY POTS BECAUSE SOMEONE WILL CALL YOU IN A LOOSE GAME.

PLAYABLE: JUST GO ALL-IN!

PROBABLE: SEE ABOVE!

FOLDABLE: DON'T YOU DARE FOLD THIS HAND!

ONLINE POKER SECRETS ♣

In the past year or two, online poker has diminished since the shut down of the major online poker sites; full tilt, absolute and poker stars. Since then, players have been playing more live poker. Even though online poker still exists, live poker is a much better game to play in as well as a better form to improve your game. Online benefits a player to see and play more hands, but live poker is the ultimate place to play poker. For those who still play online poker for money, here are some secrets to improve your skills and your bankroll.

1. Online poker is a great way to play low stakes to learn the game and slowly increase your bankroll. Lower stakes may be tedious, but it's a good way to gradually build a bankroll. The players are easy, and the flow of the game is predictable and very profitable. Ignore the glory of higher stakes and play at tables you can consistently win at.

2. A lot of player will play multi-table games. This is only effective if the stakes you're playing at are lower than what you're used to. Not being able to focus on the tables individually, you're setting yourself up to rely on position and your cards. If you're max table is $10/$20 no limit, then only play multi-tables at $2/$5 and lower. You have extensive experience at those levels,

so you know the flow of the game and the players who like to play there.

3. To be successful at online poker, use a poker tracker so keep track of the styles of how each player plays at your table. It's an easy way to track how each player plays position, preflop and postflop as well as how they play hands in different situations.

4. Building a HUD (Heads Up Display), a small one, is a good way to track how often your opponents call, raise, 3-bet, c-bet, sees flops, shows aggressions, steals blinds, folds and more, preflop and postflop. Here are some acronyms to help you out better:

i. VP$IP (voluntarily put $ in the pot)
ii. PFR (preflop raise)
iii. AF (total aggression factor)
iv. 3B (3-bet raise preflop)
v. 4B (4-bet raise preflop)
vi. FBS (fold big blind to steal)
vii. CB (continuation bet)
viii. FC (fold to flop c-bet)
ix. FTC (fold to turn c-bet)
x. FA (flop aggression factor)
xi. TA (turn aggression factor)
xii. RA (river aggression factor)
xiii. ATS (attempt to steal – the blinds)
xiv. W$WSF (win $ when seeing the flop)
xv. WtSD (went to showdown)

xvi. W$$D (win money at showdown)

Knowing how they play small ball or aggressive will be displayed in your HUD. Take notes (number of - or percentages) of each acronym for each player to understand his/her style better. With the proper adjustments you'll be able to make the correct play against almost every time.

5. Most players who play poker don't take notes while they are playing. Well they should, even in live games. There's nothing with taking notes while at the table. If your memory is bad, or you just want an advanced take on how your opponents play, then simply take notes on each player. Trust me, they won't prohibit it.

6. Since you can't physically see your opponent's movements or tells, you'll have to find other ways to have an advantage (besides knowing and categorizing each player's style). The easiest way to find it is to look at their betting patterns from different positions. Over bets with big hands, minimum raises on the river for strength and check-raise-checks for bluffs are just a few of betting patterns you'll find at online poker.

7. Try to make standard plays abnormal. Like, making minimum preflop raises, make small 3- and 4 bet raises, weak check-raises, squeeze play against tight and loose players, bet with

long shots, open your all-in calling range, over bet your big hands against weak players who show aggression and ignore position at the lowest stakes tables.

8. Undeniably focus on the simple things like, 3-betting and targeting weak players, tightening up when you're losing, try to see flops cheaply for big payouts, not taking unnecessary risks, playing tight-aggressive as often as you can. There will be a lot of aggressive and loose players playing online, so being a little tight is the right play against them. I like to set traps and make odd plays against players who have a strong understanding of them game. It's keeps them confuses and I take down a lot of uncontested pots.

YOU HAVE 19 OUTS

TURN = 76%
RIVER = 38%
TURN AND RIVER = 65%
ODDS = 0.54 TO 1

IM ALL-IN – NO QUESTONS ASKED – CAN I BRING MORE TO THE TABLE DURING THESE ODDS?

PLAYABLE: ALL-IN!

PROBABLE: ALL-IN!

FOLDABLE: NOPE! AND CAN I BET MY HOUSE AND CAR?

KNOW THE NUMBERS ♦

There are many factors in being successful in poker, which we've discussed in this book as well as in Volume 1, but it's always important to know the numbers, even if you're not really paying attention to them as often as the players at your table. Here are some charts that will better help you understand the numbers as well as how to use them in different situations. Included will be starting hands, odds of hitting hands, percentage of wins and lose and so much more.

AVERAGE WINNING PERCENTAGE (OUT OF 100) WITH PAIRS.

CARDS	Number of Opponents							
	1	2	3	4	5	6	7	8
AA	87	74	65	58	49	44	40	33
KK	83	69	59	52	44	39	34	29
QQ	81	66	55	46	39	34	29	26
JJ	79	62	49	41	35	29	26	23
1010	76	59	46	37	31	26	23	19
99	72	55	42	34	27	23	19	17
88	69	51	39	29	25	20	18	16
77	66	46	34	26	21	19	16	15
66	63	43	32	25	20	17	15	14
55	60	40	29	22	19	16	14	13
44	57	37	25	21	17	15	14	13
33	54	34	24	19	16	15	14	13
22	50	31	22	18	16	14	13	12

AVERAGE WINNING PERCENTAGE (OUT OF 100).
NOTE: SUITED CARDS ADD AN AVERAGE OF 3%.

CARDS	Number of Opponents							
	1	2	3	4	5	6	7	8
AKs	67	51	41	36	31	28	26	24
AKo	65	47	38	32	28	25	23	20
AQ	64	47	37	30	26	23	20	18
AJ	63	46	35	29	24	21	18	16
A10	62	44	34	28	23	20	17	15
A9	61	42	31	25	20	17	15	13
A8	60	41	30	24	19	16	14	12
A7	59	39	28	22	18	15	13	11
A6	58	38	28	21	17	14	12	11
A5	58	38	28	21	17	14	12	11
A4	56	37	27	21	17	14	12	10
A3	56	36	26	20	17	14	12	10
A2	55	35	25	20	16	14	12	9

CARDS	Number of Opponents							
	1	2	3	4	5	6	7	8
KQs	64	47	38	33	28	25	23	20
KQo	61	44	35	29	25	21	19	17
KJ	60	43	34	28	24	20	18	16
K10	59	42	33	27	22	19	17	15
K9	58	40	31	25	20	17	15	12
K8	56	37	27	22	18	15	13	11
K7	55	36	26	21	17	14	12	10
K6	54	35	25	20	16	13	11	10
K5	53	34	25	19	15	13	11	10
K4	52	33	23	18	15	12	11	9
K3	51	32	23	18	14	12	10	9
K2	50	31	22	17	14	12	10	8

CARDS	Number of Opponents							
	1	2	3	4	5	6	7	8
QJs	60	44	36	30	26	23	21	19
QJo	58	41	33	27	23	20	17	15
Q10	57	40	31	26	22	19	16	14
Q9	56	38	29	23	19	16	14	12
Q8	54	36	27	21	17	14	12	11
Q7	52	34	24	19	16	13	12	10
Q6	51	32	23	18	14	12	10	9
Q5	50	31	21	17	14	12	10	9
Q4	49	30	20	16	13	11	9	8
Q3	48	29	20	16	13	11	9	8
Q2	47	28	19	15	12	10	9	7

CARDS	Number of Opponents							
	1	2	3	4	5	6	7	8
J10s	58	42	34	29	25	22	20	18
J10o	55	39	31	25	22	19	16	15
J9	53	37	28	23	20	17	14	13
J8	52	35	26	21	17	14	12	11
J7	50	32	24	18	15	12	11	9
J6	48	30	21	17	14	11	10	9
J5	47	29	21	17	13	11	9	8
J4	46	28	20	16	12	10	9	8
J3	45	27	19	15	12	10	8	7
J2	44	26	18	14	11	9	8	7

ODDS OF HITTING YOUR OUTS:

1 Out = 4% on the turn and 2% on the river.

2 Outs = 8% on the turn and 4% on the river.

3 Outs = 12% on the turn and 6% on the river.

4 Outs = 16% on the turn and 8% on the river.

5 Outs = 20% on the turn and 10% on the river.
6 Outs = 24% on the turn and 12% on the river.
7 Outs = 28% on the turn and 14% on the river.
8 Outs = 32% on the turn and 16% on the river.
9 Outs = 36% on the turn and 18% on the river.
10 Outs = 40% on the turn and 20% on the river.
11 Outs = 44% on the turn and 22% on the river.
12 Outs = 48% on the turn and 24% on the river.
13 Outs = 52% on the turn and 26% on the river.
14 Outs = 56% on the turn and 28% on the river.
15 Outs = 60% on the turn and 30% on the river.

As you can see, you take the number of outs on the flop and "x" it by 4 to get the percentage of hitting it on the turn. For the river, you take the number of outs and "x" it by 2. Calculating backdoor draws or runner, runner is more complicated, but we'll get into that as well.

HERE ARE SOME PERCENTAGES WHEN FACED AGAINST A RANDOM HAND:

1. A-A = 85% (6 to 1 favorite)
2. K-K = 82% (4.5 to 1 favorite)
3. Q-Q = 80% (4 to 1 favorite)
4. J-J = 77% (3.3 to 1 favorite)
5. 10-10 = 75% (3 to 1 favorite)
6. 9-9 = 72% (2.5 to 1 favorite)
7. 8-8 = 69% (2.2 to 1 favorite)
8. 7-7 = 66% (2 to 1 favorite)
9. 6-6 = 63% (1.7 to 1 favorite)

10. 5-5 = 60% (1.5 to 1 favorite)
11. 4-4 = 57% (1.3 to 1 favorite)
12. 3-3 = 54% (1.2 to 1 favorite)
13. 2-2 = 50% (even money – accurate coin flip)
14. A-K = 67% (65% if off-suit)
15. A-Q = 66% (64% if off-suit)
16. A-J = 65% (64% if off-suit)
17. A-10 = 65% (63% if off-suit)
18. A-2 = 57% (55% if off-suit)
19. K-Q = 63% (61% if off-suit)
20. K-J = 63% (61% if off-suit)
21. K-10 = 62% (59% if off-suit)
22. Q-J = 60% (58% if off-suit)
23. Q-10 = 59% (57% if off-suit)
24. Q-7 = 54% (52% if off-suit)
25. J-10 = 58% (55% if off-suit)
26. 10-9 = 54% (52% if off-suit)
27. 10-8 = 52% (50% if off-suit)
28. 10-2 = 45% (42% if off-suit)
29. 8-3 = 41% (37% if off-suit)
30. 7-2 = 38% (35% if off-suit)

PERCENTAGES OF HITTING LONGS SHOTS:

1. Backdoor flush draw = 4.2% (23 to 1 underdog)
2. Backdoor straight draw = 3% (33 to 1 underdog)
3. Chasing for over-cards (2) = 24% (4.16 to 1 underdog) on the turn and 12% (8.3 to 1 underdog) on the river.

4. Chasing for an over-card (ace) or a gut-shot straight draw = 16% (6.25 to 1 underdog) on the turn and 8% (12.5 to 1 underdog) on the river.
5. Flopping a straight when holding connecting cards = 1.31% (76.34 to 1 underdog)
6. Flopping a straight with one gapped = 0.99% (101 to 1 underdog)
7. Flopping a straight with two gapped = 0.65% (154 to 1 underdog)
8. Flopping a straight with three gapped = 0.33% (303 to 1 underdog)
9. Flopping a flush = 0.85% (118 to 1 underdog)

RANGE PERCENTAGES:

1. **Pocket pairs in early position (top 25% of pocket pairs)** = Early position raises are made by pretty much anyone who plays poker, but the tighter players won't normally raise with a pocket pair in early position unless it's Queens or higher. A loose player may choose to raise with any pair if the table is playing rather tight. Tight-aggressive players will raise with any pair, in early position, with 7-7 or higher.
2. **Pocket pairs in middle position (top 45% of pocket pairs)** = Similar to the statement above with the exception that players will open their range up a little more when no one has entered the pot before them. You might see all players

raise in middle position with any pair. Very rarely will a player limp with a pocket pair in middle position when first to open; unless they are tight-passive, or they've been running bad prior to it. Occasionally you'll find loose players set traps with a pocket pair, when they feel the players behind him will raise. In a lot of cases they will choose to 3-bet it when it comes back to them.

3. **Pocket pairs in late position (100% of pocket pairs)** = Any player will choose to raise with a pocket pair in middle position. Very few players will limp with pocket pairs, especially when no one has entered the pot before them. In later positions, players will normally raise a larger amount preflop, no matter if someone has entered the pot before them or not.

4. **3-betting with a pocket pair (top 33% of pocket pairs)** = Almost all players will 3-bet with a pocket pair Q-Q and higher. The looser players will choose to 3-bet with smaller pocket pairs and raise large amounts. A tight-aggressive player will decide to 3-bet with any pocket pair if out of position postflop and the limpers before him can lay down hands to 3-bets.

5. **4-betting with a pocket pair (top 25% of pocket pairs)** = 4-betting is rare, but normally down with A-A, K-K or Q-Q only. The more talented players will choose to 4-bet with

weaker hands, when the player making the 3-bet is in position and is making a play by his position and the flow of the table.

6. **3-betting with a big Ace (top 16% of Aces)** = 3-betting with a big ace is just like the play made with pocket pair. Normal 3-bets with Aces include: A-K and A-Q. A-J is a rare hand to 3-bet and you'll only see that done if the table is short-handed or the player making this move is a loose-maniac.

7. **4-betting with a big Ace (top 8% of Aces)** = 4-bets are only done with A-K when the player wants to commit himself to the pot. He is willing to call an all-in with it, and most players wouldn't do that with A-Q or weaker.

8. **Raising with rags (occurs less than 20%)** = Loose and tight-aggressive players will raise with rags, but they will only do it against tight opponents and/or will be out of position postflop.

9. **3-betting with rags (occurs less than 10%)** = 3-betting with rags only occurs when aggressive players are doing it against other aggressive players, usually when a player is making a move in a standard position.

10. **4-betting with rags (occurs less than 1%)** = Similar to the statement above, but this play rarely happens unless the 4-bet is an all-in bet knowing their opponent is 3-betting with rags. Aggressive players who don't want to be out

of position or pushed around will 4-bet a 3-bet against player who is in position and has a large stack.

11. **Pushing all-in (occurs about 25% of good hands vs. less than 5% with rags)** = Pushing all-in requires making this play to either have the best hand or is trying to steal the pot with rags or a semi-bluff. The tighter the player the more likely he has a monster hand. The looser the player, the less likely he has a strong hand unless he is up against a tight player who is being aggressive. Like the previous statement a looser player may choose to push all-in trying to the steal the pot with hands less valuable than what he is thinking his opponent has but feels his opponent will fold due to lack of pot odds and variance in chip stacks.

HERE ARE SOME EV (EXPECTED VALUE) PERCENTAGES at A 9-HANDED TABLE, 6-MAX TABLE AND HEADS UP:

	HAND	9P EV	9P #	6P EV	6P #	2P EV	2P #
♠	AA	2.60	/1	2.40	/1	1.15	/1
♠	KK	1.79	/2	1.65	/2	0.97	/2
♠	QQ	1.21	/3	1.12	/3	0.87	/3
♠	AKs	0.80	/4	0.82	/5	0.47	/7
♠	JJ	0.80	/5	0.86	/4	0.71	/4
♠	AQs	0.61	/6	0.73	/6	0.42	/8
♠	TT	0.50	/7	0.63	/7	0.63	/5
♠	AK	0.50	/8	0.50	/8	0.36	/10
♠	KQs	0.43	/9	0.44	/10	0.34	/12
♠	AJs	0.38	/10	0.47	/9	0.34	/11
♠	ATs	0.30	/11	0.29	/15	0.30	/15
♠	AQ	0.29	/12	0.32	/12	0.31	/13
♠	99	0.28	/13	0.31	/14	0.50	/6
♠	KJs	0.24	/14	0.32	/11	0.25	/19
♠	QJs	0.20	/15	0.31	/13	0.20	/21
♠	QTs	0.17	/16	0.25	/16	0.20	/23
♠	88	0.17	/17	0.24	/17	0.38	/9
♠	AJ	0.14	/18	0.20	/19	0.26	/18
♠	JTs	0.14	/19	0.09	/27	0.17	/28
♠	KTs	0.14	/20	0.23	/18	0.27	/17
♠	A9s	0.14	/21	0.18	/21	0.28	/16
♠	KQ	0.13	/22	0.19	/20	0.19	/25
♠	77	0.07	/23	0.07	/30	0.30	/14
♠	A7s	0.06	/24	0.13	/22	0.17	/27
♠	A8s	0.06	/25	0.04	/36	0.19	/24
♠	K9s	0.05	/26	0.10	/26	0.14	/32
♠	KJ	0.04	/27	0.11	/23	0.17	/26
♠	66	0.03	/28	0.02	/43	0.22	/20
♠	A5s	0.02	/29	0.11	/25	0.14	/34

♠	55	0.02 /30	0.04 /58	0.11 /40
♠	AT	0.01 /31	0.08 /28	0.20 /22
♠	Q9s	0.01 /32	0.07 /31	0.10 /42
♠	A6s	0.01 /33	0.03 /39	0.16 /29
♠	T9s	0.00 /34	0.11 /24	0.15 /30
♠	J9s	0.00 /35	0.00 /44	0.13 /36
♠	A3s	0.01 /36	0.04 /37	0.14 /33
♠	K8s	0.02 /37	0.01 /49	0.10 /41
♠	98s	0.02 /38	0.00 /46	0.06 /51
♠	A4s	0.02 /39	0.08 /29	0.14 /31
♠	76s	0.02 /40	0.11 /88	0.01 /66
♠	A2s	0.02 /41	0.06 /59	0.08 /44
♠	KT	0.03 /42	0.07 /32	0.12 /38
♠	Q8s	0.03 /43	0.04 /35	0.08 /46
♠	87s	0.04 /44	0.03 /55	0.02 /62
♠	QJ	0.04 /45	0.02 /41	0.14 /35
♠	T8s	0.04 /46	0.02 /42	0.08 /48
♠	97s	0.04 /47	0.07 /64	0.00 /70
♠	J8s	0.04 /48	0.03 /53	0.08 /47
♠	K7s	0.05 /49	0.04 /34	0.06 /49
♠	44	0.05 /50	0.03 /38	0.06 /52
♠	54s	0.06 /51	0.02 /40	0.09 /96
♠	QT	0.07 /52	0.01 /47	0.08 /43
♠	33	0.07 /53	0.13 /117	0.00 /69
♠	K6s	0.07 /54	0.01 /48	0.05 /53
♠	JT	0.07 /55	0.02 /50	0.08 /45
♠	65s	0.07 /56	0.02 /51	0.09 /94
♠	53s	0.08 /57	0.09 /72	0.11 /110
♠	K4s	0.08 /58	0.04 /57	0.02 /60
♠	22	0.08 /59	0.10 /83	0.07 /90

YOU HAVE 20 OUTS

TURN = 80%
RIVER = 40%
TURN AND RIVER = 67.5%
ODDS = 0.48 TO 1

EVERYTHING I OWN I'D PUT IN THE POT WITH THESE ODDS.

PLAYABLE: YOU WIN!! HERE'S YOUR WSOP BRACELET

PROBABLE: WINNING TOO MUCH MONEY?

FOLDABLE: A BLIND MAN WOULDN'T FOLD THIS HAND!!

STEALING THE BLINDS & SQUEEZE PLAYS ♥

Stealing the blinds is crucial in any poker game, whether you're playing in a cash game or a tournament. Of course, in cash games, it counts for more, since your chips have real value, but even in tournaments, you must attempt to steal the blinds to help pay for them later when they increase. Squeeze plays is also a good way to steal the pot preflop knowing one player is trying to make the same attempt and gets a caller involved. Since the caller didn't 3-bet, you have a better chance of stealing a pot against multiple opponents, when one of them is capable of make the same moves towards the pot as you.

STEALING THE BLINDS:

Stealing the blinds in cash game are less likely to be successful, since cash games are played looser than tournaments, so people are more willing to gamble in a cash game then a tournament, but it's still possible. The best way to steal blinds in a cash game is to make large raises against loose players who will be out of position postflop. The best way to steal blinds in a tournament is when the table is playing on the tight side and the players in the blind are tight players who rarely defend their blinds. Both games require large raises; 3-bets or 4-bets if possible, but since most of the money is made postflop, I would advise you to do it more in cash game, since you're more likely to get callers and better odds to steal the pot when the flop hits.

Aggression is king in cash games, but you must learn how to play back at check-raises and other types of raises against players who are trying to take the pot from you. If they are out of position, they may choose to check-raise with nothing when a board is either scary or is a texture of rainbow. If this happens, you should, more often than not, play back at them; flat call or raise on a later street. If they are in position, then they choose to just call your bet and see how you play the turn card. They may be setting a trap, but you can't back down now. You've shown aggression preflop and on the flop, so I would suggest you continue to bet out, unless you have a strong read on your opponent, pick up a tell, or choose to check the turn and bet the river. The only downfall to checking the turn is that they may sense weakness and raise your river bet with rags. If they are capable of making this play, then make a large bet on the river or just keep showing aggression on every street.

Stealing the blinds in tournaments is just a way to increase your stack at a small risk. I personally like stealing blinds to pay for my own blinds later in the game. I like to let the stolen blinds pay for lost bets, blinds or bad beats later in the rounds. I'll keep my stack growing by making the correct plays and getting full value for my hands, but occasionally I may choose not to make standard position raises to let my opponents know I'm not always out to steal blinds and make standard plays; it keeps my opponents guessing.

SQUEEZE PLAYS:

If you know the original raise could easily be weak, even if he is not, but still holds a hand of value by having a caller, then by you choosing to 3-bet him you're stating that you have a very strong hand. As long as the players in the blinds are not loose calling stations, and the middle position caller is not known for setting traps by slowing play big hands preflop, you should be able to take down the pot more often than not.

Just like stealing the blinds, this may not work as often in cash games, then in tournaments, but it's still a play that's quite successful. I would just limit the times you do it to keep your opponents unaware of this play. Pick the right spots and you should have no problem taking down sizeable pots with any two cards. The tighter the players at the table, the more likely your move will work. If your table is filled with loose players or calling stations, then I would choose to only make this play when you feel your opponents have been watching your style as being unlucky, on tilt or one to complains a lot to himself. A tight image against tight (but aware) players will help you pull off this move in this particular game.

ADVERTISING ♠

Advertising is giving information on how you play certain hands, by showing your cards, to set traps later against players who think you're making the same play you showed earlier. Some players may show a bluff, while others only show very strong hands. The deception is to let others know either you're capable of bluffing or you only play big hands, so the next time you're involved in a pot with that person, you'll be able to mix it up and either bluff more pots or get paid off more often.

Most of the time advertising is not a good thing to display. I mean, why would you want to give away information on how you play? If you gave away all your information, all your opponents would know how to play, and you'd never walk away a winner. They would easily make the proper adjustments and make the correct plays against you every time. Luck would be your only factor of even winning one hand, or you just might only win the small pots.

Even though most players never advertise their cards or style of play, I do feel in certain situations you must give a little something away to keep your opponents guessing. The less information your opponent has on you, the more likely he'll pay you off trying to see what you're actually holding. This is good when you have the best hand, but it definitely backfires when he chooses to "pay you off" when you're bluffing.

Advertising is only beneficial at tables with players who actually pay attention to the players around them. It would be stupid to advertise against people who only plays his cards, ignores position and doesn't even think of player knowledge or adjustments. Doesn't make sense to advertise against rookies who are playing their first hand of poker, loose players who are just looking to gamble or online cash games, where players are constantly moving tables. Rarely make this play but do it if you feel your opponent is paying attention and is known for adjusting the players at the same table. You're better off not giving away any information, but if the flow of the game is not going your way; with your big hands not being called or your bluffs always being called, then I would choose to mix it up and advertise an abnormal hand to show the players around you (who are paying attention) that you're capable of making the "non-standard" play.

FOLDING BIG HANDS PREFLOP ♣

I know, I know, the title alone makes you scratch your head, but think about it. No matter how big your hand is (besides A-A), there is always a chance you are beat. Understand your true hand value against your opponents and their style can determine whether your "big" starting hand is the best. Most situations may require you to just call and see a flop, then make the proper adjustments, but when you suspect you're beat and the price is not right, then folding is your only option.

It's very hard to fold big hands preflop, because there are only a few hands that may be better and the odds of one of your opponents to be holding them is slim. Hands like:

1. K-K
2. Q-Q
3. A-K (suited or off suit)
4. J-J
5. A-Q (suited or off suit)

Other hands like:

1. 10-10,
2. A-J,
3. 9-9 or

4. A-10 suited, is not considered monster starting hands preflop, especially in a multi-way pot with aggression. I feel these hands are easy told to 3- and 4 bets. If the table is short-handed and there is a 3-bet, and I'm sitting there with one of these hands, I may choose to make a small 4-bet or push all-in. The only time I would fold in this same spot, if there are players waiting to act who haven't put a chip in the pot yet. It's always harder to make a raise with players still waiting to act. You have no information on them, so most players tend to tighten up.

Hands stated in the first list are harder to lay-down no matter how many players are involved. I think J-J and A-Q (suited or unsuited) are hands that are easier to fold, but when you're sitting there with K-K, Q-Q or A-K, your best decision is not so easy. Here are some examples where fold a big hand preflop is the best play:

K-K

Folding pocket Kings preflop, is a rare play that many players may never do ever in their career. I know I haven't. If someone is lucky enough to have pocket Aces, then I'm going to pay him off. In most situations folding Kings is not a smart, but when a tight player is 3- and 4 betting with multiple players still involved in the hand, then he most likely has the goods (Aces).

Another situation where a play has K-K beat, is when a player limps from first position at a full table, then chooses to 4-bet when someone raises in middle or late positions and invites two or more callers.

The standard play for pocket Aces preflop in first position is to limp in hopes of someone raising after you. This play is too obvious and will most likely get not action if the player making the original raise knows about this play. It's a good play if you really don't have pocket Aces, and the player at the table are aware of this standard move, forcing them to fold hands of real value. But against most players, they don't recognize this play. They feel they are just trying to steal the pot knowing they are out of position and the players still involved in the pot are capable of folding hands of value preflop, especially if the 3-bet is larger than normal.

Folding Kings postflop is a little easier to do, especially if the board is scary. But most players can't fold Kings preflop, no matter what the price is. If you sense Aces, but from players making obvious plays, either choose to call and see the flop or fold and wait for a better spot. The benefit of seeing the flop is to outplay the opponent sitting with Aces. But before calling, be aware that most players can't fold Aces postflop, even if the board shows concern for multiple made hands. If you do decide to call the preflop raise, make sure it's against an opponent who can fold big hands to postflop aggression.

Q-Q

Folding pocket Queens preflop is very similar to folding Kings, yet I feel Queens are a little easier to get away from. Even if I feel I'm against A-K, I still may choose to fold if the pot is not offering enough in return or I'm not entirely sure my read for A-K is correct. Chances are most players will not fold Q-Q preflop, unless there is a 3- and 4-bet by separate players preflop. Playing Q-Q postflop is just like playing K-K or any other pocket pair; hitting a set to continue, being in position to steal the pot on a weak board or out of position and check-raising a bet against player who is capable of position bets.

Folding Q-Q preflop in a cash game differs from a tournament. More often than not you're not folding Q-Q preflop, even to 3- and 4-bets, especially short-handed. In a tournament, on the other hand, folding Q-Q is only correct when you're still waiting to act and the player before (probably in early positions) have been extremely aggressive. Just like K-K, if there are players 3-betting and 4-betting and you're still waiting to act, then chances are your hand is no good, especially against tighter range players. If you made the original raise in early or middle position and there is a 3- and 4-bet, then a fold is probably correct. 3-bets and raises from the blinds against your late position raise, doesn't conclude with a fold. In those situations, you should just flat call and play the flop accordingly.

A-K or A-Q

I think folding A-K or A-Q preflop is a pretty easy decision to make. If the player is aggressive and labeled more on the tighter side, then it's correct to fold, even though tight players over play A-K and may choose to make 4-bets against obvious players with big pairs. Against loose players, it's good to play back at them with A-K or A-Q, but back down to 4-bets and large all-ins. I would try and see flops cheap with either one of these hands, unless you're the aggressor trying to take down the pot before the flop.

Many players overplay A-K and A-Q thinking they are hands of true value, where as most professional know, they are still drawing hands with postflop value. Theses are effective when taking pots away with players with live cards or will be out of position, and against large pots against players who are capable laying down similar hands and medium pocket pairs. Short-handed tables and late position raises are the best spots to be aggressive with these hands. At full tables you'll see players limp in early position with these hands because they feel they might not be able to call a raise with them against particular players and they know they'll be out of position throughout the remainder of the hand.

J-J

I think J-J and any other pocket pair smaller (even A-J and A-10 hands) are easy hands to get away from preflop against aggressive players with obvious big hands. Try and see flop cheap if you can with them in hopes of hitting a set. If you do not hit a set, then play the flop in ways to either save yourself money or win the pot at a cheap price. Being in position and knowing your players will determine your best play. If you raise preflop with J-J and there's a 3-bet, then a call would be correct in hopes of catching a good flop. Against 4-bets and large all-ins, folding J-J would be the correct play.

With any of these hands preflop, they must be played accordingly against different types of opponents. You should make more calls against loose players and more raises against tighter range players. Only fold against tighter players when they show aggression out of position. Fold against loose players when they choose to be aggressive with multiple players still waiting to act.

Here are some examples where your strong starting hand may be no good preflop:

1. You limp in first position with K-K and there is a raise from middle position. The player on the button decides to make a possible squeeze play by 3-betting, while the player in the big blind, who is not short-stacked at all thinks for a while then pushes all-in. Now it's up to you. Folding K-K is not a bad play. You're up against multiple opponents and there are multiple raises. Chances are someone has A-A.

2. You raise in middle position and hold A-K suited. The player in the cut-off seat makes a large over raise and the small blind calls. It's up to you but it price is not right. You know the over raise means a strong hand, because it's coming from a tight player who only raises with big hands, so instead of calling or pushing all-in, since that may be your only play, you decide to fold. In this situation you may have a hand of value to outdraw against a pair of Queens or Jacks, but there's always the possibly he is sitting there with A-A or K-K. The player who called the 3-bet is a tight-aggressive player most likely setting a trap, so folding here is probably best.

3. The table is short-handed (6-max) cash game and you raise with A-Q after a player in early position limps in. The button calls, because he is in position and the original limper decides to 3-bet. You decide to 4-bet, feeling the limper is weak trying to steal the pot and since you're sitting at a 6-max table, A-Q is a solid hand. The button folds and the limp-3-better decides to push all-in. It's only costing you a little more than the original 4-bet, but you feel you are beat. The price may be right, but you know your hand is no good. When he decided to push all-in, he knows you'll call, because of the great pot odds. In his mind, he knows you'll call, so there is no way your A-Q is way behind.

CALLING WITH WEAK
HANDS PREFLOP ◆

Calling with weak hands preflop usually only occurs when the pot is large, and you have some invested or you're trying to make a play postflop against a player who is easy to take down. Their postflop game is predictable, and you are capable of making them fold when the board is weak. Occasionally a player will call with weak hands preflop to get paid off if the board in previous hands or rounds have been sporadic. This usually happens when you choose to limp in because most flops are seen with no raises preflop. This is normally a way of playing small ball; a Daniel Negreanu style of poker.

When I refer to weak hands, I am referring to hands that most players don't normally play. One-gappers (suited and unsuited), weak Aces in early position, weak and medium Kings and Queens, and other hands that players choose not to play at a standard table:

   i.   J-8
   ii. J-7 suited
   iii. 10-7 suited and unsuited
   iv. 9-6 unsuited
   v. 5-3 suited and so on.

When choosing to play these hands, you are looking to extract a large pot when the board favors your unorthodox starting hand. You have chosen to limp in, in hopes of flopping a big hand a player wouldn't put you on. These hands are also good for calling 3-bets preflop, in position, against weak player who play postflop poker poorly. In standard situations, when trying to steal the pot with a bluff raise, which is done with these types of hands, you are choosing to do so in position against a player who is capable of folding a big hand to a 3- or 4-bet. When you decide to just flat call, you are trying to earn more money on later streets or you're trying to keep the pot relatively small to hit something big on the flop, turn or river.

I'm sure you've seen on television where a professional poker player chooses to call a raise preflop with a weak hand and the reason for this is the following:

1. They have position postflop and are capable of making a play when the board is dry.
2. They don't feel their opponent will fold to a 3- or 4-bet and wants to see a flop in hopes of maximum value.
3. The flop has been running dry or weak, and hopes the flop will continue that trend.
4. Trying to establish a loose image to your opponents that you will play any two cards.

5. It's against an opponent who plays hit or miss postflop and since you're acting first, you can steal the pot with a weak bet.

6. The pot is large and multi-way and the pot and implied odds favor your hand mathematically.

7. The players still involved are on tilt or are having a run of bad luck and will most likely fold quality hands postflop to any aggression.

A PLAYER'S RANGE ♥

	EP	MP	HI-JACK	CUT-OFF	BUTTON	SB	BB	3-BET	4-BET	ALL-IN
A/A	RW	RW	RW	RW	RW	RW/CW	RW/CW	RW, CW	RW, CW	CW
K/K	RW	RW	RW	RW	RW	RW/CW	RW/CW	RW, CW	RW, CW	CW
Q/Q	RW	RW	RW	RW	RW	RW/CW	RW/CW	RW, CW	CW	CW
J/J	RW	RW	RW	RW	RW	RW	RW/CW	CW	FOLD	CW
10/10	RW	RW	RW	RW	RW	RW	RW	CW	FOLD	CW
9/9	RW	RW	RW	RW	RW	RW	RW	FOLD	FOLD	FOLD
8/8	RW	RW	RW	RW	RW	RW	RW	FOLD	FOLD	FOLD
7/7	RW	RW	RW	RW	RW	RW	RW	FOLD	FOLD	FOLD
6/6	CW	RW	RW	RW	RW	RW	RW/CW	FOLD	FOLD	FOLD
5/5	CW	RW	RW	RW	RW	RW	RW/CW	FOLD	FOLD	FOLD
4/4	CW	RW	RW	RW	RW	RW	RW/CW	FOLD	FOLD	FOLD
3/3	CW	RW	RW	RW	RW	RW	RW/CW	FOLD	FOLD	FOLD
2/2	CW	RW	RW	RW	RW	RW	RW/CW	FOLD	FOLD	FOLD
A/K	RW	RW	RW	RW	RW	RW/CW	RW/CW	CW	FOLD	CW
A/Q	RW	RW	RW	RW	RW	RW	RW/CW	FOLD	FOLD	FOLD
A/J	CW	RW	RW	RW	RW	RW	RW/CW	FOLD	FOLD	FOLD
A/10	CW	RW	RW	RW	RW	RW	RW/CW	FOLD	FOLD	FOLD
A/9	CW	RW	RW	RW	RW	RW	RW/CW	FOLD	FOLD	FOLD
A/8	FOLD	RW	RW	RW	RW	RW	RW/CW	FOLD	FOLD	FOLD
A/7	FOLD	RW	RW	RW	RW	RW	RW/CW	FOLD	FOLD	FOLD
A/6	FOLD	RW	RW	RW	RW	RW	RW/CW	FOLD	FOLD	FOLD
A/5	FOLD	RW	RW	RW	RW	RW	RW/CW	FOLD	FOLD	FOLD
A/4	FOLD	RW	RW	RW	RW	RW	RW/CW	FOLD	FOLD	FOLD
A/3	CW	RW	RW	RW	RW	RW	RW/CW	FOLD	FOLD	FOLD
A/2	CW	RW	RW	RW	RW	RW	RW/CW	FOLD	FOLD	FOLD
K/Q	CW	RW	RW	RW	RW	RW	RW/CW	FOLD	FOLD	FOLD
K/J	FOLD	RW	RW	RW	RW	CW	RW/CW	FOLD	FOLD	FOLD
K/10	FOLD	CW	RW	RW	RW	CW	RW/CW	FOLD	FOLD	FOLD
K/9	FOLD	FOLD	FOLD	RW	RW	CW	CW	FOLD	FOLD	FOLD
Q/10	FOLD	CW	CW	RW	RW	CW	CW	FOLD	FOLD	FOLD
J/10	FOLD	CW	CW	RW	RW	CW	CW	FOLD	FOLD	FOLD

A player's range can help narrow down and determine what your opponent is holding. In this chart above, you'll see which hands you should call with (CW), raise with (RW) and fold (FOLD) with, when you're in that situation. These are suggestive hands for almost any style of player. For example, if you're in early position (EP) and you hold A-A, you will obviously raise with it (RW). And if you're holding K-10, and someone has 3-bet you, then you would make the easy fold. If someone has made a 4-bet and you have 10-10, then the best choice would be to fold. And if someone pushes all-in and you have A-Q, then your only choice would be to fold. His range is better than A-Q, so make the easy muck. If you see: RW/CW, then it's up to you to decide to call or to raise, depending on the player in the BB or SB if someone has limped in the small blind.

In the chart below (next page), you'll see the range on which type of player would play these particular hands in different situations. What a loose player (L), a tight player (T) or a tight-aggressive player (TA) will play in different positions. Any type of player outside of these guidelines, will be determined by your own instincts and understanding of that particular player.

	EP	MP	HI-JACK	CUT-OFF	BUTTON	SB	BB	3-BET	4-BET	ALL-IN
A/A	L, T, TA	L, T, TA	L, T, TA	L, T, TA	L, T, TA	L, T, TA	L, T, TA	L, T, TA	L, T, TA	L, T, TA
K/K	L, T, TA	L, T, TA	L, T, TA	L, T, TA	L, T, TA	L, T, TA	L, T, TA	L, T, TA	L, T, TA	L, T, TA
Q/Q	L, T, TA	L, T, TA	L, T, TA	L, T, TA	L, T, TA	L, T, TA	L, T, TA	L, T, TA	L, T, TA	L, T
J/J	L, T, TA	L, T, TA	L, T, TA	L, T, TA	L, T, TA	L, T, TA	L, T, TA	L, T, TA	L	L, T
10/10	L, T, TA	L, T, TA	L, T, TA	L, T, TA	L, T, TA	L, T, TA	L, T, TA	L, TA	L	L
9/9	L, T, TA	L, T, TA	L, T, TA	L, T, TA	L, T, TA	L, T, TA	L, T, TA	L, TA	L	L
8/8	L, T, TA	L, T, TA	L, T, TA	L, T, TA	L, T, TA	L, T, TA	L, T, TA	L, TA	L	L
7/7	L, T, TA	L, T, TA	L, T, TA	L, T, TA	L, T, TA	L, T, TA	L, T, TA	L, TA	L	L
6/6	L, T, TA	L, T, TA	L, T, TA	L, T, TA	L, T, TA	L, T, TA	L, T, TA	L	L	FOLD
5/5	L, T, TA	L, T, TA	L, T, TA	L, T, TA	L, T, TA	L, T, TA	L, T, TA	L	L	FOLD
4/4	L, T, TA	L, T, TA	L, T, TA	L, T, TA	L, T, TA	L, T, TA	L, T, TA	L	L	FOLD
3/3	L, T, TA	L, T, TA	L, T, TA	L, T, TA	L, T, TA	L, T, TA	L, T, TA	L	L	FOLD
2/2	L, T, TA	L, T, TA	L, T, TA	L, T, TA	L, T, TA	L, T, TA	L, T, TA	L	L	FOLD
A/K	L, T, TA	L, T, TA	L, T, TA	L, T, TA	L, T, TA	L, T, TA	L, T, TA	L, T, TA	L, T	L, T, TA
A/Q	L, T, TA	L, T, TA	L, T, TA	L, T, TA	L, T, TA	L, T, TA	L, T, TA	L, T	L, T	L, T
A/J	L, T, TA	L, T, TA	L, T, TA	L, T, TA	L, T, TA	L, T, TA	L, T, TA	L, T	L, T	L
A/10	L, TA	L, T, TA	L, T, TA	L, T, TA	L, T, TA	L, T, TA	L, T, TA	L	L	L
A/9	L, TA	L, T, TA	L, T, TA	L, T, TA	L, T, TA	L, T, TA	L, T, TA	L	L	L
A/8	L, TA	L, T, TA	L, T, TA	L, T, TA	L, T, TA	L, T, TA	L, T, TA	L	L	FOLD
A/7	L	L, T, TA	L, T, TA	L, T, TA	L, T, TA	L, T, TA	L, T, TA	L	L	FOLD
A/6	L	L, TA	L, T, TA	L, T, TA	L, T, TA	L, T, TA	L, T, TA	L	L	FOLD
A/5	L	L, TA	L, T, TA	L, T, TA	L, T, TA	L, T, TA	L, T, TA	L	L	FOLD
A/4	L	L, TA	L, T, TA	L, T, TA	L, T, TA	L, T, TA	L, T, TA	L	L	FOLD
A/3	L	L, TA	L, T, TA	L, T, TA	L, T, TA	L, T, TA	L, T, TA	L	L	FOLD
A/2	L	L, TA	L, T, TA	L, T, TA	L, T, TA	L, T, TA	L, T, TA	L	L	FOLD
K/Q	L, T, TA	L, TA	L, T, TA	L, T, TA	L, T, TA	L, T, TA	L, T, TA	L	FOLD	L
K/J	L, TA	L, TA	L, T, TA	L, T, TA	L, T, TA	L, T, TA	L, T, TA	L	FOLD	FOLD
K/10	L	L	L, T, TA	L, T, TA	L, T, TA	L, T, TA	L, T, TA	L	FOLD	FOLD
K/9	L	L, TA	L	L, TA	L, T, TA	L, T, TA	L, T, TA	L	FOLD	FOLD
Q/10	L	L, TA	L, T, TA	L, T, TA	L, T, TA	L, T, TA	L, T, TA	L	FOLD	FOLD
J/10	L, TA	L, TA	L, T, TA	L, T, TA	L, T, TA	L, T, TA	L, T, TA	L	FOLD	FOLD

218

PROFESSIONAL SECRETS ♠

Here is a list of professional secrets the best players in the world don't want you to know:

1. Always 3- and 4-bet against an opponent who is capable of folding and is out of position.
2. When a player makes a squeeze play, and is known for it, and you're sitting in the blinds, choose to 4-bet it with any two cards.
3. Check-raise frequently against a player who makes standard continuation bets, even on a scary board.
4. Represent more hands when your table is short-handed. Assure yourself you are making larger bets and have an extensive knowledge of your opponents calling ranges.
5. Be more aggressive against other aggressive players when your hand has a value stronger than your opponents.
6. Steal all pots, when in position, and look to steal orphan pots when players show weakness.
7. Weak bets usually mean a weak hand. Raising might not be the best option. Calling them down might be better to extract more chips. Raise if you feel his range consist of big draws and middle pairs with backdoor redraws. Raise more often on the turn than on the flop.

8. Always put yourself (your cards) in fold equity. You should always leave room to fold when you sense strength from an opponent. Stack sizes and the amount you bet, or raise should factor in how committed you're trying to be. But don't make small bets because you're afraid of being raised. Play your hand normally but vary your bets with the idea of folding if he plays back at you, when holding a weak hand.

9. Track all LAG (loose-aggressive players) at your table. Setting traps and getting full value for your superior hands, pay off best, against these types of opponents.

10. Learn to steal from UTG (under the gun). Most players use this position as an obvious "tell" of strength. Bluff occasionally, especially if the later positions players are considered tight.

11. Most players can steal a pot but learn how to re-steal and steal. Being aggressive when in and out of position against loose players making a play at the pot. The button, hi-jack and the cut-off seats are areas of great bluffing opportunities. Steal pots against opponents who are making plays in these spots.

12. Make small 3- and 4-bets against tight-aggressive and experienced professionals. In position or not, they will more often than not fold, deciding not to be too committed.

13. Limping and not making 3- and 4-bets with monster starting hands. Learn to mix it up and

get a greater value for your hand. Chances are they won't put you on a premium hand, since you didn't 3-bet preflop.

14. Check-raise bluffs against opponents with large stacks on a scary board and their range doesn't fall in to what he is trying to represent; medium straight and weak flushes when he was in early position preflop.

15. Call more all-ins preflop when the price is right. No matter what you're holding, call more often the pot odds are correct and your stack can afford it. This is generally geared more towards tournaments.

16. Make a minimum raise on the river when you sense your opponent is holding a medium strength hand and is capable of folding based on his knowledge of betting and position tells.

17. Occasionally "float" (calling a bet with no draw and no pair, in hopes of stealing the pot on a later street). Against better players who make c-bets, and positional bets, this play works quite well. You can choose to check-call the flop and bet out on the turn. Mix it up from time to time to keep your opponents guessing.

18. Lead out against a preflop raiser when the board is dry. Occasionally check-raise when you sense he missed the board completely.

19. Induce bluffing, with big hands, against opponents who make frequent attempts at stealing the pot.

20. Over bet the pot against predictable players playing in live games that indicate they play online primarily. Use this play when they show signs of strength, but not with a stronger hand that you are currently holding.

21. Don't be too aggressive in small pots, especially if the pot was not raised preflop. Keep it small, even with big starting hands. Extract as much as you can at a minimum price. Too many players go broke in un-raised pots, because they fail to let big hands go against opponents who vary their limping range.

22. If you're playing poker online, choose to play in games where more flops are seen. In these games, it's easier to steal pots, especially in tables of 6-max.

23. If you feel an opponent is making a play postflop, and you are in position with a monster hand, then simply call his check-raise and play the hand slow until the river.

24. Vary your bet sizes on the types of opponents you are playing against. Generally, you want to bet more against loose players and less against tight players.

25. Fold on the button from time to time to let your opponents know you don't always steal from that position. Of course, only fold when you have a very weak hand. Make similar plays when you're in the cut-off and hi-jack seat as

well. This play will help you steal more pots at various times in the game.

26. Evaluate a player's range based on his position, the players in the blinds, button and cut-off and who is being aggressive prior to your turn. Tight players in the blinds can determine the loose range for a player making a raise preflop. Same rule applies for player in later positions. Loose and aggressive player in these similar positions can determine a range that is significantly tighter.

27. Check-call doesn't necessarily mean a draw or even a hand say like, middle pair. If you raised preflop and it's against an experienced player, he could be floating. His play on the turn should determine his holdings. A bet into you on the turn could mean a floater.

28. Frequently raise a check-raise, on the flop, against an aggressive player, when the board is dry. Re-steal his attempt at trying to take the pot away from you.

29. Don't be afraid to push against a large stack when you feel he is trying to make a move at the pot. Aggressive players like to put others in situations for most, or all, their chips. Pushing against a small stack is not the best idea. Chances are they will call.

30. Use position to your advantage against players who make standard positional plays. 3- and 4-betting out of position against a player

who raises preflop in early position can make players fold, in fear of a stronger hand. If they play back at you, then simply fold.

31. Choose to play more hands out of position against players who play hit-or-miss postflop. Betting into them after the flop can help you take down more pots.

32. When playing heads up, play draws weak and made hands strong. Since the value in your holdings increase, your odds of hitting are slim, so be aggressive when you hit a good board. Using this method against a loose player will help assure a good victory.

33. Minimum raises preflop, while playing heads up poker can alter your opponent's style of play. Most players don't min-raise, so when in position, they will give up more pots than they are used to.

34. Be more aggressive against players, in a tournament, when you feel they always have a fear of getting knocked out. Players who fold frequently trying to move up a spot are sure signs of this label.

35. When a player to your left is known for making squeeze plays, and you're sitting there with premium Aces; Aces, Kings or A-K, then occasionally call and the player make this 3-bet, so when it comes back to you, you can choose to either flat call or 4-bet.

36. Pots are stolen less often than people think, so do your fair share of stealing, but make sure your bets indicate a strong hand. Most players try to steal the pot with a half size bet, where most players will call due to pot odds. Learn to bet around 80% of the pot to force most opponents to fold.

37. Attack the limpers who are known for trying to see flops at a cheap price. Make large raise to fold them out. If they do decide to call your raise, then continue to be aggressive on most boards. Any board containing multiple big cards should be played with caution.

38. Don't be afraid to take notes while playing poker during a live game. Categorize your opponents and how they play different hands in different positions. Having good memory will help, but for most, they can't remember what they had for lunch prior to sitting down. Like playing online poker, it helps you make easier decisions based on previous play a player has made. Examples are:

    a. How often does he raise preflop and check the flop?
    b. What is his range in early, middle and late position?
    c. How often does he check-raise with bluffs?
    d. Does he bet into preflop raisers?
    e. Does he slow-play or set traps?

f. Or any other play each player makes that makes his/her stand out above the rest.

39. Keep your 3- and 4-bets standard in size so your opponents don't pick up a betting pattern.
40. Always evaluate your game after each session so you keep improving your game. The game is changing every day with opponents who can mix it up with the best of them. Keeping up with accurate styles and tells can help you prolong your status as a professional.

FUTURE BETTING ♣

A lot of players will play a hand with failure to think about future betting. Future betting is when you choose to call with a mediocre hand in hopes of improving on the next street. Most players may think this is floating, but it's not. Floating is calling a bet knowing your opponent is weak, where calling a bet in hopes of improving, and ignoring the face the player will most likely bet on the next street is basically wasting your chips (if you don't improve on the next street). When you choose to call a bet on the flop, and you don't improve on the turn, your most frequent play is to check-fold. Some players may choose to check-raise, but the likelihood of that player folding is unheard of, unless you decide to go all-in.

The idea behind this flop play is to raise on the flop or fold. If you are sitting there with a mediocre hand, it is better to either fold and save your chips for a better spot or make a small raise to see where you stand. If you raise on the flop and your opponent doesn't 3-bet, then you should be able to see a turn card for free. He will most likely check the turn thinking you'll bet again. You may choose to, but I doubt he will fold. Your best play is to check as well and see if you improve on the river.

If the river helps you, then simply play your hand accordingly. If the river is a blank and he checks again, and you have no showdown value, then a large bet may force him to fold. Making a standard size bet will only induce him to call. If he bets on the river after a rag hits, then folding may be your only option. Knowing his range will help determine if your mediocre hand is good enough to call with. My guess is that he has top pair but a weak kicker. Some players may make a similar play against a player who fails to understand future betting, so a check on the turn and a river bet no matter what falls, could represent strength. Loose players are known for making this kind of play. They bet the flop hoping to steal the pot because it's short-handed and whether you raise or not may slow down to see the river. The action on the turn will resolve how he plays the river. If you checked the turn, then it's an easy play to bet the river and force you to fold with a hand possibly better than his. Loose players understand position, but will use it against typical players, and if he knows you'll fold hands of value to a river bet, even though you are last to act and should be more aggressive, then he'll use this play to his advantage.

Never put yourself in a situation where future betting could cost you more than it should have. If you have a tough decision on the flop, then knowledge of your opponents and his future betting will establish how you should play your hand. From time to time I will choose to call on the flop knowing he will bet the turn, but I will make this play to call on the turn as well knowing he likes to slow down on the river when a scare card hits. This play is normally made when we have large stacks.

OVERVALUING HANDS ◆

The idea behind overvaluing hands is depending on the person and how he plays it against targeted players with signs of obvious strength. Players who overvalue hands are usually rookies and amateurs who feel particular hands have stronger true value than they perceive.

Hands like:

> A-Q unsuited,
> A-J unsuited,
> A-10 unsuited,
> A-9 suited or unsuited,
> A-8 suited or unsuited,
> A-7 suited or unsuited,
> A-6 suited or unsuited,
> A-5 suited or unsuited,
> K-J suited or unsuited,
> K-10 suited or unsuited,
> K-9 suited, one-gap suited cards, and
> many more.

These hands should be played with more caution under optimal situations. Being aggressive first with these hands, normally do better than calling a bet or raise in or out of position.

Other hands that normally have strong value and are not overvalued like, A-K, A-Q suited, low/middle pocket pairs and more have normal strong value in most situations, but in certain spots, these hands decrease in value. Any time there 3-and 4-bets from players who are known for raising with big hands, aside from A-K, should be played with carefulness. Occasionally you should 3-bet with A-K, but the raise from the original player should be making from middle or later position. If a player chooses to raise preflop and you're sitting there with A-K in later position, then a flat call would be the best play. You would hate to 3-bet and wind up facing a 4-bet. Other hands stated early in this section that have real value in most spots should be played similar with flat calls and the rare raise but done under specific situations. Short-handed tables and loose players making the first raise is the best spot to 3-bet with A-Q, low and middle pocket pairs and other hands with similar implied odd value.

Too many players are afraid to fold hands with some value preflop even when faced with a raise. They feel if they hit the flop in any way, they should be able to win the pot. Most of the time, they will lose to a better hand. Even hands that have similar value that the original raise is holding can beat your hand in spots where the kicker plays a key role. When a player looks down and see a hand of value, they don't realize that in many spots, that they are overvaluing their hand, ignoring position and most importantly, ignoring player knowledge. I remember one time, early, during a live tournament with stacks about even, where a player raised preflop in middle position and I was sitting there with

A♠-Q♥

in the cut-off seat. I thought about it for a second trying to figure out what type of player he is as well as his range. I wanted to 3-bet to isolate the players sitting in the blinds as well as anyone trying to make a squeeze play against me. After a few minutes, I decided to fold and let the players behind me play out the hand.

The reason why I folded was because I felt the raiser was sitting there with no less than a bigger ace. Even a pocket pair would put me in a spot of a coin flip and our chips stacks didn't justify an all-in move, so folding was my best option. Even if I had a large chip stack, I didn't feel like risking too much on a coin flip at this part of the game if he chose to make a large 4-bet, and I didn't want to push him all-in, incase he was sitting there with A-K, since he seemed like the type of player who would call in that spot. The action continued with the button folding as well as the small blind. When it came to the big blind, he chose to make a large 3-bet and the original raiser called. After the board rolled out of all rags and low non-connecting cards, and the hand was over with action on every round (the big blind check-called the whole way), with a fold by the big blind on the river, the player in middle position showed his cards and flashed K-K.

Most players would have called, if not raised, with my hand preflop, but I felt he was a tighter player and his raise preflop indicated strength. Under normal circumstances, I would have played my hand aggressively, but in this spot, a fold was my best option. And I was right. Even though I would have folded to the big blinds 3-bet, I still managed to save some chips for a better spot. If for some chance I saw the flop, it would have been a check-fold against two opponents if either one of them bet.

DIFFICULT DECISIONS ♥

Difficult decisions occur when you pick up hands in the worst spot and you usually lose with them or you're put in a situation where you have no clue what to do. These spots normally take place in critical spots in tournaments and large pots, multi-way, in a cash game. I'm sure you have been in many spots where you look at your two cards, assess the situation, but still have no clue what the best move is. In this section, I will talk about these situations and what is the best move for accurate decisions.

Have you ever been late in a tournament, near the bubble, and a player from early position raises preflop and two players call? The action folds around to you, on the button, and you look down and see a middle pocket pair or even A-K. You know your only options are to fold or to 3-bet all-in. Calling is an option but in a multi-way pot, it could be even more difficult to make the right decision if the pot is all scare cards. The range for the first position raiser is probably a hand of real value. He is probably holding a big ace or a large pocket pair. Even though the bubble is near, and most players like to sit back and wait to get paid, you must be the aggressive player and force opponents to fold, so you can accumulate more chips for a better chance at not only the final table, but a chance to win the whole tournament.

The two players who called preflop most likely have hands of some value. In this spot, their range could be a wide array of possible holdings. In any matter, if you choose to 3-bet, the two callers will most likely fold. What the original player will do is undetermined. If he calls, at best you're a coin flip. Late in tournaments, it's not bet to risk it all on a coin flip. Even though you want to call and possibly win more chips to assure yourself a better position, you opt to fold and move on to the next hand.

In the actual hand, the flop came with an ace, the original better makes a large bet and the other players fold. My guess for the original preflop raiser to be holding is A-K. So, if you were sitting there with a pocket pair, chances are you would have gone broke. If he was trying to represent a big ace but was only holding a pocket pair better than 9's, then hopes for you winning is still possible. Maybe next time you'll push all-in and risk your tournament life. Either or, there is no right or wrong decision in this spot. You just hope you made the best play at the right time. If you didn't then chalk it up to experience and choose better next time.

Similar situations occur when you have a good hand preflop, in a cash game, and you're not sure what to do. Cash games, unlike tournaments, give you the opportunity to re-buy as often as you like, so making borderline calls is a little easier. Even in coin flips, if the price is right and your opponents potential range does not dominate your hand, then a call is correct. Make a squeeze play and force others to fold. Who knows, maybe the original raiser will fold as well. If he is a loose-aggressive player, then he may choose to play along with you. If you're short-stacked, then it's an easy all-in, but if everyone at the table has a sizeable stack, then I would make a smaller 3-bet to see where I stand. Depending on my hand, I would only fold if the pot wasn't offering enough in return if my opponent decides to 4-bet.

More often than not, when you're faced with a difficult decision, the best decision is to fold and wait for a better spot, even if you would have won the pot. Pot odds, players range may alter your decision to make a move, but unless the pot or table is short-handed, your best move in these difficult situations, is to fold and wait for a better spot to be the aggressor.

PART 3

EXAMPLES FROM VOLUME 2

CONTROLLING THE POT SIZE EXAMPLE ♥

Since these concepts are already explained in this book, most of the examples for them will be short and right to the point.

Controlling the pot size is crucial when you hold hand of some value, but you don't want to be priced out of the pot. Here is an example of controlling the pot size.

During a tournament, you have a medium stack and you find yourself in the money when you look down and see J♥-10♥, in the small blind. There is a raise from early position and two callers. You decide to call as well.

The flop comes: A♣-Q♥-5♥,

giving you a gut-shot straight draw and a flush draw. You decide to check and the preflop raiser makes an almost pot size bet and gets one caller. In this situation, this is an easy call, so you flat call. Even though you have a number of outs, it would not be right to raise against the preflop raiser, who most likely has a good hand, and a caller.

The turn is a 7♦.

Here is a spot where controlling the pot size would make the most sense. You have a decent hand with 12 outs, and you know if you check again, then the preflop raiser will make another large bet, possibly pricing you out of the pot. And what if the caller decides to make a move and raise on a "blank" turn card? You would have to fold in this spot as well. So, to almost assure you'll see a river card, you must control the pot size and make a bet at least half the pot size. The preflop raiser will most likely flat call, unless he if afraid of the flush draw, and the middle position caller had no choice but to either, call or fold.

In most cases, the preflop raiser will just call and see the river, especially if he has a medium ace or weaker hand himself. The middle position caller will most likely fold, if the preflop raiser calls, feeling you, and/or, the other opponent has a much stronger hand. Sometimes both players will call, depending on their range and style of play. Hopefully, if that happens, the river will improve your hand. Otherwise, you may have to give up on the hand and check it to them.

By betting the turn, you are saving yourself some chips by betting less than your opponent would bet, hoping to improve on the river. If you decided to check the turn instead, then your opponent would most likely make another large bet, to force his opponents to fold, and making the price of seeing the river too costly. Unless you know exactly the type of hands your opponent likes to play and bet with, you'll have to fold most draws when the price of seeing the next card is too much, based on your return in implied odds.

GAMBLING WHEN YOU'RE UNSURE EXAMPLE ♠

You're playing in a tournament, you're one of the short stacks, but not the shortest, and you limp in with K♦-5♦ on the button, with no raise preflop.

With 6 players in the hand, the flop comes, A♣-K♠-9♦. Everyone checks to the player to your right, who makes a standard size bet. Now, it's up to you. You have a middle pair, but there was no raise preflop. Could he really have an Ace, K-9 or a set of 9's? You could call and see a turn card and see if he makes another bet. But, what is your best play?

You decide to push all-in. Everyone else folds to the player to your right. He thinks about it for a while, and you think about what two cards he could possibly be holding.

(You're glad he didn't snap call, which means the previous hands stated he doesn't have).

1. A weak Ace?
2. King with a good kicker, but worried you have the ace (probably with a weak kicker)?
3. A draw?
4. A bluff, to take away position from you?

Your opponent decides to call and flips over K♥-10♣. You catch runner-runner for a flush and take down the pot. Did he make a good call? Or since you were the short-stack, he was willing to gamble.

It wasn't the worst call, in my opinion, but, at the same time, it wasn't a really good call. You could have easily limped in with a weak ace, and with no raise preflop, you knew if you hit the ace, your hand would be good. I'm assuming he called because you were short-stacked and was hoping you had a similar hand or weaker. I probably would have made the call myself in his shoes. If it's not costing me too much more to call, and possibly knock out an opponent, then I'll be glad to make the call with a middle pair and a good kicker.

PUSHING WITH DRAWS
EXAMPLE ♦

You're holding K♦-J♥, during the mid-levels of a low stakes cash game, and you raise preflop in middle position. You get 3 callers.

The flop comes: Q♣-9♦-4♦.

The player in position makes a medium size bet, the big blind folds. Now it's up to you, with a player waiting on the button.

You call with a gut-shot and over card, suspecting he has top pair or a draw. The button calls as well.

The turn is an 8♦. Now you have a flush draw to go with your straight draw and over card. The player in first position bets again and you decided to raise. The button folds.

The first position bettor makes a large 3-bet for almost all his chips. You don't suspect him to have 10-J for the straight, but he could have a set (4's). You could call and see if you hit the river, but you decide to show aggression since you started it preflop. If he has only queen, then you have even more outs.

The first position player folds, showing Q♠-7♠.

You flash the King of diamonds to make him think you hit the flush. If you would have called and the river was a blank, then your opponent would have most likely made another bet, and your only move would be to fold. But by you pushing with your draw, you were able to take down the pot with worst hand.

In a tournament this would be a tougher play to make, since most players play more straight forward. I still think it's a good play to make in a tournament if you know your opponent well enough. Since he didn't 3-bet preflop, there's no way he has a better hand than a set. Your call with a pair of Queens was the most likely holding he had. Since you showed aggression preflop against this type of player, it only makes sense to continue that aggression on one of the streets.

SLOW PLAYING EXAMPLE ♣

You're playing in a high stakes tournament at the Bellagio, with an average chip stack and 400 players left. The top 250 pay out, and you find yourself with 2♦-2♣ in the big blind. There is a raise preflop, two callers, the small blind folds and you call.

The flop comes: 2♥-A♦-8♣.

You check, and the preflop raiser makes a large bet. Everyone folds to the button to raises 3x his bet. You flat call. The preflop raiser calls as well.

The turn is a: 6♥. You check again, and the preflop raiser checks as well. The button makes a pot size bet. At this point, you really don't have anything to worry about, unless the preflop raiser has pocket Aces. You could raise and push out the weaker hands that could out draw you, then unless you are beat by a set (ace or 8's), you have no reason to push anyone out. If by chance you are beat, then you'll just have to pay one of them off.

The preflop raiser calls as well.

The river is a 3♠. You probably have the best hand, and you could bet to see if you're beat, or you could check and see what your opponents do.

You decide to check again, and so does the preflop raiser. The button makes a medium size bet (assuming for value). You decide to make a small raise to see where you sit. The preflop raiser folds and the button calls quickly flipping over A♥-8♥. You take down the pot with your set. The preflop raiser said he had A-K.

Most players with a set will bet or raise on the turn to push out the weaker hands, but in this pot, the board as dry of real draws, so slow-playing it to the river made the most sense. It also made you the most money.

Of course, if a heart hit the river, you would most likely have him off, unsuspecting him to catch running hearts for a flush. If you feel your opponent loves to play any suited cards, and will play them aggressively, then choose to raise on the turn to price him out.

SETTING TRAPS EXAMPLE ♥

Similar to slow-playing, this deserves a section of its own. Here is a good, but rare example, of setting a trap.

You're playing in a tournament at your local casino and it's down to one table. You have a medium stack, when you find yourself with Q♠-J♠ in late position. There is a raise from early position, but you decide to call. The big blind calls as well.

The flop comes: 9♣-8♦-10♠.

You flopped the nuts, and the big blind quickly checks. The preflop raiser makes an over bet (signs of a huge hand). You flat call, and the big blind folds.

The turn is an A♥.

The preflop raiser now checks and you make a half pot size bet. The preflop raiser, raises your bet 3x. You ponder for a moment and just call. No need to 3-bet him, unless you know for sure he has pocket Aces.

The turn is a 4♦.

The preflop raiser bets pot, and you push all-in. He snap calls, and flips over A-A. You win with your straight.

Where to start? His over bet on the flop indicated he had an over pair, but it's tough to put someone on Aces. When he check-raised the turn, you must know he had Aces, since he was being aggressive when the ace hit. Some player may over bet the flop with A-K with a weaker board, but this play is rarely done.

When he raised on the turn, you could have 3-bet him and forced him to push all-in, since he will call every time, but just in case he didn't have the Ace, you simple called and set the trap on the river for him to bet again. When he bet, it's only right to push all-in to make him call, since most players will not fold a set of Aces. Great trap play, and you definitely got the most out of your hand in a spot where you sort of knew his hand but wanted to wait until the river to extract more chips. Luckily the river didn't pair, otherwise you would have lost all your chips. But, in hindsight, whether it happened on the turn or river, you still would have made the same play, risking all your chips with the nut straight.

MAKING UNSUAL PLAYS EXAMPLE ♠

You're playing in an online tournament, and it's down to two tables, with you being the big stack. You look down and see: 10♥-10♣. You raise in first position and get 3 callers.

The flop comes: A♥-J♦-5♠.

You are first to act with 3 players waiting, so you decide to check, because you are worried about someone having an Ace. The player in middle position makes a small bet, and the player on the button calls. You call as well, to see how the turn plays out.

The turn is an A♦.

With the board pairing Aces, you decided to bet out half the pot. You get one caller.

The river is a 9♥.

With your opponent calling your bet on the turn, you are worried he must have an ace, so you check it, hoping he'll check back, and you could win on showdown value.

Your opponent bets slightly more than half the pot. What could he be possibly holding?

1. Trip Aces?
2. Jack with a good kicker?
3. A bluff?
4. A set of 5's for a full house?

You decide to make an unusual play and check-raise him all his chips. Unless he has a big Ace or a full house, he can't call. Your opponent thinks about it for a very long time. With him taking so much time, you know he doesn't have a huge hand. He either has a weak ace or a pair of Jacks. After some time, he decides to fold, not showing his cards.

In this situation your opponent could have easily has an Ace, but calling your raise preflop, I could rule him out of having such a hand. If he had a big Ace, he probably would have 3-bet preflop, unless he was worried I had a big pair, raising from my position. If he had a set, he would have played a little differently, since I didn't show aggression on the flop, so he must have known I didn't have an Ace. If I had an Ace, I would have bet on the flop, and a raise with a set, would have been the right play. His only hand is a pair of Jacks. Great read, and great play, making this an unusual play.

OPPONENTS MAKING UNUSUAL PLAYS EXAMPLE ♦

Similar to the previous section, now I'll show you an example of when one of your opponents' makes an unusual play.

You're playing in a low-stakes tournament, and you have the average stack. A loose player in early position raises preflop 3x the big blind. He gets two callers and now it's up to you in the hijack seat.

You have: K♦-K♣. You make the easy 3-bet, and the original raiser calls. One other opponent calls as well.

The flop comes: Q♥-10♦-6♠. The loose player in early position bets pot, and the player in middle position makes a minimum raise. The play is on you now.

You 3-bet preflop, and both players are betting and raising in to you. You would think since you 3-bet preflop against an early position raise, that you must have a very strong hand. Maybe you're beat in this situation, so you save your chips and choose to fold. I mean, what could they have?

1. Two pair?
2. A set?
3. Just a draw?
4. Over playing top pair?

5. Slow playing Aces?

The loose player calls.

The turn is a blank and both players check.

The river is also a blank and the loose player in middle position bets half the pot, and the player in middle position folds quickly. The player loose player flashes A-Q. The player in middle position says he had a pair of tens.

I don't know where to begin. Both players showing all this aggression against your 3-bet preflop, making you fold the best hand. Ok, I understand the A-Q play (kind of), but not the unusual play from the middle position player, that raised with middle pair, with me still waiting to act. I know some players over play top pair, but I still think his call with A-Q preflop was a little bad, and of course, the call with K-10 was even worse. They should have known I had a big hand, and when the flop hit, why were they so aggressive before the action came to me?

From time to time, you will see players making these unusual plays, and all you must do, is shake your hand and move on the next hand. I think if this was a cash game, I would be more inclined to call his bet and see how they played the turn card, but in a tournament, you protect your chips more, and fold when you feel you may be beat. Next time, just push all-in and hope for the best. You're not really worried about a hand that has you dominated, just a hand that could outdraw you.

FORCING YOUR OPPONENT TO FOLD EXAMPLE ♣

Similar to the previous section, only in reverse. Now, it's your turn to make an opponent fold, when they have the best hand (most likely).

You're playing in a mid-stakes level cash game, and your have the most chips at the table. Everyone folds to you on the button and decided to limp in with 9♥-7♠ on the button. Both blinds call.

The flop comes: A♣-Q♥-8♦.

The small blind checks and the big blinds bets half the pot. You call, floating to the turn, using your position. The small blind folds.

The turn is a: 10♣. The big blind bets half the pot again, and you decide to raise 3.5x his bet. He calls.

The river is a 3♠, and the big blind makes a value bet. You ponder for a moment and raise an almost pot size amount. The big blind thinks about it for a very long time, talking to you, trying to see if he is beat.

During this one-sided conversation, you are thinking he probably has a weak ace, and puts you on two pair or better. What your opponent should be thinking is, why did I just limp on the button? This is a play where raises come from the most. If he understands position at this level, then he must put me on a big hand, and by limping preflop, I was trying to trap my opponent and earn more chips postflop.

After a while, the big blind decides to fold, barely flashing his Ace. You show your bluff, while he shakes his head, agreeing that your limp on the button was suspicious, but he couldn't make the call. You take down the pot, forcing your opponent to fold the best hand.

What I don't understand is, if he felt I had a big hand when I limped preflop, then why was he continuing to bet into me? I know I'm able to mix up my plays, but if his instincts were saying, "FOLD" then why didn't he listen to them and give up the hand? My guess is that of what a lot of players do: They see a hand of value, and since there was no raise preflop, then his top pair must be good. What most players don't notice, is that a skilled player will limped in the right situation, trying to trap his opponents, to out play them, and win more chips postflop, forcing only the more aware players to fold their hands.

PATIENCE EXAMPLE ♥

Patience, in a poker game, doesn't really need an example (just like the next few sections, so I'll just sum up their meanings). As stated in the section, it's just a state of mind where you need to evaluate the flow of table, and assure you're making the correct decisions. Don't play outside your limits or make plays too often you're not used to. Pick your spots when playing a hand, and in the long run, you will be successful.

BEING AGGRESSIVE EXAMPLE ♠

Being aggressive is just as it sounds. Playing your hand aggressively enough to either earn more chips against an opponent with a strong hand as well, but not as strong as yours. Playing your best starting hands for full value, and choosing when to be aggressive with weaker hands, against opponents with hands of value.

If you pocket big Aces and big pocket pairs, then you should be 3- and 4-betting. If you hit big draws against weaker opponents, then should play them aggressive as well. Or, if you sense weakness, or are playing against players who can fold big hands to aggression, then you must be aggressive with that as well. Mix up your game, but when the right time comes, be aggressive and take down those large or uncontested pots.

PLAYING TIGHT EXAMPLE & PLAYING LOOSE EXAMPLE ♦

It's as simple as mixing up your game, when the flow and the players at the table ask for it indirectly. If the table is tight, then loosen up your game. If the table is loose, then tighten up your game. If the flow is one way, then switches to another, then you should be aware of this, and adjust your game accordingly. You should always base your plays around how the table is playing. I don't care what hands you are playing, just play them in a style that fits best with the table, and the players involved. Occasionally, play them in an "opposite" manner, to keep your opponents guessing.

Sometimes, I'll play a loose table, loose, or a tight table, tight, but it doesn't always work. If I feel my opponents are aware of this, then I can use this play against them. They think I'm playing at the flow of the table, but I'll mix it and play a hand, and its' style, the most unpredictable way. Most of the time it fails, but every once in a while, it'll make my opponents scratch their head. And from then on out, my game is completely unpredictable, and I'll go back to playing the proper strategy, that results in more success than failure.

ON THE BUBBLE EXAMPLE ♣

You're playing at the WSOP, and you've decided to play in the $1,000 (30-minute levels) event #45. You've been playing your best poker and it's getting close to the bubble. Since you have a large stack, you decide to play a little tighter and fold your way to the money. After a couple of hours, there is one spot left to be knocked out, then everyone will make in the money.

There's nothing worse than being knocked out on the bubble and just missing the money by one player. The blinds are high, so you still must play hands, when all-of-a-sudden, you look down and find yourself holding:

A♦-A♥,

on the button. The player in first position make a large raise, and the next three players fold. The player two seats to your right decides to push all-in. Now it's up to you.

The player in early position made a large raise, large enough to, basically, make himself committed, and you have pocket Aces. Do you dare to 4-bet, and hope the early position player folds? Or do you just call and see what he does?

1. If you call and then he calls, then you can check it down, for a safe play.

2. If you call and he pushes all-in, do you really want to risk a large portion of your chips with Ace, against two players?
3. If you call and he folds, then just hope your hand holds up.

Most players will 4-bet with Aces, even though the other opponent will most likely call. But since it's the bubble, and he may still get paid, since he has more chips than the player all-in, he may just snap call and hope for the best. In my opinion, in this spot, I would flat call and see what the original raiser does. Whether he pushes or folds, I'm playing the hand. I'm trying to win the tournament, not just make the money. So, if I have a chance to win a lot of chips, then I will certainly go for it. The only time I would 4-bet with Aces, if when there was only one raise, not two. And, the only time I would fold Aces, is if there were multiple players all-in. I wouldn't want to risk most of my chips against 3 or more players.

Whether you play tight, or loose, when the bubble is approaching, it is your call. Sometimes, I would fold my way to the money, and other times I'll be over aggressive with them, especially at a table of scared players just trying to make the money. Feel out the table, and see what play is best. We all want to make money, but most of us, want to win. And, we can't win unless we win more chips.

TOURNAMENT OR CASH GAME SPECIALIST EXAMPLE ♥

Like earlier in this section, I talked about concepts that really don't need an example. Here is another concept, as well as a few more, that just need some reclarification.

Choosing which game and style you want to be successful at is your call. Most players are naturally better at one game than the other. I'm a tournament specialist and understand that style better than a cash game. I'm trying to expand my skills to the cash game table, but that'll be a process. Play both games and see which fits you better. Normally, it's more structure and flow with a tournament, while a cash game is more aggressive and unpredictable. If your personality leans more towards one style, then I would focus on that game more often. Perfect your game to that flow, then gradually learn the other type.

IS BLUFFING UNDERRATED?
EXAMPLE ♠

We've talked about how bluffing is overrated in volume 1, and in this book, bluffing being underrated. There's no example needed for this topic. You bluff when it feels right, and not just because you get a high from it. Some players don't bluff enough, and some players bluff too much. I think you should bluff less than the average player. Pick your spots, when they can believe the story you're trying to tell. If you bluff too much, most players will start to play along with you. Bluff not enough, and you'll never get action. Balance out when you bluff, and when you feel it right, and you'll soon get action from the average players, and the loose players will start laying big hands down against you.

BLIND POKER EXAMPLE ♦

Blind poker, just like it was stated in the "Blind Poker" section, is playing a hand blind. Playing position, and the players, when making a decision. You'll be surprised how often you can play a hand blind and be successful. If you know your opponents well enough, you'll know what hands they like to play, in every position. You'll also know how they play position defensively, and what hands they will call a raise with, and what hands they will fold. Try it sometime!

ADVANCED POKER TELLS EXAMPLE ♣

You're playing in a major poker tournament, and you've made it to the final table. You have a basic understanding on how everyone plays, but since this is the final table, everyone may play differently. After a few hours of basic play, you look down and see:

> K♦-Q♠, in the hijack seat, and there was a raise from middle position from a loose-style player. You decided to call and everyone else folds.
>
> The flop comes: A♥-8♥-10♦.
>
> You have a gut-shot straight draw, and your opponent makes a small bet. You call.
>
> The turn is a: J♣. Your opponent makes another small bet, and you decide to make a small raise, to see where you stand. He calls.
>
> The river is a: 2♥. Your opponent quickly checks, and you decide to bet half the pot. The river is a little scary, completing a flush, but since he raised

preflop, and played the flop and turn weak, you don't really put him on a flush. He probably has a pocket pair, or a weak ace.

After some thought, your opponent picks up his hand like he is about to muck it. Randomly peaking at his cards again as he shuffles them around. It looks like he is about to fold, when he put his hand down, places a chip on them. And announces, "All-in."

You did not expect this play from him at all. He clearly wanted to fold his hand, but now he pushes all-in? You have the straight and the only hand you are worried about is the flush. Could he really have played his hand in such an odd way?

After thinking about it longer than you ever have before, during any poker game, you decide to call, and your opponent flips over: J♥-9♥, for the flush, and the win.

His play on the flop and turn was very odd, and the way he wanted to fold his hand on the river, make it even more likely that he had a weak hand. Not a typical way to play the hand, but at least we caught one of his advanced tells, and from now on, can use that tell against him next time. I doubt he'll do this tell again, but you never know, unconsciously, he may inadvertently make a blunder.

NOW YOU'RE A PRO EXAMPLE ♥

Here's another example that's not really required, but I didn't want to leave out any concepts from this book.

It's time to decide that you're going to play poker professionally. Do you have everything that's needed to be successful?

1. Money?
2. Time?
3. Experience?
4. Discipline?
5. Successful track records?

Like, I stated in the section, it's not east to be a professional poker, but if you have the opportunity, and the passion, then you should at least try it for a while (on a part-time basis). If you continue to be successful, as you move up in to bigger games, then gradually take the proper steps to be a full-time poker player. I consider myself a part-time player, because I don't feel I have all the requirements to a full-time player. If I had more time, or a larger bankroll, then I might pursue poker full-time. But for now, I enjoy playing when I can.

Even if you win a major tournament, doesn't mean you should be a full-time poker player. Great, you won a big tournament, and you have a large bankroll, it doesn't mean you should quit your job and risk it all playing poker. Start out slowly, and if your bankroll increases without jeopardizing anything, then consider playing professionally.

ONLINE POKER SECRETS
EXAMPLE ♠

The biggest online poker secret, and it's really not a secret, but most players don't use it, is the poker trackers software. This is an easy way to track every player at your table, and how he/she plays in every position. It tracks a statistical number of how often they call, raise, 3-bet, flop, turn and river aggression, c-bet, and so much more. Even when a new player sits down, you can look at his sheet, and see the type of player he is. Just that alone will help you make better decisions against him.

KNOW THE NUMBERS EXAMPLE ◆

Just know the numbers. Understand the math behind poker. It's as simple as that. No need for an example.

A lot of players know the numbers, but they don't necessarily use the numbers on every play they make. And that's okay. Just knowing the numbers, you'll be able to make better decisions based on what odds you have of winning and how far you are behind in the hand (in theory). Calculate the numbers in your head, when the situation calls for it. Understanding your outs, implied odds, reverse implied odds, and the chance of winning in ratio to the pot, and the numbers of players involved in the hand, and you'll start to see how the numbers even out in the end, if you follow suit, and play the numbers when it's required.

Some players will say that it's not how many pots you win, but it's about making the correct decision. This is usually referred to by the math behind poker. A lot of situations will require math as your only decision, and if you know the numbers, you'll make better decisions based off this strategy, and how much math has such an important role.

REFER BACK TO THE MATH SECTION TO REFRESH YOURSELF ON THE NUMBERS.

STEALING THE BLINDS
EXAMPLE ♣

Do you really need an example for this concept? I think it's pretty clear. If you're playing in a tournament, you must steal blinds from time to time, in order to earn uncontested chips, especially when the blinds are about to go up, or the blinds increase at a fast rate. Knowing when to steal blind will be determined by who is in the blinds and how the table has been playing. If the players in the blind rarely defend, and the table is playing on the tighter side, then it's a good spot to try and steal the blinds with any two cards. Another thing you must factor in, is if other players are thinking the same thing. If your table is filled with experienced players, they may try the same thing, and in some cases, may choose to 3-bet your raise, to force you out of the pot with your attempt to steal the blinds. Of course, they won't always know you're just trying to pick up the blinds, so they may just 3-bet trying to take control of the pot. And if they force everyone to fold, then so be it.

If you feel your opponent is trying to make this type of play, and he is capable of making this play based on previous plays, then I would attempt to 4-bet him and make him fold. Normally, loose players are the ones trying to be aggressive preflop. If you have enough chips to force him out, or he feels you really do have a hand based on your plays prior to this one, then he may just lay down the best hand.

In a cash game, blinds don't matter that much. True, the chips have real value, but in a cash game, trying to steal blinds is usually done in position (on some occasion, out of position) against a player who is trying to run the table. Look for the players who are not doing so well, they are the ones trying to steal the blinds against an opponent who is running well, without having his cards shown.

ADVERTISING EXAMPLE ♥

Like it was stated in the section, advertising is just a way to show your hand, in order make your opponent's think on way about how you are playing. I am not a big fan of advertising, but in some situations, I think it's necessary. It can definitely make your opponent think you're playing one way, so you can use that against him later in the game.

Advertising your hand is to show them either:

i.   You're not bluffing, so you can bluff them later.
ii. You have a big hand and want to protect it.
iii. You're not always trying to steal the blinds.
iv. You're raising often, to show you that you really are catching cards.

There are so many ways to advertise your hand, which was all stated in the concept section. I just wanted to give you a refresh. If you never want to show your hand, then don't. But, if you want to show your opponents' one style, so you can mix it up later, then go ahead and advertise. But a word from the wise, don't advertise too much. It could give away too much information.

FOLDING BIG HANDS
PREFLOP EXAMPLE ◆

Folding big hands preflop is not an easy thing to do, especially when you hold Aces or Kings (or sometimes Queens. Even though I have folded Queens before preflop to a standard 3-bet and my opponent showed pocket Kings). Here is an example of folding A-K preflop.

You're playing at the WPT, and you've made it to the final table. There are 5 players left. You have a big stack and are holding A♦-K♥ in the small blind. The player in middle position limps in and the player on the button decides to raise 4x. You decide to 3-bet for a large amount. After some deliberation, the player who limped in, decides to push all-in. The player on the button calls, and now it's up to you.

First, the player in middle position, we know of his suspicious limp, but we didn't think anything of it, until he pushed all-in. The player on the button first raised, then called a 4-bet. He must have a big hand, but as long as either one of them doesn't have Aces or Kings, you're A-K is a good hand to play. You could call and hope for the best, but I think it's best to fold, and let your opponent's play it out.

You decide to fold, and both players flip over their hands at the same time. The player in middle position who limped in, shows K-K, while the player who called the all-in bet, shows J-J. The board runs out and the pocket Kings win.

Whether an Ace hit the board, or not, it doesn't matter. I think you made a good laydown, and in some people's eyes, folding A-K in this spot was a bad move. You had a nice chip stack, and was able to, possibly knock out two opponents, but you chose to fold. I think in some cases I would call with A-K, if I felt my opponent who limped was trying to make a play. For him to just limp in that position, was a little odd. If he would have raised, and the player on the button called or 3-bet, then playing A-K more aggressively would have been the right play. Every situation requires a different play, and if the hand was played a little differently, then I would have risked most of my chips with A-K, against even two opponents. With my chips stack, I would have liked to have been the aggressor, and put them to a decision for all their chips with a big re-raise.

CALLING WITH WEAK HANDS
PREFLOP EXAMPLE ♣

Calling with weak hands preflop, is similar to the previous section, only the complete opposite, and usually not calling all-in bets. I could give you an example of this, but I think at this point, you have a clear understanding what this mean, especially if you carefully read the concepts section earlier in this book.

When you decide to call with a weak hand preflop, it only means one of two things:

1. You plan to outplay them on the flop or
2. You're hoping to catch a big flop and get paid off.

Players who call preflop with weak hands, whether there was a raise or not, are trying to be unpredictable, all in hopes of flopping a huge hand. They know they can get full value against another big hand, just slightly weaker than theirs. Sometimes, the flop can be so dry, that a player with a weak hand will represent its likelihood and play it aggressively. This is usually done when there was no raise preflop.

If you decide to play a hand, like, K-5 suited and the board is A-7-2 rainbow, and there was no raise preflop, then you can easily represent having the Ace and bet out. You'll only get called by hands with weaker pairs and weak draws. Even if you do get called, I would continue betting on the turn. Most likely your opponent will then give up.

Choose your battles carefully when playing a weak hand preflop. If the price is low and you're more of a postflop player (like myself), then you can easily outplay your opponent and win some nice pots. If an opponent plays back at you, then you make the call on the play he is trying to make. He could be trying to steal the pot.... or as stated before, he could have limped in with a monster. Watch out for limpers, and pots that are unraised. They could be traps.

A PLAYER'S RANGE EXAMPLE ♠

A player range is just the type of hands he/she will play in different spots. There are millions of examples I could show you, but I think the best thing to do, is just let you come up with one on your own. Every player is different, and every player will play different hands in different situations, sit there and think about a good example of a players' range, that you, yourself, have played against.

Ask yourself:

1. Was it a standard play?
2. Did he play the same hand differently this time?
3. Does he like to play different hands the same way?
4. Did he just play a hand outside his range?
5. Is position an important factor in the hands he plays?
6. Do other factors play a role in his range?

   a. Chip stacks
   b. Player knowledge
   c. Table flow
   d. Payouts?
   e. Tilt?

Answer these questions and any other you can come up with to determine his/her range. If you know what type of hands they like to play in different position and situations, you'll be able to make better decisions against them, and walk away more successful.

PROFESSIONAL SECRETS
EXAMPLE ♥

Here is one of the examples from the "Professional Secrets" section. A hand that includes a "squeeze play" (one of the concepts in this book), and how you can play against it.

You're playing in a major poker tournament in Vegas, and you've been playing solidly the entire time. You're in the money, and with three table left, you look down and see:

J♣-5♠, in the big blind.

A loose player in middle position raises 3x the big blind bet and gets a caller to his left. The "professional" in late position decides to 3-bet, while the rest of the players fold, and now it's up to you. You clearly don't have a good hand, but this play seems too standard to what they call a "squeeze play." Of course, the professional could have a good hand, as well as the original raiser, but with your playing style, and image during this tournament, and the type of players involved in this hand, you could make the daring choice and make a 4-bet.

You decide to make a large 4-bet, hoping both players will fold. Even if they, or just one of them, calls, you will be first to act, and making a large flop bet, would be your obvious best choice. True, you are out of position, but most players will give a lot of respect to a player making large raises out of position, especially against two players who have already shown aggression.

If they do call preflop and raise your bet on the flop, then simply fold, unless you hit a hand of value. Chances are, they will both fold preflop, unless they have a very strong hand. Even hands, like, a medium or weak ace, or even small to medium pairs, could be folded. With your aggressive play, and being out of position, they must put you on a very strong hand. A lot of players will even fold, A-K and pocket 10's, in this spot.

Knowing when to make the right move, is critical in any poker game. If you are aware of a player(s), making a move similar to a squeeze play, then it's your job to be aware of this, and take a chance by being the more aggressor. A player's style and image, with the way he has been playing prior throughout the tournament, will help you determine if he/she is trying to make a move. Things, like, position, just lost a big hand and could be on tilt, or even as simple as the blinds are about to go up, and their stack is getting shorter, will help determine his next potential play. If you take note of this throughout the tournament, you'll be able to a professional play yourself, and take down more pots than you expected, which is extremely helpful in tournaments.

FUTURE BETTING EXAMPLE ♦

A lot of players don't think about future betting. They see their hand of value and play it accordingly. They don't think about what a player may do on the turn or river. They just call the flop bet, and hope to improve on the turn, or in some cases, pray their opponent won't make another bet on the turn. You always must think about what your opponent may do on the next streets. Here is an example of future betting.

You're playing in an online tournament and you find yourself with, A♥-4♥, in the small blind. A player limps in early position as well as one in middle position. The button calls, you limp, and the big blind checks.

The flop comes: 4♣-9♦-9♠.

You check and so does the player in the big blind. The player in early position bets half the pot and the middle position player calls. The button folds, and now it's up to you. At this point, you could have the best hand, since there was no raise preflop, but at the same time, one of your opponents could be holding a hand, like, 5-5 or A-9.

If you call the bet, and with you being out of position the entire hand, you will have no information on your opponents. They could check the turn, if neither of them has a 9, but that's a risky play against two opponents. So, to eliminate the guessing work on your opponent's hand, you decide to fold, and retreat from their future betting.

If you're thinking about making a different play, be aware. Betting in first position is just as bad, since you still don't have any information on your opponents. If you think check-raising is a good play, you're wrong! Unless they specifically put you on trip 9's, they will not fold. Most players will call with a hand of value against this flop. And, who knows, one of the players may already have a 9, and they won't fold to any bet or raise. With a bet and a caller, you don't stand a chance in your spot. Save your chips for a better situation.

OVERVALUING HANDS EXAMPLE ♣

Overvaluing hands is a common mistake, especially for newer players. The section on this topic is covered quite well, and it gives a good explaining on the hands, and the situations, where players will overvalue their hand. I could give you an example, but I think you should read the concept again. Just because you have a hand of some value, it doesn't mean you have the best of it. Some hands look good, but are played, not only, badly, but have a higher rate of failure. These hands should be played under optimal situations, and should only be proceeded in the perfect scenario, where you have control of the pot.

DIFFICULT DECISIONS EXAMPLE ♠

There are many situations where you must make a difficult decision, but one of my favorites is should you fold K-K preflop? I have never done it before, but I have seen players do it, and they were right. Of course, it does determine on the game you are playing, as well as the players involved. In a cash game, I would never fold pocket Kings preflop, but folding this hand in a tournament is a little more common. I'll probably never fold Kings preflop in a tournament, but I guess, in the right spot, it's an easy fold. Here are some situations where you could make the difficult decision in folding K-K preflop:

1. If a tight player limps in first position, you raise, and then he 3-bets, then it clearly seems like he as Aces. In this spot, you could fold Kings.
2. If there are multiple raises (including an all-in), before it gets you, then you could fold Kings.
3. If a player folds every hand ever dealt to him, then he chooses to raise, then your Kings are probably beat.
4. If a player raises, you 3-bet, he 4-bets, you 5-bet and he pushes all-in, then your Kings could be beat.
5. You're in a tournament with two all-ins, before the action is on you, you could fold your Kings.

PART 4

ADDITIONAL STRATEGIES

POKER WEBSITE ◆

From my (old and unfortunately rarely updated due to time consumption) website, www.ryansleeper. webstarts.com, I have included some of the hands I have played in myself (live games and on the Internet), and some poker advice to help you become a better player with learning how theses concepts work in real life situations. Plus, they're interesting stories of bad beats and big wins.

The poker advice is just some extra lessons for hold'em (and other forms of poker) success. If you haven't seen my website, then this information will be new and exciting for you. If you have, then simply re-read the information to better remind yourself how I handled different hands in different situations.

HERE ARE SOME HANDS I PLAYED IN MYSELF.

HAND #1 - I was playing in an online STT (single-table tournament), and in the middle rounds of it, I was first to act and decided to limp in with pocket Kings. Everyone folds to the big blind and she decides to raise. I thought about just calling, but I wanted to be more aggressive, in case she was holding a weak Ace, so I re-raised. I know, I know, the typical limp, then 3-bet play, but this time it was with pocket Kings, not pocket Aces. She calls instantly. The flop comes: 3♥-J♣-7♦. She is first to act and bets pot. At this point,

I know she has at least a pair of Jacks, hopefully not pocket Jacks. I ponder for a minute, to display a level of weakness, then I push all-in, and she calls quicker than I could ever imagine. She has Q-J off suit and I'm a 4 to 1 favorite (81% -19%). Turn is a Q, giving her two pair and the river is an Ace. I lose the pot, and I'm knocked out of the tournament. I guess she ignore the typical limp 3-bet play, when most players make this play with big pocket pairs.

HAND #2 - A few months ago, I was playing in an online MTT (multi-table tournament) on either Fulltiltpoker.com or Ultimatebet.com, and during the later stages of it, I was moved to another table, and they sat me next to WSOP bracelet winner, Brandon Cantu. Moments later, he got knocked out. And, about 30 minutes after he did, I got knocked out. It was cool to play against him. It was even cooler to get a better payout than him.

HAND #3 - Tonight I suffered a bad beat in a live poker game. It wasn't a major bad beat, but it crippled my chip stack. I raised in middle position with pocket Aces. I get 3 callers. Flop is all low cards, with two diamonds. I bet about the size of the pot and the player to my left makes a minimum raise. Everyone else folds. I felt like folding quickly, because she is a loose player, but tight when it comes to raises. I checked her chip stack and saw she only has a few chips left. So, after a few minutes, I decide to push all-in. She calls holding a flush draw (K♦-Q♦). The turn is a diamond and I lose the pot. Half my stack was gone on that hand.

HAND #4 - I won a STT on Fulltiltpoker.com today and on one of the hands, I raised preflop with pocket Jacks. I get one caller. The flop is: K♦-Q♣-3♥. My opponent was first to act and decided to push all-in. His call preflop was odd, because he put almost half his chips in. Why didn't he just push all-in preflop? After he pushed all-in, I decided to think about his possible holdings. I felt, with the type of player he is, he didn't have a monster hand. If he did, he would have pushed all-in preflop or check-raised on the flop. I decided to call. He shows 10-J for an open-ended straight draw. The turn and river were blanks and I took down a huge pot, knocking him out of the tournament.

HAND #5 - I won a six-person STT today (online). When it got down to heads up action, I only had about 1700 in chips, while my opponent had about 7300. I managed to make our chips stacks about even by slowing playing a lot of hands. He was very aggressive. Towards the end of it, he limps in, and I check in the big blind with pocket Kings. There is an Ace on the board, so I check-called all the way down. I ended up winning the pot, while he folds a pair of 10's (Q-10). The very next hand I get pocket Aces. I limp in and he raises. I decide to 3-bet. He pushes all-in and I call. He has pocket 10's. I win the pot and now have a huge chip stack. A couple hands later, I win with A♥-5♣ against his K♠-8♦, when the board is all rags.

HAND #6 - One of the hands during this STT (online), I was playing in, was played extremely well (by me). I'm on the button and I call a raise with J-10 of diamonds. The raise was from middle position, from a player who is playing kind of loose. The flop comes: A-K-Q. The King and Queen were diamonds, meaning I flopped the nut straight and a flush draw. The raiser bets pot and I decide to raise, since there are all big cards out there. He calls. The turn comes a blank (6♠) and he check-raises me. I just call. River is another blank and he pushes all-in. I call with the nuts and take down the pot. He shows two pair (A♠-6♣).

HAND #7 - During the final three people of this less-than-normal number of players MTT (online), I limp in on the button with Q-J off suit. The big blind checks. The flop is: 5♥-2♦-7♣. We both check. The turn is an 8♣ and I check. The big blind pauses, then checks. I felt this was a suspicious pause. The river is a Q♠ and I check again. He bets pot and I fold quickly (with my top pair). He shows a straight (4♥-6♦). I told him I folded a Queen and he responds by saying that he was hoping I had one, but unfortunate for him, I'm a better player than that and made the correct fold. Sadly, to say, I only took 2nd place in that tournament.

HAND #8 - From the beginning of this STT (single table tournament), I was the chip leader. When it got down to heads up, I had about a 3 to 2 chip lead. Almost every time my opponent was on the button, he would push all-in. Of course, I continued to fold until I found a good hand to call with. And any time we saw a flop, it was too easy to steal, so mainly it came down to catching cards while I was in the big blind. Finally, I catch pocket 6's. My opponent, once again, pushes all-in. I call, and he shows J♥-9♥. Flop is: 3-J-4 (all diamonds). I don't have a diamond (of course neither did my opponent), so I am drawing to 2 outs (the two remaining 6's). Turn is another 4. If I don't catch a 6 on the river, he will win the pot and have a huge chip lead. Then comes the river........a 6, and I win the tournament.

HAND #9 - I was playing on Fulltiltpoker.com's "RUSH POKER", and during it, some guy raised on the cut off seat. I was sitting in the big blind with A-K suited and decide to 3-bet. He thought for a minute and decided to push all-in (which was a huge re-raise). I thought about what he could be holding: either a pair lower than Kings, or a weaker ace, so I called. He flips over A-Q. I couldn't believe he re-raised me all-in with only A-Q. I mean, in rush poker, most players only play the biggest starting hands possible and this guy wanted to push all-in after my 3-bet with only A-Q. Of course, I liked the call, but unfortunately for me a Queen hit the river. It just shows how many players today over value certain hands in certain situations, while relying solely on luck.

HAND #10 - During a live tournament today, I was sitting in second position preflop when the player in first position moves all-in. I was holding A-K of spades and decided to call. He had more chips than me, but I felt I was in a good spot to double up, based on his previous plays. Everyone folds to the player in the big blind. He decides to call as well. The player who moved all-in shows pocket 4's, I show my A-K suited, and the player in the big blind, for some reason, flips over 7-2 of diamonds. I walked away from the table completely confused. When I started to return to see what the results were, someone yells "I can't believe 7-2 wins with the straight". I looked at the board and saw that I was beaten by 7-2.

HAND #11 - Come on!! No more bad beats. During a live game (with a huge field), I raised in early position with 7-2 of hearts. I have my (advanced) reasons for making that particular play. I get two callers. The flop is 7♣-5♠-2♦. Dream flop for a bluff-raise preflop. The player in first position (Mr. Tight) bets about the size of the pot. I know he has a hand, but it's unlikely he has a set, so I push all-in. He calls instantly flipping over J-J. The turn is a blank, but of course the river is not; it's a Jack. I made the perfect play preflop and the on the flop, and I don't fault playing 7-2 at all-in that spot because, like, I said before, I had my reasons. But as always, the river kills me. If you read this section again, you'll see why I made this play in that spot. Think about it.

HAND #12 - I took 4th place tonight at a charity poker tournament, with a nice turn-out, and nice payout. I was playing extremely well until I got rivered on the last hand. I think one of the better hands all day, where I check-raised with a straight draw. The guy pondered for moment but ended up mucking. I put him on middle pair. Another good play, was when I limped in the small blind with K-J suited. The flop was all low cards, I was first to act with 3 or 4 players still waiting to act and I decided to push all-in. I got no callers. With the blinds increasing and the ante's kicking in, it was a nice pot to pick up at that particular spot. But, I think the best play was laying down the second nuts. I just knew he was sitting there with the King high flush. The board had 4 clubs to it, including the Ace and a Queen. I was holding the Jack of clubs. The way he plays and how he bet, made it clear I was beat. I'm glad he showed; he really did have the King of clubs.

HERE ARE THE BAD BEATS

<u>Bad Beat 1</u>. I flop a set and a player calls my check-raise with top pair. He catches runner, runner.

<u>Bad Beat 2</u>. An opponent catches runner, runner, again.

<u>Bad Beat 3</u>. One player all-in and he gets 3 callers, including myself (I have Q-J). Flop is Q-J-2. First position goes all-in, I raise all-in, and other guy calls. I'm holding Q-J (huge favorite to win). The first position player holds J-2 (only has 2 outs - two 2's). The caller has A-Q (only has 3 outs - three Aces), and the all-in player shows A-10 (Only has 4 outs - four Kings). I'm a huge favorite, but of course, a 2 hits the turn (the two outer) and a King hits the river. J-2 wins the main pot and the side pot, and the all-in player, hits the gutshot straight, but loses (but he would have beaten me anyways).

<u>Bad Beat 4</u>. I'm all-in with A♣-J♣, and a player calls with J♦-10♥. I'm a huge favorite (3 to 1) to win again. The flop is rags, but the turn is a 10 and I lose when the river is a blank. I made a couple great calls, and lay downs, throughout the tournament to kind of help last longer, like, calling an all-in bet with just middle pair. I knew he only had a flush draw. And folding pocket 10's to an all-in bet preflop. Player showed pocket Kings. Bluffing at the pot anytime I could and calling with nothing on the flop to steal them on the next street. As well as calling an all-in bet against a tight player with A♦-10♠. Still, taking those bad beats was hard to recover from, but I knew I still had work to do and I wasn't going to give up. Finished in 8th place, which is not bad, but it would have been nice to at least make the money. By doing so, I could have put the bad beats behind me.

NOW BACK TO HANDS I PLAYED MYSELF

HAND #14 - Took 3rd place tonight (in a live game), losing to a 3 outer on the river.... again. I was in the small blind with J-4 of hearts and limped in. The big blind checked. The flop comes: J♦-4♠-3♥ and I check. The big blind bets the minimum and I push all-in. He calls. He has J♣-5♦. I'm a huge favorite again, but of course, a 5 hits the river for a higher two pair. 3rd place paid decent, but it's never enough when you catch sick beats day after day. You play well all day...all week...all month and continue to get outdrawn to a player with only a few outs. It wasn't as bad as the other day, so I'm okay with the outcome. It happens. I'll deal with it.

HAND #15 - LIVE GAME: Are you serious? I limp in first position with pocket Kings. I didn't want any alarms going off that this hand was the first time I raised. Six other people call, and the big blind, which raises with any 2 cards, raises as planned. PERFECT. Exactly what I wanted, so I re-raised all-in. Everyone folds to the big blind. He thinks about for a few and decides to call. He shows 9-7 off suit. WHAT? And of course, he hits a pair of 7's on the flop and two pair on the turn. River is a blank and I storm out.... quietly!!! An absolutely weird call that made no sense at all, risking half his chips, and out draws me!

HAND #16 - Tonight I took the bubble (in a live game). Very frustrating. Final hand was A-J vs. K-J. I was holding A-J and pushed all-in and was called by K-J, and of course a King hits the flop, and the turn and river were blanks. Played extremely well, but I guess I couldn't pop the bubble. Better luck next time.

HAND #17 - Playing in a tournament online tonight and there were about 10,000 people playing. After hours and hours, it got down to fewer than 600 people. I'm below the average chip stack, so I must make a move soon. The player in first position raises and I decide to 3-bet all-in with A-K suited. Everyone folds, and the original raiser thinks for a second, then calls. He shows A-8 suited. I'm confused on his call. His chip stack is about equal to mine, yet he chooses to call almost all his chips with a weak hand in obvious comparison to mine and our positions. The flop is nothing, and so is the turn, but as usual, the river is an 8, and he wins the pot, knocking me out of the tournament. I'm baffled on his call. Last this long and decide to call an all-in bet when you know you're obviously beat, if not, dominated, which made no sense to me. I'm 3-betting a first position bet, it's clear that A-8 is way behind. Damn rookies and their suited cards and weak Aces.

HAND #18 - I decided to play a satellite on Fulltiltpoker. com for a chance to win a seat in the qualifying WSOP MAIN EVENT (10k buy in). I played well all the way down to heads up, and I'm sitting there with the chip lead. A few hands later I knock my opponent out and won the tournament. Now, I have a seat in the next event, which takes place next Monday. If I win that tournament, I win a free seat in the 2010 WSOP MAIN EVENT, for a chance to win millions of dollars. Unfortunately, I came up short on winning that seat, by about 150 spots.

HAND #19 - Just won a multi-table satellite for tonight's tournament, where the top payouts are huge. I've been running really well lately, so hopefully it will follow me into this next tournament. I've been known to get extremely unlucky, but I don't want to jinks myself tonight. During the multi-table tournament, I was playing solid poker; not getting unlucky. When it got down to heads up, my opponent had a 3 to 1 chip lead on me, but I knew it wasn't over. I battled back playing quality heads up poker, like, I normally do.

One hand really sticks out above the rest, is when I raised on the button with 6-6 and he just calls. The flops come: A♣-x-x. He checks, and I bet almost 2/3 the pot. He check-raises all-in. I type "flush draw?" And after a few second, I decide to call and put my tournament at risk, with my strong beliefs he only had a draw. I was right. Thankfully the turn and river were blanks and I doubled up. After some aggressive bets and raises, I was able to get a nice chip lead on him. And about 10 hands later, I was a 2.5 to 1 chip leader, and I took him down with A-K against his Q-J when an Ace hit the flop ....and I was on my way to the next tournament later tonight. (UPDATE: Made the money, but just short of 1st place)

HAND #20 - I was playing in an online MTT poker tournament, and the first hand, I limped in on the button with 5-2 of hearts, after one player limped in, in early position. The small blind folded and the big blind checks. The flop comes: 6-K-7 rainbow. Everyone checks. The turn comes another King. Everyone checks again. The river is an Ace. Both players checked, and I bet 2/3 the pot, since I couldn't win the pot if I checked it down. The big blind folds and the player in middle position check-raises. I decided, after some serious thought, that he was bluffing, since he didn't make a value bet on the river, so I decided to re-raise. He folded instantly, and I took down the pot.

HAND #21 - During a tournament, the middle rounds or so, I decide to just limp in with J-10 of diamonds. A few callers after me and the big blind raises. The big blind is a tight player who only raises with big hands, but I decided to call. I had position and not a bad hand to possibly out draw a big pair. The flop comes: K-8-5 (two diamonds). The big blind bets and I call with my flush draw. The turn is a 9. Now I have a flush draw and an open-ended straight draw. The big blind makes a big bet. At this point, I feel she has a good hand, since she is continuing to bet, but I still wanted to raise to cover up my hand, and if I hit my hand on the river, I'll definitely get paid off. After a few minutes, I decided to just call. I would hate to raise and have her re-raise me, forcing me out of a large pot, even though I have a good number of outs. The river is a Q, giving me the nut straight. With a board of: K-8-5-9-Q. She makes another big bet on the river and I go into my "fake" thinking mode. Now, I am clear she has a strong hand, so I make the most aggressive move there is, hoping she would call: ALL-IN. She thinks for a while and decides to call. She flips over A-K of diamonds as I show my nut straight. Thank god, I didn't hit my flush.

HAND #22 - During a live NLH poker tournament, I limped in with a medium Ace in the small blind, with no raises before me. The flop comes: A♠-3♦-8♥. Everyone checks. Turn is a 7♥ and I bet about half the pot. Everyone folds, except for the player who limped in second position, who makes a standard raise. When it comes back to me, I instantly fold, showing my top pair. He shows me a set of 7's. I hated giving him a free turn card, but at least, I was able to fold to his raise without any hesitation. The type of player, and the position he was in, helped me make an easy fold.

HAND #23 - During the late stages of a STT, I managed to limp in with J♣-9♠ in the small blind, with no raise and only one limper. The big blind checks. The flop comes: K♥-8♠-7♦. Everyone checks. The turn card is a 10♥, giving me the nut straight. I bet half the pot and the small blind raises about 20 times that. The limper calls, so I push all-in, for only a few hundred more. They both call. The limper has K♦-7♠ for two pair, the big blind has 10♣-8♦ for two pair as well, and I'm sitting there with the nut straight. As long as the board doesn't pair, I win. The river is a 2♠ and I take down a huge pot.

HAND #24 - (Satellite free roll) Down to the final three people in an online STT, and I'm sitting there in the small blind with pocket 4's. The button limps in and so do I, while the big blind checks. Flop comes: 4♦-Q♣-4♠, and of course I check it all the way down. Unfortunately, so do the other players. The turn and river are blanks and I bet on the river, about half the pot. Sadly, to say, no one called.

HAND #25 - During this 90-person tournament, I noticed the player to my right likes to slow play. On this one hand, he just limps on the button (no one has limped before him). I am in the small blind with Ace-Jack and decide to just call. The big blind checks. Flop is: 7-A-9 (two hearts). I check (possibly to check-raise), the big blind bets pot and the button calls. I think for a minute and decide to fold. What a sick fold to no raise preflop (or on the flop). On the turn (a rag hits), and the big blind goes all-in and the button calls. River is a blank and the button (the person who loves to slow play) shows Ace-Queen for the win.

I felt he was slow playing his hand, since he would normally raise on the button, when no one has entered the hand before him. I made a very tough lay down, but I felt I was beat, so I folded. How many players can make that kind of fold? My guess would be: not too many. Sometimes you got to play your opponent and ignore the strength of your own hand. I ended up making the final table, but only taking 3rd place for my efforts. I'm happy with my results, except for the bad beat I took on the final hand. Pocket Kings (me) cracked by pocket 10's. Board: A-Q-J-K-5.

HAND #26 - During an online cash game, everyone folds to the player on the button, who makes a standard position raise. The small blind folds and I decide to just call with A♦-J♠. The flop comes: A-A-A. Of course, I check it down, but unfortunately my opponent checks as well. Turn is a 5♦ and the river is a K♥. I had to make a bet on the river for some value, but my opponent folds and I win the minimum. There's nothing, like, flopping quads and winning a very small pot.

HAND #27 - Today my pocket Aces got cracked by pocket 4's, just shy of the final table. But, the hand of the day was my fold, earlier in the tournament. I limped in on the button with A-3 of spades. I and four other players saw a flop. The flop is 7-A-9 (two hearts). Everyone checks to me, so I bet about 2/3 the pot. A tight player in the big blind decides to check-raise. Everyone folds to me. Now, it's only costing a small percentage, but there is no way my top pair (weak kicker) is good. Plus, I'm kind of short-stacked. I've been watching this guy play, and he would only do that with a hand better than mine. I think about it for a second and decided to fold face up. Everyone was shocked that I folded top pair to a small raise, but I knew I was beat. The player didn't show his hand, but there is no way I had him beat. I mean, by making that play he knew that I had to call, so his hand must have been of greater value than top pair with a weak kicker. Even though it would have only cost a little more in chips (almost double the original bet), I knew I was beat. Why give away more chips, when it's obvious I'm beat?

HAND #28 - During tonight's live poker tournament, I was playing really well, making it to the final 2 tables, but of course I got outdrawn on the turn to a three outer. But, one of the hands that really stuck out was during the middle stages of it. A tight-aggressive player raised in middle position and got two callers. I folded before he raised, but as always, I try to figure out what my opponents potentially raise with. The flop was K♦-K♠-3♣. Both players checked and the preflop raiser goes all-in (which was an over bet). Now, most over bets mean they are sitting there with a monster hand, usually the nuts, but in this spot, I felt he wasn't holding trip Kings. Both players folded, and I announced out loud, "What do you got, pocket 8's?" And he flipped over his cards showing 8♥-8♠. What a read.

HAND #29 - Made two good plays today; one on the Internet and the other in a live game. Of course, in the live game, I didn't make it too far, but on the Internet, I took first place (it was STT - single table tournament).

1. LIVE GAME: A player limped in first position (some old guy), and I raise in second position with pocket 10's. I get two callers, and the limper decides to 3-bet all-in. I ponder but end up folding. I know what a limp/3-bet means. He had pocket Queens. I told him I folded pocket 10's. I think he was surprised I folded.

2. ON THE INTERNET: Four players left in the tournament and the player to my left is being very aggressive, betting and raising any time he can. Of course, everyone folds until they have a hand, but once I got sick of him stealing pots, I decided to play back at him. With no raise preflop I check-call all the way to the river. He is betting on every street and I'm holding nothing but hopes of stealing it. The river comes, and I check again. He decides to bet pot (big bet at that point). I decide to check-raise with nothing (high card), and he folds instantly. Sorry, buddy, you can't steal all the pots. It's my turn. Since that pot, I stayed aggressive, and took down first place against that same guy. Once it got down to heads up, it was no match. He was too easy to read.

HAND #30 - I was playing Omaha H/L on Fulltiltpoker. com. I enjoy Omaha almost as much as I do Hold'em. Plus, I feel Omaha cash games are a little easier, resulting more outs when holding more possibilities, so risking my money on less valuable hands is easier to do, as long as I have a lot of outs and my read on my opponents are correct. On the first hand, I hold:

A♥-A♠-2♠-J♦; a monster hand for high-low, so I raise. I get two callers. Flop comes with an ace and the turn pairs the board (giving me a full house). As one player folds, the other player calls me down with two pair (he had the other Ace).

On the very next hand I hold: J♥-J♦-8♥-5♠. The flop comes: Q♠-8♦-8♣. I check-raise and a player in middle position calls, while another player re-raises. I instantly fold. The other player calls and is all-in. The re-raiser had Q-Q-x-x. Flops a boat, leaving me the easy fold with only trip 8's. I had a feeling that's what he had.

HAND #31 - Today, playing in a live game, I decide to limp with 8-6 in middle position. The players are playing soft, plus the blinds were weak players, who rarely raise preflop. The flop comes: A-K-Q, all hearts. Everyone checks to the player on the button, who makes a standard bet. Everyone folds to me. I feel at this point that, this player is just making a "feel" bet, to narrow the field and to see where he stands against anyone with a flush or flush draw. So, with my read, I decide to check-raise. He utters "Well, I don't have an Ace or a heart, so I must fold" - showing K♦-J♣. Hate showing my hand, but I decided to show my complete bluff and say, "Neither do I". WHAT A READ!

HAND #32 - LIVE TOURNAMENT: Today, I get short-stacked and pushed all-in with pocket Queens. I get two callers and end up winning the pot. The very next hand, I get pocket Queens again. I raise and a girl in middle position 3-bets all-in. It's folded around to me and I ponder what her possible holdings could be. Earlier, I saw her just call a raise with A-Q, so that eliminates a hand like that, so I must put her on a big pocket pair. After a few minutes I decide to fold and show my pocket Queens. She shows pocket Kings. The whole table is shocked I folded that hand, while someone utters "You know, you're probably the only person here who would have laid that hand down." I respond with, "I felt I was beat". Sometimes, you have to play your opponents and not just your cards."

HAND #33 - Playing a Pot-Limit Omaha cash game on Fulltiltpoker.com and I'm playing extremely well. During a rush at this one table, I pick up 7♣-7♦-x-x on the button. A player raised in middle position, and the player next to him calls. I call as well. The flop comes: 7♥-J♦-Q♠. The player who raised preflop bets pot and the next player raises all-in. I felt at this point, I could very easily be beaten. Of course, if they are on a draw, then I should have the best hand. But in Omaha, having the best hand on the flop isn't always a good hand to play, even to one bet - let alone a raise. I decide to fold, thinking someone has a higher set. I was right. The preflop raiser called the all-in and showed a set of Jacks. The all-in player had top pair, top kicker (which is extremely weak in Omaha) and a gut-shot. The turn and river were blanks and the set of Jacks won the pot. Looks like I made another good lay down. It's horrible

Ryan Sleeper

to lay down a set, even in Omaha, but when you know you're beat, and you can't force your opponent to fold, then folding your hand is the only option.

HAND #34 - WHAT A CALL (during a live game)! I limp in first position with 10♣-10♠. A player in middle position raises preflop. He has been raising a lot during the early rounds of this live tournament, so I can put him on a wide range of hands. The player in the big blind calls the raise, and so do I. The flop is J♥-6♣-8♦. The big blind checks "blind", and I check as well. The preflop raiser pushes all-in, which is a little less than pot. The player to my right calls. Now it's up to me. I don't feel the player in middle position has a pair of Jacks or better and I don't think the caller has one either (my instincts are telling me this). If he did, he would have raised. That's just the type of player he is. After a few seconds of pondering, I call. Cards are flipped over and I'm holding the best hand. The player in middle position has a flush draw and the caller had middle pair. The turn and river were blanks and I triple up.

HAND #35 - Just missed the money in today's live tournament. One hand early in this tournament really sticks out above the rest. I am in first position and choose to limp with Q♥-Q♠. Four other players call. The flop comes: K-Q-7, all hearts. I flop a set, but I must play it semi-cautiously in case someone has the flush already. The blinds check, and I bet almost a pot-size bet. The next player folds and the middle position player pushes all-in. Everyone else folds, and now it's up to me. OK, it's obvious this guy has the flush (as I tell him out loud), but I feel it's my turn to get lucky, and I call. He flips over 3-4 of hearts. Turn is another Queen and I have quads and take down the pot. I knew I was beat, but I wanted to rely on luck. I felt I'll either go big or go home. Thankfully, luck was on my side.

HAND #36 - During an online one-table tournament, it gets down to five players. Everyone is playing well, setting traps and bluffing at the right spots. With blinds at 100-200, I'm sitting in the small blind with Q♥-Q♦. One player limps in, in early position, and so does the button. I decide to limp in as well. The big blind checks. The flop is all low cards: 9♦-5♥-2♦. I check and the big blind bets half the pot. The limpers fold and the button calls. I decide to check-raise pot. Both players call. The turn is a 5♠. I bet a little less than 2/3 the pot. The big blind player raises all-in and the button calls. I fold instantly. I was more worried about the button call than the big blind players raise. The big blind shows top pair (9's), while the button flips over K♦-K♠. The river is a blank and Kings hold up. What a lay-down by me.

HAND #37 - Today was a good day for sit n go's. Of course, this past week has been great. I've cashed in almost all of them; taking 1st and 2nd place more often than 3rd place. Today, two hands came up that deserved to be in here. During the middle stages of one, a player to my right (the button) raises preflop and I decide to flat call with A♥-J♣. The player in the big blind calls as well. The flop is 5♦-8♠-J♠, giving me top pair, top kicker. I check, thinking I might check-raise. The big blind bets pot and the preflop raiser goes all-in for a little bit more. I think for a second but decide to fold thinking someone has a set or an over pair. I was right. The preflop raiser had K♦-K♥ and ended up winning the pot. Another great lay-down by me.

HAND #38 - During another sit n go, in the early stages of it, the player to my right (in 1st position) limps, as do I with A-K, thinking about setting a trap. A player in middle position raises, and the original limper on my right, 3-bets all-in. Another typical limp, then 3-bet, which states he has A-A (maybe Kings). I fold without a blink and the original raiser calls, showing A-10. The all-in player showed A-A, just like I suspected, and his Aces win the pot, when rags hit the board. I made another great, and easy fold. Positional raises (with or without limpers) are great tells of strengths or weakness.

HAND #39 - During an online multi-table tournament, the following hand came up, that really helped make the final table, and take 2nd place, because it gave me a good size chip stack with only 13 players to go. I'm sitting on the button with 10♠-10♣, while the player in first position raises preflop. No one calls when it gets to me, and I decide to just call. His early position raise, more often than most, means he has a strong starting hand. So, I wanted to play it safe and see what kind of action he displays after the flop. Plus, I had position on him, so I could possibly push him off the pot, if I felt he blanked. The flop comes: Q-3-7 (two spades). He is first to act and decides to push all-in, which is an over bet to the pot. I think for a second on the possible hands he could be holding. After a few minutes, I felt he had a big ace, but not A-Q, or maybe even a small or medium pocket pair. I decide to call, and he flips over 9♥-9♣. The turn and river are blanks and my 10's hold up. My read wasn't 100% accurate, but it was close enough.

HAND #40 - During a MTT (multi-table tournament), I notice the guy in seat 4 is a loose, weak player. I already took a huge pot off him earlier, but how this hand played out, really sticks out in my mind. A player in middle position limps in, and so do I with 4♥-4♠. He is in the small blind and calls, while the big blind checks. The flop comes: 3♣-J♣-A♠. Everyone checks. The turn is a 2♣. Now there are three clubs on the board and the weak player bets almost pot. The big blind folds, but the middle position player calls. I call as well, thinking the better is weak and the caller is on a draw. The river is a 9 of hearts. The weak player in first position bets again, and the middle position player folds. Now it's up to me. After a few minutes of thinking, I couldn't put him on a big hand - or any hand of real value. With the board being: 3♣-J♣-A♠-2♣-9♥, I decide to call with just my pair of 4's. My hand is good as he shows 10 high. What a read!!!

HAND #41 – Today, during a multi-table tournament, I get dealt K♦-K♥ in late position. Two players limp in and I decide to raise four times the big blind. I get one caller. The flop comes: 8♦-6♠-8♣. He checks, and I bet half the pot. He calls. The turn comes a 7♥. He checks again, and I decide to check as well. I feel he is way behind and will most likely make a river bet. The river is a 2♣, and he thinks for a while, then pushes all-in (an over bet to the pot). I instantly call. He shows Q♥-10♠ for a total bluff and I take down the pot. I induced a river bluff and it worked.

NOW SOME POKER ADVICE ♠

(also taken from my website – in all forms of poker, not just Hold'em)

1. Poker tells are important to know on every opponent, but your instincts should be the major factor in your final decisions.

2. Adjusting to your opponent's style (loose or tight), and the game at hand, is one of the most important skills to have at the poker table. You'll end up folding more against a tight player, who is showing aggression, and call (or raise) more often, when a loose player is making all the moves. Occasionally, you'll slow play against a loose player to set a trap, when your hand is very strong.

3. Rarely play just your cards. Play your opponent(s) more often.

4. Never be afraid to fold any hand at any time. If you feel you are beat and are forced out of the pot to a big bet or raise, then simply fold and play another hand.

5. Any time you sense weakness, you must attack with a big bet or raise.

6. Mixing up your plays is crucial in playing a successful game of poker. Prior to playing a hand, look to see who is in the blinds and who is short-stacked. The tighter the player is, the easier it will be to steal the blinds. If the players are loose, then a limp 3-bet

might be your best play, because you know a loose player will most likely raise.

7. *"You have to be in it to win it, but you can't win them all."* So, choosing to play too many hands, is an option, if your plans are to ultimately lose your entire bankroll. Sometimes, just sitting back and waiting for big hands, is a good way to evaluate your opponents game and style for proper adjustments later in the game. Once you have a feel the how everyone is playing, then you can loosen up your game, and play more hands.

8. In some cases, bluffing is overrated. You should strive more on making accurate reads and plays, and less on bluffing.

9. Too many players waste big pocket pairs preflop, by raising too much, in hopes of just stealing the blinds, because they are afraid of being outdrawn. Learn to get full value for every big hand you acquire. Every hand can beat every other hand, so why not try and get the most you can with it? Sometimes you'll win, and sometimes you'll lose, but that's poker. You can't always assume pocket Aces should win every time.

10. Poker is about being unpredictable and making the correct plays. So, to keep your opponents guessing, you should learn how to make "new moves". For example, instead of check-calling with a flush draw, you should bet out, or even, check-raise. Or, when you hit middle pair and back door draws on the flop, you should not fold, but raise. But make

sure when you make these new plays, you are making them against the right opponents; players who understand position, player knowledge and are capable of folding weaker hands of value.

11. To be successful, you must understand the right games to pick to assure yourself great success. Don't play stakes too high or too low. Pick a game you can afford and have experience with. A game where you know the players style, the flow of the level and you've done well there before.

12. A value bet is only successful when you know your opponent will call. A value bet bluff is even more successful when you do against a player who has a higher knowledge behind the meaning of a value bet. A tight-aggressive player is the one player, where your value bet bluff will work more often.

13. Take your time in every move you make. If you rush a bet, then your opponents may think it's a bluff. If you rush a raise, then your opponents will know you're holding a strong hand. If you take your time on every hand, your opponents will rarely be able to put you on a hand. Also, by taking your time, you'll be able to put the story together more accurately and be able to make the right decision almost every time.

Many times, I have taken my time in difficult situations, and when I was able to put the story together more clearly, I could sense my opponent being weak, so I raised or re-raised. I can't count how many times I made an opponent fold to my long process to raise. In some cases, I was probably beat.

14. Budget your poker money, for wins and losses, over a long period of time. Not daily. By doing so, you'll have a better understanding where, and which games you do better at, on a more accurate status in your pursuit as a professional.

15. You can't always rely on catching good cards and hitting monster flops, turns and rivers. You also can't always fold when you know you're beat. Sometimes you must play weaker hands, in and out of position, and call big bets and raises, hoping to get lucky.

16. An over bet, especially when playing online poker, usually means a very strong hand. Every once and a while you'll see an over bet bluff, but more often than not, it's a "tell" of strength. I've seen over bets in live poker, and it usually means strength as well.

17. An act of disinterest, then a raise, usually means a strong hand as well.

18. Someone who is staring at the flop for a really long time, then makes a quick bet, usually means a bluff. Of course, this tell is usually the opposite when someone decides to raise.

19. Betting patterns are one of the best form of information a poker player can use for success, specifically, while playing online. Of course, this "tell" is important, it's almost as important as knowing your opponents game and how he plays every hand in different positions. Betting patterns

are important in live games as well, but since you can't see your opponent's face, or movements, their bets are extremely helpful, when understanding the hand, they are trying to represent.

20. The phrase: "Out of Position", refers to acting first (postflop). This is a bad spot, especially against a preflop raiser. You rarely want to act first when a player has raised preflop, because if you miss the flop and he bets, which he will normally do, you will have no information on him and end up folding more hands than you should. This results in more lost pots. Acting last (or later) is always better for information and proper (successful) plays.

21. When the pot is multi-way and the player in first position bets strong, he most likely has a big hand. Only the loosest player at the table would bet in first position with a weak hand or draw. The tighter the player is, the stronger their hand is. In this situation, he is most likely holding 2 pair or better.

22. When playing Omaha, you must not always treat your hand, like a, Hold'em hand. Preflop, you should play it like two hold'em hands and play it with position and having both "hands" of strength; while postflop you must play it like Omaha is naturally played. Draws are the best hands to have in Omaha (especially lock draws). Over pairs, top pair, and similar hands are weak in Omaha. Normally, two pair or a set is the bare minimum to win the pot in Omaha, unless it's short-handed. Be careful playing a paired board in

a multi-player situation. Full houses are common in those spots.

23. In Omaha, folding the non-lock flush draws are a safe bet, when two or more players are making big bets and raises. But, at the same time, big bets and raises could mean made hands, not draws, meaning your flush draw could be good if you hit it. Knowing your opponent's game and the positions they are in, will help determine the meaning of their bets.

24. Rarely chase for over cards or a gut-shot straight draw. Chances are it will cost too much with the ratio of return versus how much you put in over a long period of time. Short-handed pots are optimal for chasing over cards when the pot is large, and you can outplay your opponent. Gut-shots are only valuable when it's multi-way and the pot is large compared to the original bet. You must also factor in the implied odds, when playing a gut-shot.

25. Respect raises and re-raises against tighter players. Even if you have top pair, chances are your hand is no good. In some cases, folding open-ended straight draws and flush draws is correct when tighter players are 3-betting and 4-betting.

26. Watch for players making unusual plays. For example, a certain player always raises on the button. When it comes down to short-handed, he continues to make his button raise, but every once and a while he will just limp in. When he makes this kind of play he is most likely holding a big hand

and is waiting for you to raise, so he can re-raise. He is setting a trap, and trying to avoid the blinds to fold, so he can get full value for his hand. I see a lot of times when a player is on the button, he will either fold or raise. When he limps in, I know he has a big hand. This advice only really works against a player who is newer to the game and is considered a loose player. A tight-aggressive player can mix it up and limp with weaker hands only because he has position.

27. In 7-card stud, you can almost tell exactly what your opponent is holding by the plays he makes in the early rounds of the hand. On the first round of betting, if your opponent bets out, he most likely has a pair in the hole, especially if there are over cards to the one showing on his board. In other situations, he may be holding a monster draw. If there are raises early on, then your opponent is holding a strong hand and wants to protect it. You can narrow it down to a few possible hands, of which he is raising with, by the cards showing from the remaining players still involved in the hand.

28. Poker tells are being displayed constantly at a poker table. It's your job to find them and use them to your advantage. Tells of strength are: acting weak, acting disinterested, asking the dealer if it's up to him, asking how much the bet is, when a player sighs, hands movements of an act of "whatever", rubbing of the hands, moving closer to the action etc.

Tells of weakness are: acting strong, acting quickly, aggressive bets or raises with small valued chips, long stares at the flop - then betting etc. Once you can establish these tells as for what they really are, you must act on them properly. Don't be afraid to raise when you sense weakness, or fold when a player is obviously showing strength.

29. Understand true value of starting hands and the probability of its true earnings. Folding medium Aces (and Kings), and small pocket pairs, against obvious players who raise in early position. Even in situations where you are forced to go all-in or fold.

I remember one time, during a tournament, I was short stacked and was waiting for a good hand to push all-in with. Finally, I get pocket 5's in middle position. A player in early position calls and now it's up to me. I look around the table and realize that the limper, the small blind and the big blind (and possibly the button - who was the chip leader) would most likely call my all-in bet; meaning the true value of my hand in this spot, is weaker than normal. So, it's an obvious fold. In any other situation, I would push all-in; for example, I was on the button with no limpers before me.

A small pocket pair has no true value or a high probability against multiple opponents. The result on that hand previously mentioned? The button had pocket 9's and I would have lost.

Even hands like, A-10, K-J or even Q-10 suited decrease their true value when up against multiple opponents, especially when players are aware of your short chip stack and are willing to play a hand in early position.

30. Stealing pots are crucial in successful poker. More often than most, a player will try and steal the pot postflop when everyone has checked to him, and he's last to act. On some occasions, this attempt to steal the pot will be made preflop, but this usually happens when a player has a weak hand and knows the other players will fold. Of course, many times this player will get some action.

    The more advanced way to steal, a larger than normal pot, preflop is when a player is raising trying to steal the blinds, while another player (who knows this action) is 3-betting the "pot stealers" bet. NOW, is the time to re-raise him. You know the original player is raising to steal the blinds and, in this case, the re-raiser is raising because he knows this action as well. If you choose to re-raise both players, you'll most likely take down the pot. Let's hope neither player actually has a hand. If the stacks are similar, then pushing all-in, is probably your best play to win the sizeable pot against blind stealers.

31. When a player checks, and then calls a bet and a raise. He usually has one of two potential hands, depending on the board. If there is a flush draw on the board, then he most likely has the nut the flush. If there no draws on the board, then he most likely has a strong hand, and is choosing to slow

play it. The only exception would be, if the player is a weaker status player; then he probably has top pair with a very good kicker. Occasionally a player will call a bet and raise, after he checks, holding a weak straight draw. With the pot offering him great implied odds, he feels if he hits his draw, then he'll most likely get paid off. In most cases, he is right.

32. A rule of thumb for positional tells of strength is this: The more people waiting when a player bets, raises or check-raises, the stronger his hand is.

33. A lot of players will wait until the turn, in hold'em, to raise. When a player knows you have a good hand, because you raised in early position, or re-raised someone's original raise preflop, and then calls your big bet on the flop, beware on how he plays the turn. You might want to check to turn in hopes of him checking as well. If you make another big bet and he chooses to raise (most likely all-in), he just may have you beat. If you're sitting there with an over pair or worse, then folding might be the best play. He could easily have a bigger pair or a set. Two pair is common, but sets are even more common, in this type of play. Unless you have monster draws or a monster hand yourself, then folding should be your only option.

34. When a scare card hits the turn or river, in a game of hold'em, don't always assume your opponent just hit his hand. His position preflop, and how he plays postflop should help you determine his potential

holdings. For example, you are involved in a 3-way pot and you hold top pair with a great kicker and is last to act. The flop rolls out and there is a flush draw, and both your opponents check, so you bet. They both call. The turn is a rag and you bet again. They both call again. The river completes a flush, and this time one of your opponents bets out. If the first player makes this bet, he usually has the flush, assuming the other player, and yourself have big chips stacks (meaning you'll most likely call, since it won't damage your stack). If the second player bets out, then he might not have the flush, but still a hand of value, and doesn't want to call a big bet by you on the river, so he is controlling the pot size with a medium strength hand. If you have two pair of better, you should make the call, as long as there no other draws out there. And, I would only call the bet by the first player is he is known to bluff in spots like this.

35. During a multi-way pot, in hold'em, and you bet out on the flop with half your stack, no matter if you raised preflop or not, and someone just calls you, then that person most likely has a big hand. He probably has you beat. He knows you're short stacked, and pot-committed, but he wants more value for his hand, so he just calls, hoping other people will call as well. Of course, you have no choice but to go all-in on the turn. Even if you check the turn and he bets more than you have, you're still going to have to call. Folding would be

a huge play, but not a lot of players can do it. I've only done it a few times and every time, they've shown me a set, or the nuts, while I only had top pair or an over pair. One time, I think I had two pair.

READING HANDS QUIZ ♣

1. You're playing a 6-max tournament and you get to see the flop, with 4 players, on the button with K-7, with no raise preflop. The flop is: J-8-2 and everyone checks. The turn is an Ace, and everyone checks again. The river is a 3, and this time the player in first position bets half the pot. What does he have?

    a. A bluff? – possibly but unlikely
    b. A monster hand? Very unlikely
    c. A weak pair? Maybe but I doubt it
    d. A pair of Aces? Yes!!! A lot of players will check the turn when they hit a good pair/hand on the turn. And they check to gain more information. Since everyone else checked, he knows a bet on the river will gain some value.

2. You're playing a in a one table tournament and a tight player in middle position raises preflop and gets 2 callers. The flop is: K-7-7 and it gets checked around. The turn is a 4 and it gets checked to the player in last position, who makes a good size bet, and everyone folds to the preflop raiser to decides to check-raise. What does he have?

    a. Aces? It's possible but he most likely would have bet the flop.

b. Kings? Yes! He checked the flop to induce a bet from an opponent. Even though he had to wait until the turn to gain a bet.

c. A bluff? Very unlikely. A c-bet bluff would have been more affective.

3. During an online tournament you notice everyone is playing kind of tight. You're sitting in the small blind with K-Q off suit and decide to limp in after 5 players have limped before you. You check blind and the flop gives you the nut straight with 2 diamonds (you have the kind of diamonds). A player in middle position bets half the pot and he gets one caller. You decide to make a larger check-raise to put both opponents to a decision. The player who made the first bets thinks about it for a while and decided to call, which is odd because that is most of his chips. The other player folds. What does he have?

a. The nuts? No!

b. 2 pair? No!

c. A flush draw? Yes!! A lot of players will call raises with a flush draw versus any other hand that needs improvement. If he had anything else, he would have pushed all-in or folded.

d. A pair with a straight draw? No!

4. You've made to the final table and you're sitting on the button with pocket 5's. There was a raise preflop, you called, and so did 3 other players. The

is K-J-2 and the preflop raiser bets a small amount. Everyone folds except you, thinking you could have the best hand, if not, you have position. The turn is a J and he decides to check. You check as well. The river is a 3, and this time he bets half the pot. What does he have?

a. A bluff? Yes! He played the hand like, a missed draw, or a hand that needed to hit.

b. The nuts? Maybe, but unlikely most players would play the hand differently and a little more aggressive with the nuts.

c. Top pair? Possibly, if he had a weak kicker, but my gut is saying call with your pocket 5's and don't be surprised if you take down the pot.

5. During a tournament with high blinds, you have Q-J, and you see a flop with a weak raise from middle position. The flop is K-Q-5. The preflop raisers bets minimum and only you call. The turn is a blank and he bets the minimum again. You call to see the river. The river is another blank and he makes the same bet. What does he have?

a. The nuts? Looking for a value? Nope!

b. A bluff? Possibly, but unlikely. A bluff bet would have been bigger.

c. Middle pair, just like you? Probably but, with you calling, he'd probably check the river for showdown value.

    d. Top pair? Yes! His kicker is probably weak and doesn't want to risk too much.

6. A tight player, during a cash game, decides to play a hand from early position, but didn't raise. No one did, and it's multi-way. The flop is 2-4-7, and it gets checked around to the player in late position who makes a large bet. The tight player decides to check-raise. What does he have?

    a. Pocket Aces? Maybe, but unlikely. I feel he would have made a bet on the flop to protect his hand.

    b. Pocket Kings? Same answer as above.

    c. A bluff? Unlikely. Even though he is a tight player and his image would perceive him as having a big hand, it's unlikely he would make this play in a multi-way pot.

    d. A set? Yes! A strong hand, looking for value, so by check-raising, he earns an extra bet.

7. A frequent bluffer and position raiser, during a live tournament, decides to limp on the button. You have A-J in the small blind and decide to just limp in. The big blind checks. The flop is A-10-7. You check, thinking you might check-raise, and the big blind checks as well. The player on the button bets 2/3 the pot. What does he have?

a. A set? Possibly, but unlikely. A raise preflop with a pocket pair would have made more sense.

b. A bluff? Maybe, but I doubt it. Unless he knows for sure the blinds are being aware, a bluff is less likely to happened after just limping on the button.

c. Top pair with a big kicker or pocket Aces? Yes! Even though you have a similar hand, he probably has you beat. This hand happened to me and I folded my A-J. the hand played out with big blind and the player won the hand on the river, showing A-Q. Watch for those loose players who just limp.

8. During a tournament, you decide to raise in middle position with K-K. The player on the button and the blinds decide to call. The flop is: 10-J-Q. The player in first position bets out a little more than half the pot. The big blind folds and now it's up to you. You think for a second and decide to flat call. The button folds. What does the bettor have?

a. Top pair? Unlikely. Against multiple opponents and a preflop raiser, this would be a risky bet.

b. A bluff? No! Horrible play if it was.

c. A set? Maybe. With a scary board and the preflop raiser waiting, this would be a good time to bet into him with a big hand.

d. 2 pair? Yes! A set would be a good play to check-raise to disguise your hand better, but in most pots, I've seen, the bettor has 2 pair. This situation happened to me, and we both saw an Ace hit the turn and after she bet, I raised all-in knowing she might call. I told her, after the hand, I know you have 2 pair.

9. During a high stakes cash game, a player decides to check-call every bet to the river, where the river card would complete the flush, and this time he makes a large bet into you. What does he have? (mind you, you have a strong hand, but a flush beats you)

   a. A flush? If you were making large bets all the way to the river, then he most likely doesn't have the flush, unless he is a rookie-style player.
   b. A pair (or even 2 pair)? It's possible, depending on what cards are out and what his range is.
   c. A bluff? Most likely. He is trying to represent the flush, hoping you would fold. His style will determine is he is bluffing or not. My guess is either 2 pair or a bluff. I've seen both, with more bluffs. Just depends on the board and the type of player he is. If he knows you're capable of folding, then a bluff would be the more likely answer.

10. During a tournament, you and 2 other players get to a see an unraised flop. The flop is Q-10-6 with two clubs. The player in first position bets and the player in middle position decides to raise. The

player in late position just flat calls. What does this player have?

a. Top pair? Possibly, but not my first guess.
b. A straight draw? Maybe, but most players will fold a straight draw against 2 aggressive players.
c. The nuts? Unlikely. A 3-bet would be the best play against 2 people.
d. The nut flush draw? Yes!! I can't count how many times I've seen this with a player calling a bet and a raise with the nuts flush draw.

11. During a high stakes cash game, you're holding pocket 4's and raise preflop. You get one caller from the small blind. The flop is 2-3-5. The small blind checks and you bet half the pot. He calls the turn is an ace. He checks again, and you make another half pot size bet. He calls again. The river is another ace and this time he bets out 2/3 pot. What does he have?

a. A bluff? No! too risky with that board with potentials strong hands.
b. A straight, just like you? Possibly but I doubt it. What kind of hands would call out of position holding a 4?
c. A full house? Most likely. If he feels you have the straight by the way you played, then a bet with a better hand would make sense.

12. During the late stages of a tournament, you have 9-9 and call a raise from early position. The flop is 3-4-8. You decide to check and the preflop raiser makes a large over bet. What does he have?

   a. A-K? maybe but unlikely. A standard size bet would have been more likely he has A-K.
   b. A set? Doubt it. He would have made a normal bet to keep you in.
   c. An over pair? Yes! He absolutely has an over pair. And even though you do as well, you must make the fold. A lot of players will over bet their big hands to make the most they can from it. Obvious tell of strength.

13. During a low-stakes cash game, you decide to raise preflop with 9-9. You get one caller, who plays very loose. The flop is Q-3-3. The loose player check-call. The turn is another Q. The loose player check-calls again. The river is a 4. You check the river for showdown value and the loose player bets half the pot. What does he have?

   a. A bluff? Possibly. With his image and your check on the river, it's a great time to steal the pot with a bluff.
   b. A Queen? Maybe. Even though he is loose, if you keep betting, then there is no reason to raise, unless you feel he is capable of raising

with any two cards and you're known to call down based on his range.

c. A 3? Unlikely. Even though he is loose, I wouldn't put him on a hand containing a 3.

d. Pocket 4's? Nope! Sure, this hand is possible, but I feel he would raise before the river hit with a pocket pair. My guess is a bluff, since you showed weakness on the river. If you can't win by checking it, then a bet makes the most sense.

14. During a tournament you find yourself with A-K in late position, against a raise in first position. You decide to call. Everyone else folds. The flop comes: A-10-2 with two hearts. Your opponent bets and you flat call. The turn is a blank and it goes check, check (even though you should make a bet on the turn, you decide t to check to induce a river bluff). The river is a 7 of hearts (which completes the flush), and your opponent makes a large bet. What does he have?

a. The flush? Maybe, but unlikely. His first position preflop raise doesn't strike me as holding two suited cards.

b. Pair of Aces? Possibly, which would lose to your kicker.

c. A bluff? Most likely, unless he as a smaller pair. In either case, I feel this would be an easy call.

15. You're playing in an online tournament, and you make the easy raise with A-A, in middle position, and you get two callers (one from the small blind and a player two seats from your right). You are last to act when the flop rolls out as: K-Q-8. The player in first position bets 2/3 the pot and the next player to act raises 3x. Now it's up to you. What do they have?

    a. A bluff? Nope! You raised preflop and they are taking control of the pot postflop. There is no way either is bluffing.
    b. Top pair? The player in first position may have top pair, but the raiser has at least two pair.
    c. A set? Possibly, but either way, your hand is no good. Make the easy fold.

16. You're playing at a loose table where every player has a wide range and likes to be extra aggressive in pots. You look at your hand, in late position, and find A-3 suited. A player in middle position makes a very large raise preflop and you decide to call. Everyone else folds. The flop is 7-J-5. The preflop raiser bets half the pot and you call. The turn is a blank and you both check. The river is a 10 and the preflop raiser bets 2/3 the pot. What does he have?

    a. The nuts? Unlikely. He would have been more aggressive with it against a player who called his larger than normal raise preflop.

b. A pair? Possibly, but you know a raise could push him off it.

c. A bluff? More than likely, yes! I would put in a raise to see where you stand. If he raises you back, then I would push all-in if your stack is large enough. In some cases, you may just flat call with ace high, and it could be good.

CONCLUSION ♥

Unfortunately, this is the end of this book. But I'm sure by now you have all the necessary tools to become a great poker player with a successful future. If you've read volume one prior to this book, then I have no doubts in your success at the poker table. You have just completed the course of poker knowledge, on how to make the correct decisions on and off the poker felt, assuring you on which games to play correctly, how to play proper hands in different situations, making the proper adjustments against the endless number of styles and plays each player makes at the table, and how to handle your money to accumulate even more over your poker career.

In the future, I plan to bring more education to the average player out there today, and who knows, there may be a volume 3. I think the information combined in these volumes are sufficient enough to make any player successful. But as times change, so do the players, so we all must find ways to improve. Books on poker is a great way to improve, so the information I have provided here, hopefully has improved your game already. I'm sure the next book I publish will help the next generation of players. Of course, I won't discount this book to that generation, simply because we all know, the more knowledge you have, the better you are.

Continue your education of poker, in books, and at the tables, to establish levels that are constantly changing. Factor in everything you've learn and use it at the poker table. Sometimes you'll win, and something you'll lose, but hopefully in those pots, those sessions, or all the tournaments you play, where you've come up short, you'll be able to learn from them. I've had my series of back beats, losing sessions and tournaments, where I felt like I didn't know what I was doing. And, on the other hand, I've had days, weeks and months, where I felt I was the best player in the world. How to handle these situations will help you secure a more successful career in poker.

Everyone gets two cards, and we all must make decisions that are tough, but if we continue to learn, and continue to grow as, not only players, but as people, in the end, the better players, and the ones making better decisions, will have all the money. Luck is always a factor, but skill will take us father. If we want to be a long-term success in the game of poker, then we must make better decisions more often than the other players at the table.

I think by reading this book and Volume 1, you are ahead of the game. I may be a lesser known author, but my books have proven success rates to the average player. If you want to become a successful poker player, then don't be ashamed that you've learned something from someone who is unknown in the poker world. I've done well for myself in lower stakes (while gradually moving up into higher stakes), and now it's time to play with the best players in the world, at the WSOP. Hope to see you all there!!

GLOSSARY ♦

Some of these words you may not find mentioned in this book, but it's important to know them. A few of them are just alternate sayings with the same definition.

3-Bet:
> To re-raise someone's raise.

4-Bet:
> To raise someone's 3-bet.

Advertising:
> To display one image or style of play to switch it up in future hands. Showing a bluff early on to assure value for a later hand. Or playing tight and only showing big hands to pull off a bluff later in the game.

All-In:
> Having all of one's money in the pot. To bet everything you have in front of you.

Back Door:
> The term is used for a hand made on 4th and 5th street that a player wasn't

originally trying to make. It also means catching runner-runner.

Bad Beat:

Having a hand that was the big favorite defeated because of a lucky draw.

Bankroll:

The amount of money you have available to wager.

Belly Buster:

A draw to an inside straight; also called "gut shot." If the flop is 2-3-5 and you hold an Ace and a 6, only the 4 will give you the straight, so you're on a belly buster or gut-shot draw.

Bet:

To put money in the pot before anyone else has.

Bettor:

The first person to put money in the pot, on any given round.

Bet for Value (aka value bet):

To bet, and to be called, by a lesser valued hand. You are betting to make money, not to make your opponents fold, because you know you have the best hand.

Blank:

A card that is not of any value to a player's hand.

Blinds:

A forced bet that one or more players must make to start the action on the first round of betting. The blind rotates around the table with each new deal.

Bluff:

A bet or raise with a hand you do not think is the best hand. Normally betting or raising with no pair or draw.

Board:

The community cards in the center of the table.

Bottom Pair:

Pairing the lowest card on the board.

Button:

The Dealer.

Buy-In:

The minimum amount of money required to sit down in a particular game.

Call:

To put in the pot the amount of money equal to an opponent's bet or raise.

Call a Raise Cold:

To call a double bet (a bet and a raise).

Caller:

A person who calls the bet or raise.

Chase:

To continue a hand trying to outdraw an opponent's hand you are quite sure is better than yours. A lot of players like to chase for an over card. If the flop is 3-6-9 and your opponent is holding A-Q he might call you "chasing" for an over card (Ace or Queen).

Check:

To decline to bet when it is your turn, passing the action to the player next to act.

Check-Raise:

To check and then raise after an opponent bets.

Cold Deck:

A situation where it seemed like the deck was stacked. Multiple players with big hands that are rarely seen at the same time. For example, one player has pocket Aces against 2 opponents with pocket Kings or Queens. Also, called a "cooler."

Community Cards:

The cards dealt face up in the center of the table that is shared by all the active players.

Continuation Bet (c-bet):

Making a bet postflop after you have raised preflop, no matter if you hit the flop or not.

Dead Hand:

A hand a player may not continue to play because of an irregularity. Usually when a player violates a rule. Examples: (1) showing a hand to an opponent before all action is completed. (2) Turning your cards face up before an opponent calls or before a turn or river card is exposed.

Dead Money:

Money put in the pot by players who have already folded their hands.

Drawing Dead:

Drawing to try to make a hand that cannot possibly win because an opponent already holds a bigger (made) hand or the nuts.

Draw Out:

To improve your hand so that it beats an opponent who had a better hand than yours prior to your draw.

Double Belly Buster:

Four cards to a straight, which can be made with cards of two different ranks. If the board is 7-9-10-K and you hold Q-8, then a 6 or Jack will give you the straight. Giving you 8 outs instead of 4 outs, like, a gut-shot would.

Early Position:

A position on a round of betting in which you must act before most of the other players.

Edge:

An advantage over an opponent.

Expectation:

The average profit or loss of any bet over the long run.

Favorite:
> A hand that has the best chance of winning.

Family Pot:
> A pot: in which most or all the players at the table are involved.

Fifth Street:
> The fifth and final community card on the board. Also called "The River."

Flat Call:
> To call a bet without raising.

Flop:
> The first 3 exposed community cards, which are dealt simultaneously.

Flush:
> Five cards of the same suit.

Fold:
> To drop out of a hand rather than call a bet or raise. To "muck"

Four-Flush:
> Four cards to a flush.

Four of a Kind:

> Four cards of the same rank. Also called "quads".

Fourth Street:

> The fourth community card on the board. Also called "The Turn."

Free Card:

> A card that a player gets without having to calling a bet.

Free Roll:

> A situation where two players have the same hand but one of them has a chance to make a better hand. Ace King off suit vs. Ace King suited, meaning they have the same hand but the suited Ace King has a chance of winning with a flush. The player with the suited cards is "free rolling"; especially when the board has given the suited cards a flush draw.

Full House:

> Having three cards of one rank and two cards of another rank. Three of a kind and a pair: 3 threes' and 2 twos' in one hand.

Giving a Hand Away:

> Playing your hand in such a way that your opponents should know what you have.

Good Game:

> A game in which there are enough players worse than you for you to be a substantial favorite.

Gut Shot:

> When you're drawing to an inside straight. Also called "a belly buster." You're holding 8-9 and the board is A-5-6, meaning you need the 7 (4 outs) to catch your straight. A card, in the middle of the draw, that will complete it.

Heads-Up:

> Playing against only one other player.

Hourly Rate:

> The amount of money a player expects to win per hour on average.

Implied Odds:

> The ratio of the total amount of money you expect to win if you make your hand to the bet you must now call to continue in the hand.

Kicker:

A side card. If the board is 2-4-6-7-10 and you hold A-10, while your opponent holds King-10, then you win because you have a higher kicker with your Ace to his King.

Late Position:

Positions on a round of betting in which you act after most of the other players have acted.

Limit:

The amount a player may bet or raise on any round of betting.

Limp In:

To call a bet rather than raise. (Preflop Action)

Live Cards:

Having 2 cards not matching your opponent(s) cards. All-in preflop and you have Q-J. Your opponent has A-K. You have live cards because none of your cards match any of your opponent(s) cards.

Live One:

A loose, weak player with a lot of money to lose.

Lock (also look up "nuts" or "pure nuts"):
A cinch hand. A hand that cannot lose.

Long Shot:
A hand that has little chance of being made.

Loose:
Playing more hands that normal.

Loose Game:
A game with a lot of players in most pots.

Middle Pair:
Pairing the second highest card on the board.

Middle Position:
A position on a round of betting somewhere in the middle.

Muck:
To discard you hand. To "fold".

Multi-way Pot:
A pot in which two or more players are involved.

Nuts:
The best possible hand at any given point in the pot. If you flop the nut

straight, it means the flop is 10-J-Q and you're holding A-K. You have the best possible hand (or nuts) on the flop.

Odds:

The ratio of the amount of money in the pot to the bet you must call to continue with the hand.

Off-Suit:

Two cards: Not of the same suit.

On Tilt:

Playing much worse than usual because you've come emotionally upset. Usually happens when you have bad beat. Also called "steaming."

Open-Ended Straight:

Four consecutive cards to a straight, which can be made with, two cards of different ranks. If you fold 9-10 and the flop is 2-8-J, then you have 8 outs to give you the straight. A 7 or Queen will complete it. The ends of a straight.

Outs:

Cards left in the deck, which will improve your hand.

Over-call:

A call or bet after another player has already called.

Over-card:

A card higher than any other card on the flop or any card higher than those in your hand.

Over-pair:

A wired pair that is higher that any card on the board.

Pair:

Two cards of the same rank.

Pass:

To check or fold.

Pay-Off:

To call a bet or raise when you don't think you have the best hand.

Position:

The spot in the sequence of betting in which a player is located.

Pot:

The total amount of money wagered at any point in the hand.

Pot Committed:

Forced to call a bet when most of your money is in the pot. I don't believe in pot committed, because I feel you can fold any time you know you're beat no matter how much is in the pot.

Pot Odds:

The ratio of the amount of money in the pot to the bet you must call to continue with the hand. When your opponent bets $50 into a $200 pot, then you're getting 4 to 1 on your money. 200 divided by 50 = 4.

Preflop:

The action that is taken place before the flop. The action once everyone has his or her 2 cards down.

Put Someone on a Hand:

To determine as best as you can the hand(s) an opponent is most likely holding.

Pure Nuts:

> The BEST possible hand. Usually referred to after the river card is dealt.

Rag (brick):

> A card that doesn't complete any possible draws. Also called a "blank".

Raise:

> To bet an additional amount after someone else has bet. A raise must be at least double the original bet.

Raiser:

> A player who raises.

Rake:

> An amount retained by the casino (or house) from each pot.

Represent:

> To make your opponents believe you have a better hand than you really do.

Re-Raise:

> To raise after an opponent has raised.

Reverse Implied Odds:

> The ratio of the amount of money now in the pot to the amount of money you

will have to call to continue from the present round to the end of the hand.

Round of Betting:

A sequence of betting after one or more cards has been dealt.

Royal Flush:

An ace-high straight flush. The best possible hand in poker.

Running Pair:

Fourth and Fifth Street cards of the same rank. For example, you hold A- 7 and the board is 8-9-Q. To catch a running pair, you'll need both the turn and river to be either 7's or both Aces'.

Rush:

Several winnings in a short period of time.

Second Pair:

Pairing the second highest card on the board.

Semi-Bluff:

To bet with a hand, which you do not think, is the best hand but which has a reasonable chance of improving to the best hand.

Set:

Three of a kind, when you hold a pair and a third one hits the board. For example, you're holding pocket 6's and the flop is 2-6-10.

Short-Stacked:

Playing in a game with a relatively small number of chips remaining.

Showdown:

The turning up of all active players' cards at the end of the final round of betting to see who has the best hand.

Side Pot:

A second pot for the other active players when one player is all-in.

Slow-Play:

To check or just call an opponent's bet with a big hand in order to make more money on later rounds of betting.

Slow Rolling:

To delay an easy call. You know you have the best hand, but you take longer that you should to make the call or show your hand.

Small Ball:

A strategy of seeing flops cheaply to either win a big pot by connecting with rags or a small pot by outplaying weaker opponents without risking too much.

Starting Requirements:

The minimum initial hand, a player considers he needs to continue in the pot.

Start the Action:

To make the first bet in a particular hand.

Steal:

To cause your opponents to fold when you probably do not have the best hand. Could also be labeled as a bluff.

Straight:

Five cards of mixed suits in sequence.

Straight Flush:

Five cards of the same suit in sequence.

Structure:

The limits set upon the ante, forced bets and subsequent bets and raises in any given game.

Sucker:

A player who can be expected to lose money. An inexperienced player.

Suited:

Two or more cards of the same suit.

Tell:

A mannerism a player exhibits that may give away the strength or weakness of his hand.

Three of a Kind:

Three cards of the same rank. Also called "Trips"

Tight:

Playing fewer hands than the norm. Playing only premium hands and playing just your cards and not your opponents.

Tight Game:

A game with a small number of players in most pots.

Tilt:

When you don't play your normal style after taking a bad beat. You let your emotions take over the game, making too many bad decisions.

Top Pair:

Pairing the highest card on the board.

Trips:

Three of a kind.

Turn:

The fourth community card. Also called "The Turn."

Two-Flush:

Two cards of the same suit.

Underdog:

A hand that does not have the best chance of winning.

Under the Gun:

The first person to act on the first round of betting.

Value:

What a hand is worth in terms of its chance of being the best hand.

Value Bet:

> Making a small bet into a large pot to gain an extra bet.

Walk:

> To be in the big blind (preflop) and everyone folds to you. Winning the pot uncontested.

Wired Pair:

> A pair in the hole. Also called a "pocket pair."

Printed in the United States
By Bookmasters